WORLD WAR II
TANKS

ORBIS PUBLISHING · LONDON

WORLD WAR II
TANKS

Eric Grove

With a foreword by
Field Marshal Sir Michael Carver GCB CBE DSO MC

Special illustrations by
The County Studio, Coleorton, Leicester

Endpapers: *A T-34 (right) and T-26 (left) supporting Soviet ski troops during the counteroffensive of December 1941 to March 1942 (Blitz Publications)*
Page i: *A Tiger II (RAC Tank Museum)*
Overleaf: *An L 3/35 Lf showing off its spectacular capabilities during the siege of Tobruk (Zennaro)*
Opposite page: *A Cromwell VII (RAC Tank Museum)*

© Orbis Publishing Limited London 1976
Printed in Italy by IGDA, Novara
ISBN 0 85613 200 4

Contents

A typically mixed column of well-camouflaged
Japanese tanks on the move in the Philippines
(Fujiphotos)

Foreword

by Field Marshal Sir Michael Carver GCB CBE DSO MC

In this book, Eric Grove has provided a description of the tanks and other armoured fighting vehicles developed and used by the principal participants in World War II, which will be of great value to those already expert in the subject, to students of war and all military enthusiasts whether or not they specialize in the subject of tanks.

In all the countries covered, a similar trend in the development of armour and armoured warfare can be seen. Starting from the initially diverging concepts of a siege machine, of which the original World War I tank was an example, and alternatively a replacement for horsed cavalry, both in its reconnaissance and its 'shock action' roles, it lead to the development of one type which could combine the functions of the siege machine, shock action in battle and also the mobile role of a force employing far-ranging mobility as the main instrument of decision.

The British were the first to develop the ideas, but were slow to turn them into suitable vehicles, partly due to the demands of more traditional arms and partly to lack of resources. Nevertheless, the Matilda II and the Cruisers of 1940–1 were good tanks for their day. But there were too few, and the Cruisers were unreliable and lacked potential for development. The Germans, like the British and the Americans, wasted effort initially on light tanks, mechanical representations of the horse, but eventually produced vehicles of great potential in the *PzKpfw* IIIs and IVs and most of all in the *Panther*. The *Tiger* was a siege machine, like the Churchill, though a more formidable one. The Russians were the first to develop the full possibilities of the tank arm. To have had 20,000 in service in the 1930s when others were talking in terms of hundreds, was a remarkable achievement, as it was to have produced over 87,000 tanks and more than 25,000 other armoured fighting vehicles during a war in which half of their country was a battlefield.

Ironically, the Russians' battle-winning tank, the *T-34* from which the Germans derived the *Panther*, was itself a development, as was the British Cruiser, of the Christie – a private American venture rejected by the United States Army. The American tank story is itself an ironic one. After World War I, tanks were assigned to the infantry and a fast mobile vehicle was not considered necessary. When the United States entered World War II, the basic infantry tank was the M3, designed as a siege-train machine. On the other hand, the M4, or Sherman, which followed, was, like the *T-34* and the *PzKpfw* III and IV and *Panther*, a truly 'universal' or as it would now be called a 'main battle' tank. The cavalry had had to be content with a light tank, but they had a very good vehicle in the Stuart, equivalent in armour, firepower and mobility, except for range, to the British Crusader. French, Italian, Polish and Japanese tanks are also dealt with in this book, although their importance and influence both on design and in the battlefield were not of the same order.

Here, gathered together in one handy volume, is a storehouse of information on the subject, of particular value as a reference book to those studying the campaigns in which these vehicles were pitted against each other or the history of their development, as well as to all tank enthusiasts.

Michael Carver

FM

Acknowledgements

A comprehensive reference work on armoured vehicles must draw heavily on the prolific literature in the field. The following authors' books and articles have been of particular use but the list is not exhaustive:

B. Barclay, J. Bingham, G. Bradford, P. Chamberlain, G. Chapman, S. Clayton, L. Covelli, D. Crow, B. Culver, M. Dario, W.J.K. Davies, H.L. Doyle, N.W. Duncan, D.P. Dyer, C. Ellis, F. Fatutta, U. Feist, G.W. Futter, T.J. Gander, A.J. Gooch, H. Guderian, T. Hara, O. Holub, A. Horne, R.J. Icks, T.L. Jentz, J.J. Kegler, A. Kikuchi, B.H. Liddell Hart, K. Macksey, J. Magnuski, J.F. Milsom, M. Norman, R.M. Ogorkiewicz, D. Orgill, B. Perrett, N. Pignato, A. Seaton, T. Segar, A.L. Sohns, C.F. Sperber, W.J. Spielberger, Y. Takani, F.M. von Senger und Etterlin, F. Vos, B.T. White, T. Wise, S. Zaloga.

A specially good source of information on this subject is the journal of the AFV Association, *AFV News*. Details of membership can be obtained from G. Bradford, RR No 2, Preston, Ontario, Canada.

I must also acknowledge the help of Richard M. Bennett, H. Herbert and Michael Ginns for the useful information they supplied, together with the generous assistance of Colonel P. Hordern, Major-General N.W. Duncan, the other staff of the Royal Armoured Corps Tank Museum, Bovington and Michael Chapman, Librarian of the Britannia Royal Naval College, Dartmouth.

Finally my thanks are due to my mother who typed the manuscript and my wife for her general forebearance and advice.

Photographs

Pages 2–4, RAC Tank Museum, Bovington; 4–5 Blitz Publications; 6, RAC Tank Museum; 6–7, Staatsbibliothek, Berlin; 8, RAC Tank Museum; 9, Signal/Nicole Marchand; 12–16, Blitz Publications; 17, H. Le Masson; 18 (top), RAC Tank Museum; 18 (bottom), Blitz Publications; 23, RAC Tank Museum; 26–29, Blitz Publications; 30, RAC Tank Museum; 31–33 (top), Blitz Publications; 33 (bottom), Imperial War Museum; 35, Keystone; 36–39, US Army; 40–43, RAC Tank Museum; 44–46, Zennaro, Rome; 48–49, RAC Tank Museum; 50, Zennaro, Rome; 52–53, Imperial War Museum; 54–55 (top), RAC Tank Museum; 54–55 (bottom), Bibliothèque Nationale/Dorka; 55, RAC Tank Museum; 56–57, Imperial War Museum; 58–59, Fujiphotos; 60–63 (top), Imperial War Museum; 63 (bottom), RAC Tank Museum; 64–65, RAC Tank Museum; 66–67, Blitz Publications; 68–70, RAC Tank Museum; 71–72, Blitz Publications; 73, RAC Tank Museum; 74, Fox Photos; 76–79, Blitz Publications; 81, Fox Photos; 82–89, RAC Tank Museum; 90, La Société Jersiaise (Archives); 92, Agence France-Presse; 92–3, RAC Tank Museum; 93, La Société Jersiaise (Archives); 94–5, Imperial War Museum; 96, Blitz Publications; 97, RAC Tank Museum; 98–99, Imperial War Museum; 100, RAC Tank Museum; 102–3, Novosti Press Agency; 104, Blitz Publications; 105–6, RAC Tank Museum; 108, Novosti Press Agency; 110, RAC Tank Museum; 112, Novosti Press Agency; 114, RAC Tank Museum; 115, Novosti Press Agency; 116 (top), RAC Tank Museum; 116 (bottom), Blitz Publications; 119–21, Novosti Press Agency; 122–23, Blitz Publications; 125 (top), RAC Tank Museum; 125 (bottom) – 126, Blitz Publications; 127, Holmès-Lebel; 129 (top), RAC Tank Museum; 129 (bottom), US Army; 134, Blitz Publications; 135–37 (top), US Army; 137 (bottom)–138 (top), Blitz Publications; 138 (bottom), US Army; 139, RAC Tank Museum; 141–43, Blitz Publications

Right: *A PzKpfw III on guard in Toulon, 27th November 1942 (Bundesarchiv, Koblenz)*

GERMANY

Despite their lack of interest in armoured operations during World War I, German views changed in succeeding years. With an army reduced to 100,000 men by the Treaty of Versailles, a favourable climate was created for soldiers like Heinz Guderian to find ways of substituting technology for manpower. Versailles also forbade the Germans any tanks, and development had to be carried out in secret in Sweden and Russia as well as Germany itself. Inspired by the writings of British progressives, such as Colonel Fuller, the idea of an armoured division – a combined 'all arms' formation based around brigades of tanks and moving at their speed – began to evolve. In 1931, Guderian was appointed Chief of Staff to the Inspectorate of Motorized Troops and the stage was set for the organization of a modern German armoured force. Planning began for new light and medium tanks which eventually became the *PzKpfw* III and IV but for short term training lighter *PzKpfw* I and II – originally designated agricultural tractors to disguise their true purpose – were decided upon.

With the selection of Hitler as Chancellor in 1933, German armour gained a powerful advocate, and two years later with the renunciation of the Versailles Treaty open re-armament began. The Motorized Troops Command became the Armoured Troops Command and three *Panzer* (armoured) divisions were formed,

the second under Guderian himself. Each had an establishment of a tank brigade (562 tanks, later reduced to 276–324), a reconnaissance battalion, infantry brigade, field artillery regiment and other support units, all motorized.

Everything did not immediately go Guderian's way. The Fourth Tank Brigade was set up as an infantry support formation and the cavalry formed four Light Divisions each with a single light tank battalion for screening duties. However, the occupation of Austria in 1938 illustrated not only the mechanical weaknesses of the new German tanks but also the advantages of their remarkable long-range mobility – Second Panzer Division of Guderian's Corps covered 420 miles (675·78 kilometres) in 48 hours. With this vindication of their utility two more *Panzer* divisions were formed, the Fourth and Fifth. Hitler had by now assumed personal charge of the armed forces and appointed Guderian head of Mobile Troops.

The first full scale demonstration of blitzkrieg warfare in 1939 was more than enough to overwhelm Poland, although, due to delays in development, the majority of the tanks used were *PzKpfw* Is and IIs. After this victory in the East the four Light divisions were up-graded to full *Panzer* status (up to 218–29 tanks).

Shortages remained, however, and when Germany invaded France and the Low Countries, out of a total of 2,574 tanks over half were still

PzKpfw Is and IIs. Most of the available heavier German armour was concentrated in the hands of the three *Panzer* divisions of Guderian's XIX *Panzer* Corps, which, together with two mainly Czech equipped *Panzer* divisions of XLI *Panzer* Corps, made the decisive breakthrough around Sedan and drove to the Channel coast by the end of the month. Armoured warfare, properly conducted over short distances and in relatively easy terrain *could* humble a more conventional army; the doubts of the German High Command, which had almost succeeded in holding back the progress of the race across France, were stilled and the number of *Panzer* divisions was ordered to be doubled.

Armour appeared to offer victories that were cheap in industrial and economic resources as well as lives and time. The output of the apparently mighty German war machine remained limited and tank production during 1940 was only 1,460 – an increase over the previous year's 249 but hardly enough for requirements. If more divisions were needed available tank strength would have to be spread more widely and the tank component of the *Panzer* division was lowered to one regiment of 150–200 vehicles.

In February 1941 an *ad hoc* group of elements of Third *Panzer* Division was sent to Africa as the Fifth Light Division; this was followed by a full *Panzer* division, the Fifteenth, in April and these two formed *Deutsche Afrika Korps*

whose exploits under Rommel again demonstrated German expertise in armoured warfare. In September 1941 Fifth Light became Twenty-first *Panzer* Division and *DAK* the *Panzergruppe Afrika*. In 1942 Rommel's whole Axis army became *Panzerarmee Afrika* for the final push on Egypt that ended at Alamein.

By then, events in this theatre, were overshadowed by those elsewhere. With their French experience the German army was confident of quick victory against Hitler's major target, Russia. Over 3,200 tanks were committed in the initial onslaught in 17 *Panzer* divisions.

But over much greater distances and against individually superior Soviet tanks the weapon that had crushed France proved inadequate. As the *Panzer* divisions pushed deeper into Western Russia so the logistical problems became more and more difficult. Winter made the situation even worse and the bid for a lightning victory finally stalled at the gates of Moscow. Recriminations followed, and Guderian was reduced to the reserve.

Tank production was increased for a renewed offensive in 1942 but there were still insufficient vehicles for all the *Panzer* divisions which now numbered 25; only those formations which spearheaded the attack in the south were fully equipped, each with three battalions of *PzKpfw* III and IV, about 170 tanks. This could only be done by stripping the formations on other parts of the front and these were reduced to one or two understrength tank battalions. These redeployments were rewarded by more massive tactical victories in the 1942 summer offensive but as the focus shifted from the Caucasus to Stalingrad so the stage was set for disaster. By the end of January 1943 an entire German army had been forced to surrender at Stalingrad.

With the total available German tank strength down to only 27 tanks per division, Guderian was recalled as Inspector General of Armoured Troops with wide powers to put Germany's armoured forces back on their feet. It was only now, after her first major defeat, that the German economy was fully mobilized for war. By 1944 Guderian planned to have all the *Panzer* divisions on a four tank battalion basis, 400 tanks in all.

Despite all efforts – 12,151 AFVs being constructed in 1943, half of which were tanks – this was an impossible target to achieve. In addition, the major German offensive of 1943, the assault against the Kursk salient, was stopped dead in its tracks after some of the heaviest armoured battles of all time, with equally large-scale casualties. German problems were not helped either by arguments over the control of vehicles and by the creation of new *élite* formations, such as the Nazi Party's own army the *Waffen SS*, which got priority in the allocation of equipment. The average *Panzer* division had only two tank battalions, one of *PzKpfw* IVs and one of *Panther* tanks, each composed of a total of four 17–22 tank companies.

When the Western Allies opened the second front in the west, the German forces were caught between two well-equipped opponents. Despite the largest production figures yet – 8,328 tanks and 10,659 other armoured fighting vehicles being produced in 1944 to 1945 – and also flashes of the old skill in armoured operations on both fronts, the Germans were finally overwhelmed by superior resources and the Allies' command of the air.

Between 1939 and 1945 the Germans produced some 23,500 tanks and 17,445 other armoured fighting vehicles, the majority after 1942. These were impressive figures but do not compare well with other major combatants' production. The Germans were unprepared for the length of the war they had begun and they mobilized their industries too late. Nor did they help themselves by their passion for technological improvement and plans for new vehicles, often highly impractical, which delayed and complicated production. Strategic insight and, latterly, technological superiority could be significant and sometimes decisive but they could not overcome administrative and managerial failures.

Left: *Three of the five 'Neubaufahrzeug' experimental multi-turreted heavy tanks built in 1934–5*

PzKpfw I and II

The *PzKpfw* I and II – originally designed as stop-gap, light, training tanks – formed the backbone of the German *Panzer* forces until well after the beginning of World War II. The *PzKpfw* I dated back to 1932 when a specification for a simple tank, to train the new armoured divisions, was issued to MAN, Krupp, Daimler Benz and Rheinmetall Borsig. Krupp, using knowledge gained in Sweden and from a Carden Loyd tankette, produced an *LKA* chassis with four coil-sprung road wheels each side and a trailing idler touching the ground. A rear-mounted, 57-hp, Krupp M305 petrol engine drove through the front sprockets. This two-man vehicle mounting two 7·9-mm MG 13 machine-guns in a small turret on the right-hand side was chosen for production, with Daimler Benz superstructure, under the pseudonym

Landwirtschaftschlepper (*LaS*) – agricultural tractor – to disguise its intended purpose.

Production began in 1934 on an initial order for 150 chassis with smaller wheels and an external girder each side to carry the leaf-spring suspension of the rear three wheels and idler. Troop trials showed that the new tank was underpowered and the IB *LaS* May was developed with a new larger 100-bhp Maybach NL 38 TR engine. This improved the tank's power to weight ratio and ability to cover difficult ground but the already disappointing range of 91 miles (146 km) was reduced slightly to 87 miles (140 km). Weight was also increased and length from 13 feet 2 inches to 14 feet 7 inches (4·02 m to 4·42 m). Height remained 5 feet 8 inches (1·72 m), width 6 feet 10 inches (2·06 m) and armour was also unchanged at

13 mm maximum, enough to protect against small-arms fire only. The new engine necessitated a lengthened suspension with five wheels and a raised idler.

In 1935, with open rearmament, the need for subterfuge disappeared and the two tanks became *Panzerkampfwagen* I (MG) *Ausführung* A and B; about 300 and 1,500 respectively were built. Despite their lack of firepower and protection, due to delays in the development of the *PzKpfw* III and IV production continued until 1941; while at the outbreak of war they constituted over a third of Germany's tank force.

Many fought in Poland in 1939 and they also appeared in Norway and Denmark the next year. In the French campaign 523 were still on the strength of the *Panzer* divisions where good logistics made up for deficiencies in range. As

late as the invasion of Russia and the campaign in the Western Desert *PzKpfw* I *Ausf* A and B were still in first-line service although by the end of 1941 most were relegated to their original training roles or had been converted.

Between 1936 to 1938, 200 *PzKkfw* Is (mostly *Ausf* B) were converted to *Kleiner Panzerbefehlswagen* (small armoured command vehicles) *SdKfz* 265. These had a high, fixed, 30-mm armoured superstructure, mounting a single machine-gun, and extra radio equipment for control of armoured operations – a vital component of the blitzkrieg concept. Ninety were with the *Panzer* divisions that moved on France in May 1940.

In order to provide mobile artillery for the *Panzer* and motorized divisions the *PzKpfw* I *Ausf* B chassis was used for two pioneer self-propelled guns, both developed in 1939 by Alkett of Berlin. One carried the 47-mm Czech *PaK* 36 (*t*) anti-tank gun in a small, three-sided open mount. A total of 132 were on strength

by July 1941 and the type saw service in tank destroyer battalions in France, Russia and North Africa. The other modification was a large 150-mm heavy infantry gun (*sIG* 33) in a massive three-sided 10-mm armoured box on the front of the chassis; 38 of these clumsy vehicles were produced and they provided direct gunfire support for motorized infantry in the Polish, French and Russian campaigns.

An attempt was made to convert the *PzKpfw* I into an eight-ton *Ausf* C fast reconnaissance vehicle but only one *VK* 601 prototype was built. Another, much heavier (18-ton) modification, *Ausf* D (*VK* 1801) with 80-mm armour and a heavy interleaved suspension was developed for infantry purposes in the summer of 1940. With its two machine-gun armament and a speed of only 15 mph (24 km/h), this design – an aberration in German armoured ideas – reflected the continued power of the traditional arms although only 30 were built out of a total order for 130 tanks.

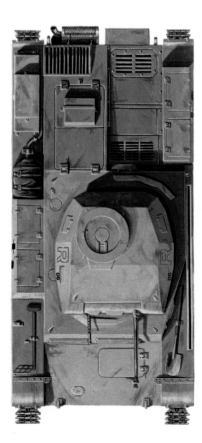

PzKpfw II Ausf F
Weight 9.35 tons (9.5 tonnes)
Crew three
Armament one 20-mm KwK 30 gun with 180 rounds and one 7.92-mm MG 34 machine-gun with 2,550 rounds
Armour hull nose 35 mm, driver's plate 30 mm, sides 20 mm, decking 10 mm, belly 5 mm, tail 15 mm; turret front 30 mm, sides 20 mm, rear 15 mm, top 10 mm
Engine one Maybach HL 62 TR inline six-cylinder liquid-cooled petrol, 140-hp
Speed 25 mph (40 km/h)
Range 118 miles (190 km)
Trench crossing 5 feet 7 inches (1.7 m)
Vertical step 1 foot 4½ inches (42 cm)
Fording 3 feet (90 cm)
Length 15 feet 9 inches (4.81 m)
Width 7 feet 6 inches (2.28 m)
Height 6 feet 8 inches (2.02 m)

Left: A PzKpfw Ausf F captured from 10th Panzer division in Tunisia. It is painted sand yellow and the turret markings are those of a headquarters vehicle of one of the division's Panzer regiments. A Panzer regiment HQ had up to five such reconnaissance tanks. Note the Ausf F recognition features: the wide full-length driver's plate with dummy right-hand aluminium visor to confuse hostile gunners searching for a vulnerable spot, the conical rear idlers and the lack of turret stowage bin

The *PzKpfw* II dated back to 1934 when a specification was issued for an improved light tank to fill the gap caused by the delay in development of heavier vehicles. Krupp offered an *LKA* II prototype based on their previous tank but this time the MAN offering was chosen. This new *LaS* 100 chassis had six small road wheels each side, sprung in pairs between the sides of the tank and an outside girder. A 130-hp Maybach engine drove the seven-ton vehicle via the front sprocket. The driver steered using the normal clutch and brake system as on the earlier *LaS*. A turret mounting a 20-mm *KwK* 30 automatic gun, together with an *MG* 34 machine-gun was fitted and maximum armour thickness was 14·5 mm. For this period the 20-mm weapon had an acceptable armour piercing performance: 24 mm of vertical armour at 500 yards (457 m).

Limited production began in 1935 and the first 25 1/*LaS* 100s entered service as the *PzKpfw* II (2 cm) *Ausf* a1 (*SdKfz* 121). A further 25 a2 and 50 a3 followed with minor improvements to engine and suspension. A new larger (140-hp) engine was fitted to the next 100 *Ausf* bs with 30-mm nose armour which upped weight to nearly eight tons. With the next limited pre-production series, *Ausf* c, a new suspension of five medium-sized, elliptically-sprung road wheels was adopted which became standard for the remainder of the series. With larger tanks still in short supply, full-scale production began in 1937 by MAN, Famo, MIAG and later Wegmann. The first production model was the *Ausf* A which had a new, angular, welded nose instead of the previous rounded casting and this was followed by the *Ausf* B and C with turret cupolas instead of periscopes. Extra 14.5-mm frontal armour was added.

In 1939 there were 1,226 *PzKpfw* IIs of all types in service, although by this time the deficiencies of the tank in armour and firepower had already become clear – the armour was not thick enough to withstand modern anti-tank guns and, perhaps more important, the 20-mm gun was becoming increasingly useless against more modern tanks. Nevertheless, the

Opposite page: *An example of the last PzKpfw II model to see service, albeit in small quantities, the Ausf L 'Luchs' (Lynx) reconnaissance tank. This photograph shows one of the tanks of a Waffen SS reconnaissance unit captured in France*
Above: *In the first winter on the Russian front PzKpfw II and III were still operating together as main battle tanks. The interesting PzKpfw II Ausf F on the right, appears to have had its puny 20-mm gun replaced with a more powerful weapon, possibly a captured French 37-mm SA-38. The cupola is also modified*
Below: *Another use for the PzKpfw II chassis was as a carriage for the 150-mm sIG 33 heavy infantry gun. This example is seen knocked out in the Western Desert*

PzKpfw II proved adequate in Poland and even in France as the major single type (950 tanks) in the *Panzer* Divisions that struck on 10 May. As with the *PzKpfw* I strategic and tactical prowess made up for technical deficiencies.

This initial success perhaps distorted the perspective of the High Command, which kept the *PzKpfw* II in production; although only 15 had been built in 1939 and 9 in 1940, 233 appeared in 1941. These were of a new version, *Ausf* F, with redesigned frontal plating up-armoured to 30·35 mm, but speed was reduced by 10 mph (16 km/h) due to the extra weight. A few had a new 20-mm gun, the lengthened *KwK* 38. Two more similar types, *Ausf* G and J appeared with the addition of a storage-bin to the turret. All these later models had a new, conical rear idler. Over 1,060 *PzKpfw* IIs were available for action during the opening weeks of the invasion of Russia but over such vast distances, and against a more heavily armed and armoured enemy, the weaknesses of the design were even more apparent. In order to make good the vehicle's deficiencies a few *PzKpfw* IIs received new armament, some being fitted with what appears from photographic evidence to be a French 37-mm *SA* 38. By April of the next year the number in action had slumped to 866 despite continued production, and increasingly they were relegated to reconnaissance duties.

From 1942, large numbers of *Ausf* A, B, C and F chassis were used as the basis for self-propelled guns armed with the new 75-mm *PaK* 40/2 which could penetrate the latest Soviet armour. These *Panzerjägers* were designated *Marder* II (*SdKfz* 131). During 1942 and 1943 531 were converted and issued to the tank destroyer battalions of *Panzer* and infantry divisions. The most numerous SP on the standard *PzKpfw* II chassis was the *Wespe* (Wasp – *SdKfz* 124) with a 105-mm *FH* 18/2 field howitzer, with muzzle brake, which was mounted in a high

Wespe
Weight 11.5 tons (12.1 tonnes)
Crew five
Armament one 105-mm le FH 18/2 (L/28) field
howitzer with 32 rounds and one 7.92-mm
MG 34 machine-gun with 600 rounds
Armour hull nose and driver's plate, glacis 10 mm,
sides 15 mm, decking 10 mm, belly 5 mm, rear
8–15 mm; superstructure front 12 mm, sides
10 mm, rear 8 mm
Range 90 miles
Height 7 feet 8 inches (2.32 m)
Other details as PzKpfw II Ausf F tank

rear superstructure. Some 682 were converted during 1943 and 1944, mostly by Famo in Warsaw and they saw wide service in the self-propelled artillery battalions of the *Panzer* and *Panzer Grenadier* divisions.

The *PzKpfw* II *Ausf* D and E were special (35-mph or 56-km/h) versions built in 1938–9 by Daimler Benz as *Schnellkampfwagen* (fast fighting vehicles) for the light divisions. These 250 vehicles had torsion-bar suspension and large wheels of the Christie type. Apparently few reached the formations for which they were intended and went instead to *Panzer* Regiment Eight – part of independent *Panzer* Brigade

Four until the latter's formation into Tenth *Panzer* Division in 1939. The new suspension had a disappointing cross-country performance and, in 1940, 95 were converted to *Flammpanzer* II flamethrower vehicles (sometimes called Flamingo) with two forward-mounted flame-guns and a small machine-gun turret. This chassis was also later used as a mount for the Soviet 76·2-mm gun in an open shield, on top of a high box-like superstructure. Both the un-modified weapon designated *FK 296* (*r*) and the *PaK 36(r)*, modified with a muzzle brake to take German length cartridge cases, were used. Known as the *Panzerjäger* II *Ausf* D or E *für 7·62 cm PaK 36* (*r*), this was given the ordinance number *SdKfz* 132 and was also sometimes called *Marder* II. Some later vehicles had the later *PaK 39(r)* weapon or the German *PaK* 40/2. Alkett converted 185 in 1942; some *Flamm-panzer* chassis were used latterly as the former conversion had not been entirely successful and the need for mobile anti-tank defence was more pressing. The tank destroyers were mainly used in Russia where they provided for a time the only means of giving the German divisions proper mobile protection against Soviet armour.

A lightened *PzKpfw* II prototype, designated *VK* 901 had been built in 1939 with an inter-leaved wheel suspension but neither it, nor a more heavily armoured infantry support *VK* 1601, was accepted for mass production. A compromise *VK* 1300 series development (*VK* 1303) was finally accepted in 1943 as the *PzKpfw* II *Ausf* L, later *Panzerspähwagen* II *Luchs* (Lynx), a reconnaissance tank issued to the *Panzer* divisions; but few were built due to other production priorities. This was the final *PzKpfw* II derivative to see action.

Above: One of the most important German self-propelled guns of the war – the Wespe (Wasp)
Left: Although unsuccessful as tanks, the PzKpfw II Ausf D and E chassis, with their special large wheel suspensions, found a new lease of life in 1942 as chassis for the captured Russian PaK 36(r). They were the forerunners of the large number of Marder II tank destroyers which utilized the more conventional PzKpfw II chassis

PzKpfw III

In 1935, after experience gained with the design of smaller tanks had been consolidated, a specification was issued for the larger 15-ton 'light tank' which Guderian intended to be the major weapon of his armoured divisions. It was to have a high-velocity gun and have a five man crew – gunner, loader, driver, wireless operator and commander – to enable each member to concentrate on his own tasks. For maximum liaison, communications between driver, wireless operator and commander were connected to the external radio. There was considerable debate over the armament of the new vehicle. The Mechanized Troops Inspectorate wanted a 50-mm weapon but the Ordnance Department felt that the standard infantry 37-mm anti-tank gun would be sufficient. The latter view eventually prevailed and the smaller weapon was chosen but it was also decided that the turret ring would be made large enough for up-gunning should it become necessary.

In 1936 the first prototypes appeared designated *Zugführerwagen* (*ZW* – platoon commander's vehicle) from MAN, Krupp, Rheinmetall Borsig and Daimler Benz. The last-named version was chosen and the first ten production vehicles, designated 1/ZW *Ausf* A, built. The initial suspension consisted of five, large, coil-sprung road wheels each side, but the development of the tank was seriously delayed by a long search to find a better design. It was only just before the outbreak of war, after three years' time-consuming development that the definitive suspension was fitted to the *Ausf* E using torsion bars connected to six medium-sized road wheels each side. A completely new, advanced Maybach pre-selector transmission was also fitted with ten forward speeds and one

reverse; gear change and steering were both power-assisted. The design of the front plate was improved with new driver's visor and machine-gun mounting, but armour thickness (30 mm) and the engine, a 120 TR of 320 hp, were the same as the *Ausf* D. Some 41 *Ausf* E were built and after successful trials this design was standardized as the *PzKpfw* III (3·7 cm) (*SdKfz* 141); in September 1939, 98 of the above *Ausf* D and E pre-production tanks were available for service with the *Panzer Lehr* (Demonstration) Battalion and a few examples with the Panzer Divisions for the invasion of Poland.

To speed up production, manufacture of the *PzKpfw* III was spread out among several firms – Alkett, Wegmann, Daimler Benz, Henschel, Famo, MAN and MNH – and the hull of the *PzKpfw* III was divided into four prefabricated welded assemblies – hull, front superstructure, rear superstructure and turret. But output was slow as the concerns chosen for the programme were unused to the mass-production of motor vehicles and others such as Ford and Opel were not considered due to the fact that they were not nationally owned. The first major production

PzKpfw III Ausf E
Armament one 45-calibre 37-mm KwK gun with 120 rounds and three 7.92-mm MG 34 machine-guns with 3,750 rounds.
Other details as PzKpfw III Ausf F

Above: *A PzKpfw III Ausf E as used in the conquest of France in 1940. Note the 45-calibre 37-mm gun with internal mantlet and lack of turret stowage bin. The camouflage is based on the standard contemporary dark 'Panzer Grey' with green patches added for combat service. With this model and earlier types two 7.92-mm MG 34 machine-guns were usually mounted co-axially with the main armament; 120 rounds of 37-mm ammunition were carried. Only 41 of this type were built and they constituted the last of a long line of pre-production variants. The Ausf E introduced the standard PzKpfw III torsion bar suspension. PzKpfw III Ausf E tanks were later fitted with 50-mm guns*
Below: *A PzKpfw III Ausf J loaded down with extra stowage bins finds its wider tracks useful in the final unsuccessful push for Moscow in December 1941. A national flag is draped over the turret for identification*

PzKpfw III Ausf F
Weight 20 tons (20.3 tonnes)
Crew five
Armament one 50-mm KwK L/42 gun with 99 rounds and two 7.92-mm MG 34 machine-guns with 3,750 rounds
Armour hull nose 30 mm, glacis 25 mm, driver's plate 30 mm, sides 30 mm, decking 17 mm, belly 16 mm, tail 21 mm; turret front, sides and rear 30 mm, top 10 mm
Engine one Maybach HL 120 TRM V-12 water-cooled petrol, 300-hp
Speed 25 mph (40 km/h)
Range 109 miles (175 km)
Trench crossing 7 feet 7 inches (2.3 m)
Vertical step 2 feet (60 cm)
Fording 2 feet 7 inches (80 cm)
Overall length 17 feet 9 inches (5.41 m)
Width 9 feet 7 inches (2.92 m)
Height 8 feet 3 inches (2.51 m)

Above: *The Ausf F was the first major production variant of the PzKpfw III. Note the 42-calibre 50-mm gun in an external mantlet, turret ventilator and stowage box. Early Ausf Fs had similar guns and mantlets to the Ausf E illustrated previously. This particular tank is one of those sent to Africa to form Deutsche Afrika Korps: note the palm tree and swastika marking on the left hull front. Next to it is the divisional sign of the 15th Panzer Division, sent to reinforce Rommel*

PzKpfw III Ausf M
Weight 20.8 tons (21.13 tonnes)
Armament one 60-calibre KwK 39 gun with
98 rounds and two 7.92-mm MG 34 machine-guns
with 2,550 rounds
Armour hull nose 50 mm, driver's plate 50 mm
and 20 mm, tail 50 mm; turret front 57 and
20 mm, sides and rear 30 mm
Range 93 miles (155 km)
Overall length 21 feet 6 inches (6.55 m)
Width 9 feet 9 inches (2.97 m)
Other details as PzKpfw Ausf F

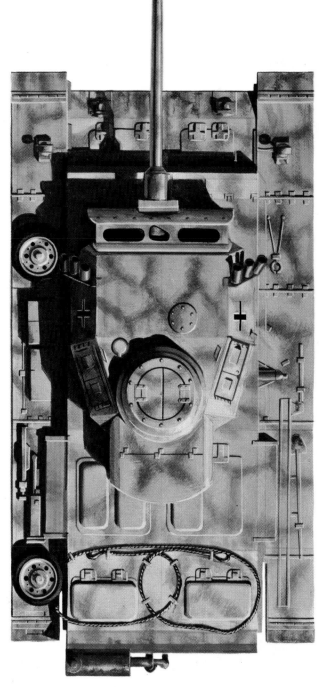

Right: *A PzKpfw III Ausf M showing the several*
differences between this late vehicle and the earlier
Ausf F opposite. Note extra spaced armour added
to the mantlet and re-designed thicker driver's
plate, new 60-calibre KwK 39 gun, improved
cupola, absence of side escape hatches, new driving
sprockets and idlers, re-arranged return rollers
and wider tracks. The re-designed engine access
hatches and new exhaust system were introduced
on the Ausf M to allow wading up to 5 feet (1.52 m)

mark was the *Ausf* F, little changed from the E except for improved brake ventilation and a slightly derated 300-hp TRM engine.

By the end of 1939, 157 *PzKpfw* IIIs of all types had been built and by May 1940 there were 349 available to take part in the French invasion. Another 39 converted to armoured command vehicles enabled higher commanders of *Panzer* formations to stay up with their leading troops, a vital aid in blitzkrieg operations. On 10 May, 1940 the majority of *PzKpfw* IIIs were concentrated in Guderian's XIX *Panzer* Corps, whose task it was to make the decisive break-through in the Ardennes. Here their success was due more to the *PzKpfw* IIIs good crew layout, which assisted well co-ordinated mobile operations, than to its rather poor armament and protection. The L/45 37-mm gun with a muzzle velocity of 2,500 fps (762 m/s) could not penetrate any but the least protected enemy tanks and 30-mm armour was little protection from most Allied guns. The shortcomings of this gun had become apparent long before and in 1939 orders had been given to Krupp to develop a new 50-mm tank gun for the *PzKpfw* III. Forty *Ausf* Fs, with the new 50-mm *KwK* L/42, were rushed into action before the end of the French campaign but had little effect on the outcome.

After the lessons of France, Hitler ordered the up-gunning of the *PzKpfw* III with the longer L/60 50-mm anti-tank gun; but to save time the Army continued fitting the L/42. *Ausf* Es and Fs were retro-fitted with this gun which was in a new external mantlet. New Fs and, from October, *Ausf* Gs with slightly modified cupolas and driver's visors, were fitted as new – although the first Gs had 37-mm guns as the 50-mm remained in short supply. Some Gs were fitted with air filters and improved ventilation as *Ausf* G (*Tp*) (Tropical) and these served in the Western Desert. In this theatre, although the *PzKpfw* III was vulnerable to the British two-pounder (40-mm) gun (at least until later increases in protection) its armament proved effective against all British tanks except the Matilda. Although the 50-mm gun's AP performance was less good

in actual penetration, its projectile carried a high explosive charge, inflicting more permanent damage on enemy armour than that of the British two-pounder's (40-mm) solid shot. High explosive shells were also carried, useful for action against anti-tank guns; it was a particular weakness of British tanks that their two-pounder (40-mm) guns did not have this facility.

At the end of 1940 yet another new version appeared, the *Ausf* H which embodied the results of combat experience in improved armour protection. Extra 30-mm plates were bolted and welded to the hull front; wider tracks of 400 as against 360 mm were introduced to compensate for the extra weight and there was a new manual gear-box with only six forward speeds as the older one had been unnecessarily complex. Older models were retro-fitted to the new standards. There was also a command

version (*Panzerbefehlswagen* III *Ausf* C, later H) with a dummy gun. Used in North Africa from 1941 the up-armoured *PzKpfw* IIIs (both *Ausf* H and *Ausf* G modified in the field) proved unexpectedly difficult to defeat with the two-pounder (40-mm) gun, previously effective against the 30-mm plates.

When the Germans invaded Russia 1,440 *PzKpfw* IIIs were available for service. Initially, 965 were used and they were the backbone of the strongest *Panzer* divisions' tank regiments, equipping two out of the three companies of each of their tank battalions. In addition to the standard vehicles there were others fitted for deep wading which were used in the initial offensive across the River Bug and later across the Dnieper. The *PzKpfw* III was adequate for dealing with the older Soviet tanks but the KV and *T*-34 tanks with their thick well-shaped

Above: *All types of PzKpfw III from Ausf F onwards fought in North Africa. The protection of this early Ausf J with short 50-mm gun has been modified to Ausf L standard with extra 20-mm spaced armour on the driver's plate and mantlet. The tank was knocked out during the battles around Alamein in 1942*

Left: *One of the 75-mm armed PzKpfw III Ausf N gunfire support tanks attached to the 501st Heavy Tank Battalion of Tigers knocked out in Tunisia. This PzKpfw III model was sometimes known as the Sturmpanzer III and was designed to provide a suitable infantry support tank for the Panzergrenadier divisions*

armour and powerful guns proved difficult to defeat. Up-gunning could no longer be postponed and as Hitler was furious that his orders had been ignored, plans for the development of a tank version of the longer L/60 50-mm weapon were at last put in hand.

The new *Ausf* J (*SdKfz* 141/1) was built with heavier armour of 50 mm all round, which was stronger than the 60-mm welded appliqué armour of its predecessors. The driver's visor was again changed and a new ball-mounting

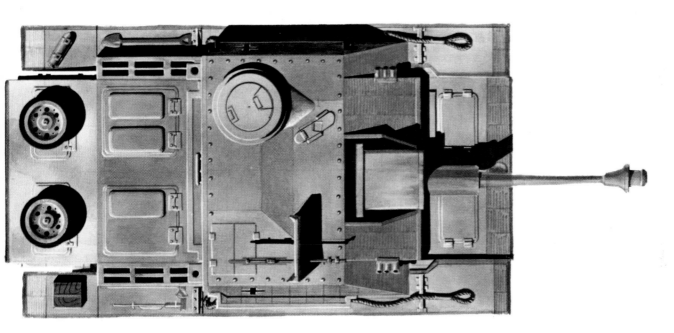

for the hull *MG* 34 adopted. Mechanical steering was fitted and other details changed to assist mass-production. From November the new L/60 50-mm gun began to be fitted and 40 *Ausf* Js were constructed by the end of the year with this weapon. The *KwK* 39 L/60 had a muzzle velocity with normal AP rounds of 2,700 fps (822 m/s), or 3,835 fps (1168 m/s) with *PzGr* 40, but even this was soon found to be insufficient. These first 'Mark III Specials' only reached the Western Desert in May 1942.

Only 862 *PzKpfw* IIIs had been built in 1940 and when the invasion of Russia boosted demand to 7,992 vehicles for 36 *Panzer* divisions (twice the total existing German armoured fighting vehicle strength) German industry, demobilized from a not very high level of war production after the fall of France, was hard pressed to meet its targets. Plans to develop a replacement 22 ton *VK* 2001 (DB) or *ZW* 40 tank were soon dropped and another factory MIAG was brought into the *PzKpfw* III programme. Still only 1,713 tanks of this type were built in 1941 and even by 1942 production targets of 190 vehicles a month were not being met. Some of these were of yet another model, the

Ausf L, also L/60 armed. To increase protection at low cost, a spaced 20-mm armour plate was added to the mantlet and hull front. A special *Ausf* L *(Trop)* was developed with improved ventilation, filters and hatches; these were widely used in North Africa from mid-1942.

Some 2,605 *PzKpfw* IIIs were built in 1942 (1,907 with the *KwK* 39) as German industry at last began to mobilize itself for total war. In order to simplify production the next *Ausf* M dispensed with the vision ports and escape hatches in the hull sides and it was also modified to wade up to five feet (1·52 m). By the end of the year the *PzKpfw* III was outmoded as a battle tank and the final variant appeared as the *Ausf* N (*SdKfz* 141/2) close support tank with low velocity L/24 75-mm guns taken from *PzKpfw* IVs. This gun had inferior AP performance to the 50-mm L/60 but it was a better weapon for HE support and the N was designed to provide the vehicles for the tank battalions of *Panzergrenadier* divisions. Some were also allocated to *Tiger* heavy tank battalions. The first were *Ausf* L modified to N standard and saw action by the end of 1942; 660 were converted or built new up to August 1943.

Sturmgeschutz III Ausf G
Weight 23.5 tons (23.9 tonnes)
Crew four
Armament one 75-mm StuK 40 (L/48) gun with 54 rounds and one 7.92-mm MG 34 machine-gun with 600 rounds
Armour nose 80 mm, driver's plate 50 and 30 mm, sides 30 mm, decking 11–17 mm, belly 16 mm, tail 30 mm
Range 105 miles (169 km)
Overall length 22 feet 2½ inches (6.77 m)
Width 9 feet 8½ inches (2.96 m)
Height 7 feet 1¼ inches (2.15 m)
Other details as PzKpfw III Ausf F

Above: *These Sturmgeschutz III Ausf G assault guns, were widely produced from late 1942. Originally under the control of the artillery arm, they were first organized into 18-gun assault gun battalions each of 3 batteries of 6 vehicles. These were later enlarged into army assault artillery brigades of up to 45 assault guns (3 batteries of 14 with 3 HQ vehicles) and a small infantry component. Assault guns were the élite troops of the artillery with an impressive record against enemy armour – 20,000 enemy tanks claimed by early 1944 alone*

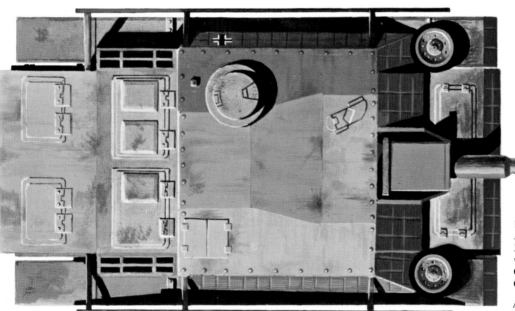

10.5-cm Sturmhaubitze 42 Ausf G
Armament one L/28 105-mm howitzer with
36 rounds and one 7.92-mm MG 34 machine-gun
with 600 rounds
Overall length 20 feet 1½ inches (6.13 m)
Other details as StuG III Ausf G

Above: *The 10.5-cm Sturmhaubitze 42 Ausf G is
basically the same as the StuG except for the
L/28 105-mm howitzer. This model has Schürtzen
protective plates fitted as was commonly done on
StuG vehicles and late model PzKpfw III tanks.
Early StuH 42s had muzzle brakes and later
StuG and StuH were fitted with better-shaped
rounded mantlets. Muzzle brakes of a new design
were adopted with some of these later StuH 42.
A 1944 type army assault artillery brigade would
contain one platoon of StuH 42 in each of its
three batteries, a total of 12 assault howitzers
per brigade. These, together with the 33 75-mm
armed StuG III, gave a powerful high velocity
armour piercing/low velocity high explosive mix
of capabilities to the unit*
Left: *A typical StuG III Ausf G fully fitted out
with protective Schürtzen abandoned to the
enemy. Note the extra armour fitted to the nose
and superstructure front*

Construction of *PzKpfw* III tanks ceased in order that production resources could be concentrated on the production of *Sturmgeschütze* (assault guns). These originated with infantry demands for an armoured close-support artillery vehicle, very necessary if all tanks were to be concentrated in the *Panzer* divisions. Daimler Benz developed a vehicle based on the *PzKpfw* III chassis with a low 50-mm armoured superstructure in which was mounted a limited traverse 75-mm L/24 tank gun. Thirty were ordered for troop trials and some took part in the invasion of France in May and June 1940 helping to clear the roads through the Ardennes. These operational tests were successful and the vehicle was ordered into production as the *Gepanzerte Selbstfahrlafette für Sturmgeschutz 7·5-cm Kanone* (*SdKfz* 142), normally shortened to *StuG* III. The *Ausf* A version was mounted on an *Ausf* F (5/*ZW*) tank chassis with no side escape hatches. Alkett, the major *PzKpfw* III contractor, had built 184 by the end of 1940. With the introduction of the new *Ausf* H tank chassis the model letter changed to B, – the C and D assault gun models were basically similar. An E version was developed as a commander's vehicle with extra radio facilities. Although production was concentrated on the *PzKpfw* III tank, 548 of these assault guns were produced in 1941.

In September, Hitler, to whom the concept appealed for its economy of resources, demanded that *StuG* vehicles should be up-armoured and up-gunned. As an interim measure some were fitted with a 33-calibre 75-mm gun but by February 1942 a version of the L/43 75-mm gun

of the contemporary *PzKpfw* IV had been fitted and demonstrated to the *Führer* as the 7·5-cm *Sturmgeschutz* 40 *Ausf* F (*SdKfz* 142/1). After 119 vehicles the weapon was changed to the L/48 gun and this changed the designation to *Ausf* F/8. At the end of 1942, again in accordance with Hitler's wishes, 80-mm armour was fitted by means of bolting on an extra 30-mm plate over the existing 50-mm base. This produced the *Ausf* G which also had a commander's cupola and, often, a shield-mounted machine-gun. Production of these continued until the end of the war. These assault guns were in reality turretless tanks and increasing numbers were produced by Alkett, MIAG and Krupp as Germany's need for large numbers of mobile, armoured high-velocity guns outstripped her tank building capabilities. In 1942, 791 *StuG* IIIs of all types were constructed, no less than 3,041 *Ausf* Gs in 1943 and 4,850 in 1944 – 123 were produced in 1945.

With such a large amount of German resources going into assault guns and given the German tendency for competing authorities it was natural that a struggle should break out over their control between the artillery to whom they were first allocated and Guderian who wished to utilize the *StuG* IIIs to spin out his limited armoured strength and provide better anti-tank protection for the infantry divisions. The artillery strongly resisted the Inspector General of Armoured Troops' claim and it was not until the end of 1943 that assault gun units came under full armoured control.

In addition to the 75-mm gun *StuG* there was

a version mounting a 105-mm howitzer with greater HE power though at the expense of armour penetration capability. These first used the *Ausf* F superstructure but the production vehicles were 10·5-cm *Sturmhaubitze* 42 *Ausf* G (*SdKfz* 142/2). Nine 105-mm *StuH* IIIs were constructed in 1942 (including prototype), 204 in 1943 and 904 in 1944. Another assault variant mounted the 150-mm sIG 33 infantry gun. In all 15,350 *PzKpfw* III chassis were built.

PzKpfw IIIs were supplied to Hungary and friendly neutrals such as Spain and Turkey also received them. Captured examples were used by the Free Polish forces for training in the Middle East while the Soviets converted others into assault guns with 76·2-mm guns (with or without muzzle brake) in a slightly higher superstructure than the *StuG* III. As the *SU* 76*I* this served against its former owners and some were recaptured by the Germans and used 'third hand'! The *PzKpfw* III survived the war in the armies of Eastern Europe.

The *StuG* III was also supplied to allies, Finland, Rumania and Bulgaria receiving examples from the Germans and some were even acquired by Syria after the war.

Below: *When captured by Soviet forces PzKpfw III and Sturmgeschütze were often pressed into service against their former owners. Some PzKpfw III tanks were re-armed with 76.2-mm guns and others were converted by the Russians into assault guns. This Ausf J, however, appears to be in its original condition, as are the StuG IIIs supporting it in the usual Soviet style*

PzKpfw IV

The *PzKpfw* IV was the only German battle tank to remain in production throughout the war years and it became the major such vehicle of the German army. This, however, had never been intended. Originally the IV was seen as an artillery support vehicle only to the lighter tanks in the *Panzer* Division, equipping one company in a battalion. Hence a low-velocity, relatively high-calibre gun was fitted in order to obtain a good high-explosive capability.

The first prototype appeared in 1934 from Rheinmetall-Borsig under the pseudonym *Bataillonsführerwagen* (battalion commander's vehicle) and used a version of that firm's standard tractor. Both Krupp and MAN also produced prototypes with advanced interleaved wheel suspensions but, in order to get the tank into production quickly, the various features were combined together with the leaf-spring coupled bogie suspension of the Krupp design for the *Zugführerwagen* specification, and the result was produced by the latter manufacturer as the *I/BW Ausf* A.

The specification had called for a tank of no more than 24 tons due to the limitations of the standard German bridge although the first vehicles only weighed just over 17 tons. The

suspension, which remained standard for the whole series, was composed of four pairs of wheels and there were four return rollers; a standard 250-hp Maybach HL 108R petrol engine was fitted, driving through the front sprockets and producing a speed of 18·2 mph (30 km/h); and the five-man crew were dispersed in the same efficient way as in the *PzKpfw* III, with similar communication equipment. The L/24 75-mm gun was mounted in the turret with a co-axial MG 34 machine-gun; a second machine-gun was in the hull front, set back a little from the driver's position. The turret had electrical traverse. Again, as in the early III, hull armour was thin, a mere 14·5 mm on the hull and 20 mm on the turret. Production and troop trials were dilatory and only 35 were constructed during 1936. In the following year 42 *Ausf* Bs were manufactured and 140 *Ausf* Cs in 1938. These introduced new HL 120 engines and 30-mm armour on hull (B) and turret (C) fronts. Together they were sufficient to produce a medium allocation to the tank battalions of existing *Panzer* divisions and production decreased to 45 in 1939; the majority of these were *Ausf* D with 20-mm side and rear armour.

Combat experience showed that although the

type was basically sound and could finally be officially adopted for service as the *PzKpfw* IV (7·5-cm) (*SdKfz* 161) it needed further up-armouring if it was to act as a real back-up to the *PzKpfw* III. Hence the next model, the *Ausf* E, production of which began in December, had a thicker nose and appliqué plates added to the front and sides to bring protection up to 50–60 mm; older models were retro-fitted. On the *Ausf* E a new type of visor and cupola was adopted and the latter was moved forward in the turret. In February production of the definitive version began, the *Ausf* F. This reverted to a single, and therefore stronger, 50-mm front plate; a new ball machine-gun mount was fitted and the driver's visor was altered again; weight was up to over 22 tons and wider tracks were fitted (400 mm instead of 380 mm) which necessitated a widened front sprocket.

Below: *A PzKpfw IV Ausf E knocked out and captured in December 1941 near Sidi Rezegh. Note the extra armour on the superstructure front (30 mm) and the sides (20 mm) and the new lower cupola. The Afrika Korps badge is on a patch of Panzer Grey left when the tank was roughly camouflaged in desert yellow*

PzKpfw IV Ausf D
Weight 19.7 tons (20 tonnes)
Crew five
Armament one 75-mm KwK L/24 gun with 80 rounds and two 7.92-mm MG 34 machine-guns with 2,800 rounds
Armour basic: hull nose 30 mm, glacis 20 mm, driver's plate 30 mm, sides 20 mm, decking 11 mm, belly 10–20 mm, tail 20 mm; turret front 30 mm, sides and rear 20 mm, top 10 mm
Engine one Maybach HL 120 TRM V-12 water-cooled petrol, 300-hp
Speed 26 mph (42 km/h)
Range 125 miles (200 km)
Trench crossing 7 feet 7 inches (2.3 m)
Vertical step 2 feet (60 cm)
Fording 2 feet 7½ inches (80 cm)
Overall length 19 feet 4½ inches (5.91 m)
Width 9 feet 7 inches (2.92 m)
Height 8 feet 6 inches (2.59 m)

Above: *By 1943–4 most PzKpfw IVs in action were fully equipped with long 75-mm guns and Schürtzen plates, 8 mm around the turret and 5 mm on the sides. These new Ausf H vehicles (note the single cupola hatch) advancing through the outskirts of a Russian town have only the extra turret protection*

Right: *The PzKpfw IV Ausf D was introduced in 1939. Its external mantlet for the 75-mm gun and re-adoption of 7.92-mm hull machine-gun distinguished it externally from the preceding Ausf C. The side armour was also increased over the older model. Tanks of this type were progressively up-armoured and fitted with new long 75-mm guns to bring them up to the latest standards. After this model, a new type of cupola was adopted. This tank is in the condition in which it might have fought in the French campaign of 1940, or in the opening year of the campaign in Russia. The fitting under the gun is a deflector to protect the tank's aerials from the blast of the short weapon*

Altogether 278 *PzKpfw* IVs of various models were available with the medium companies of the ten *Panzer* divisions that attacked France in 1940. They provided some useful support being just able to defeat the armour of most Allied tanks. The later models were hard to penetrate at long range, and, despite their small numbers, their presence was often decisive.

Limited production continued at Krupp in 1941 and by the time Germany attacked Russia about 580 *PzKpfw* IVs were available. Demand was stepped up with the proposed expansion to 36 Armoured Divisions in July but by April 1942 the number of *PzKpfw* IVs in service had barely risen above the numbers available the year before; more factories were brought into the programme and numbers finally increased from 480 in 1941 to 964 in 1942. But this was still hardly enough as it was becoming apparent that the *PzKpfw* IV was the only German tank capable of up-gunning to penetrate the well-shaped armour of the *T*-34s and KV-1s. A long 75-mm gun, the *KsK* 40 L/43 tank gun was produced and fitted from March 1942 to the new *Ausf* F2 version of the *PzKpfw* IV – the earlier *Ausf* F now became F1. With a muzzle velocity with ordinary shot of 2,428 fps (740 m/s), and a penetration against 30-degree armour of 89 mm, this gun allowed *Panzer* units to face up to the Soviet tanks on equal terms.

A further model, the *Ausf* G, appeared in 1942 with slightly improved protection and an improved double-baffle muzzle brake on the gun. Older IVs were brought up to the latest standard as they returned to Germany for overhaul. In March 1943, in accordance with Hitler's orders of the previous year, the *Ausf* H, with 80-mm armour and an L/48 75-mm gun (2,461 fps) was introduced. To increase protection from infantry thin, 5-mm *Schürzen* (side plates)

were fitted and with Guderian's encouragement production increased: 3,073 *PzKpfw* IVs were built in 1943 and 3,161 more in 1944 to 1945. From March 1944 these were the last model, the *Ausf* J, with the electrical turret traverse replaced by a purely manual arrangement. As well as simplyifying production this also allowed an extra fuel tank to be fitted, boosting the range to 200 miles (322 km). Wire mesh *Schürtzen* were fitted to lower weight and material demands, and a new idler was also fitted. *Ostkette* wide tracks also began to be adopted from the late summer of 1944 to improve mobility.

Below: 'Guderian's Duck'. This side view of an early L/48-armed Jagdpanzer IV illustrates well both the vehicle's low silhouette and the differences between the standard vehicle and the interim model based on the normal tank chassis illustrated in the drawing on the opposite page

Bottom: Something of a rarity, this Bergepanzer IV recovery vehicle was knocked out in North Africa. Indeed, this may well have been the only PzKpfw IV chassis, an Ausf D, so modified. An extra weapon, possibly a flame-thrower, appears to have been added in the driver's visor, giving this specialized vehicle a useful combat capability

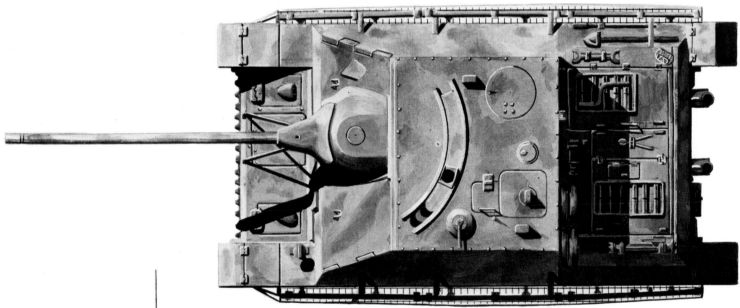

PzKpfw IV/70 Zwischenlösung (Interim)
Weight 27.6 tons (28 tonnes)
Crew four or five
Armament one 75-mm StuK 42 (L/70) with 60 rounds
Armour hull nose and driver's plate 85 mm, glacis 20 mm, sides 30 mm, decking and belly 10 mm, tail 20 mm, superstructure front 80 mm, mantlet 120 mm, sides 40 mm, roof 20 mm, rear 30 mm
Speed 24 mph (38 km/h)
Range 200 miles
Trench crossing 7 feet 3 inches (2.2 m)
Fording 3 feet 3 inches (1.00 m)
Overall length 27 feet 8 inches (8.44 m)
Width 9 feet 7 inches (2.93 m)
Height 7 feet 8½ inches (2.34 m)
Other details as PzKpfw IV Ausf D tank

Above: *This special (interim) version of the PzKpfw IV/70 (Jagdpanzer IV) was designed to overcome production difficulties by utilizing the standard PzKpfw IV Ausf J chassis with new superstructure based on that of the normal Jagdpanzer. Both Alkett and Vomag built prototypes and the former was chosen for production*

In June 1944 Hitler ordered that production of the *PzKpfw* IV should be abandoned to concentrate on its tank destroyer derivative, the *Jagdpanzer* IV, which had the 3,068 fps (935 m/s) L/70 gun of the *Panther* in a limited-traverse mounting. This vehicle dated from 1942 when a request had gone out for a new heavy assault gun with 100-mm armour. Guderian was against the project from the start; he was satisfied with the development capability of the *StuG* III and was loath to diversify production of the *PzKpfw* IV which he regarded as the mainstay of the armoured forces. Development of what was to be nicknamed 'Guderian's Duck' was slow and an interim assault gun on the IV chassis with a standard *StuG* III superstructure and an L/48 75-mm gun was designed. On some of these *Sturmgeschutz* IV assault guns (*SdKfz* 163) concrete armour was added, particularly over the driver's compartment where it could be up to 100 mm thick. About 1,000 were built in 1944, on *Ausf* H and *Ausf* J chassis, and issued to both tank battalions and artillery assault gun battalions.

The *Jagdpanzer* IV had meanwhile been developed with the same L/48 gun as it took time to develop a suitable L/70 weapon. Frontal protection was 60 mm with 30-mm armour fitted at the sides. Early vehicles carried a muzzle brake on the gun but as it was mounted so low – only four feet seven inches (1·40 m) above the ground – this led to a great deal of dust from the deflected blast and later vehicles had this deleted. The L/70 was eventually adapted and armour thickness was also increased to 80 mm (front) and 40 mm (sides).

Small numbers of *PzKpfw* IV/70, as the up-gunned *Jagdpanzer* IV was redesignated, were in action by August 1944. Its armament made it a formidable defensive weapon, particularly in the west against less well-protected British and American armour. However, despite ambitious production schedules only 1,531 *Jagdpanzer* IVs of all types were constructed. They usually served with the tank destroyer battalions of *Panzer* divisions.

Later examples were built with a slightly modified chassis incorporating features from the *PzKpfw* III tank, notably three return rollers instead of four. This reflected a final abortive attempt to rationalize the production of the two basic German tracked AFV chassis and

develop a common III/IV chassis on which various vehicles could be mounted. For example, Alkett designed a *Geschützwagen* (gun carriage) III/IV on a front-engined *PzKpfw* IV chassis with the sprockets and final drive of the III. There were four return rollers and the gun was carried in a lightly armoured superstructure at the rear. The most numerous vehicle on this chassis was the *Hummel* (Bumblebee) (*SdKfz* 165) which mounted a 150-mm FH 18/1 heavy field howitzer. The prototype vehicle had a muzzle brake and was mounted on a standard *PzKpfw* IV chassis but production vehicles had a clean barrel and the III/IV modifications. From 1942, 666 were built and they equipped the heavy batteries of the artillery battalions of favoured *Panzer* divisions.

From 1943 another version of the III/IV gun carriage appeared, mounting the 71-calibre 88-mm *PaK* 43/1 anti-tank gun. This heavy new weapon needed a self-propelled platform in the difficult conditions of the Eastern Front; the *Nashorn* (Rhinoceros) gave heavy tank destroyer brigades a new mobility, although for a direct fire weapon armour protection was poor. Some 150 chassis were completed as gunless ammunition carriers for both the anti-tank gun and also the howitzer variants.

Due to a mixture of conservatism and the tactical disadvantages of existing vehicles, with their high prominent superstructures and limited-traverse mounts, the artillery arm was not very happy with the concept of the self-propelled gun. Development, therefore, began on a series of *Waffenträger* (weapon carrier) vehicles which allowed the gun to be dismounted if necessary and also provided the lighter weapons with all round traverse. Two models mounting the 105-mm Le FH were produced, the *Heuschrecke* (Grasshopper) built on a slightly lengthened version of the *PzKpfw* IV chassis and a less specialized version using the III/IV gun carriage. Both proved difficult to operate and were never put into production.

The need for a heavy assault howitzer had become apparent during the severe street fighting in Russia in 1941–2 where existing tanks and armoured assault guns had insufficient high-explosive capability to deal with well-protected buildings and fortifications, and existing heavy howitzers were too lightly protected. Hitler felt the problem could be solved by a much more

Panzerjäger III/IV Nashorn (Rhinoceros)
Weight 23.6 tons (24 tonnes)
Crew four
Armament one 88-mm PaK 43/1 (L/71) gun with 40 rounds
Armour hull nose and driver's plate 30 mm, glacis 10 mm, sides 20 mm, decking and belly 15 mm, tail 22 mm, superstructure 10 mm
Fording 3 feet 3 inches (1 m)
Overall length 27 feet 8½ inches (8.44 m)
Width 9 feet 8 inches (2.95 m)
Height 9 feet 7½ inches (2.94 m)
Other details as Ausf D tank

Above: A total of 473 of these heavy tank destroyers were constructed on the Geschützwagen III/IV, a front-engined PzKpfw IV chassis with the transmission and final drive of the PzKpfw III. The vehicle's earlier name was Hornisse (Hornet) but this was changed at Hitler's insistence to the more aggressive Nashorn (Rhinoceros)

heavily armoured mounting for the 150-mm *sIG* 33 heavy infantry gun which would have to go on the *PzKpfw* IV chassis. The vehicles were ordered in October 1942 and in service by April of the next year as *Sturmpanzer* IV *Brummbär* (Grizzly Bear) *Sdkfz* 166. Early Grizzly Bears were on the *Ausf* F and *Ausf* G chassis with a relatively high armoured superstructure with 100-mm sloping plates at the front and 70-mm protection at the sides, with a new version of the infantry gun the *SturmHaubitze* 43 L/12 in a ball mounting in the frontal plate. Later models on the H and J chassis had several differences, notably a modified gun-mounting with longer 'collar', a new driver's compartment with periscopes and in the last production run a new roomier superstructure with a machine-gun, lack of which had proved a serious weakness. A total of 313 Grizzly Bears saw service with the infantry gun companies of *Panzergrenadier* regiments and artillery units in Russia, Italy and France. They were powerful, if specialized, vehicles in the infrantry support role but reliability could be erratic due to the chassis being overloaded.

As the war progressed so the Germans began to lose air superiority and their armoured units became very vulnerable to Allied air attack. Suitable protection was urgently required and from 1943 *PzKpfw* IV chassis were diverted to become *Flakpanzer* IV anti-aircraft vehicles. Hitler demanded a *Flakpanzer* with twin 37-mm guns but as an interim measure either a single

Sturmpanzer IV Brummbär (Grizzly Bear)
Weight 27.7 tons (28.2 tonnes)
Crew five
Armament one 150-mm StuH 53 (L/12) howitzer
with 38 rounds
Armour hull nose 80 mm, sides 30 mm, decking
and tail 20 mm, belly 10 mm; superstructure
front 100 mm, sides 30–70 mm, top 20 mm,
rear 20–60 mm
Speed 24 mph (38 km/h)
Trench crossing 7 feet 3 inches (2.2 m)
Fording 3 feet 1½ inches (95 cm)
Height 8 feet (2.44 m)
Other details as Ausf D tank

Right: *A middle production Brummbär built in*
1944 after the success of the first 60 built in late
Spring 1943. Note the long 'sleeve' on the howitzer
barrel and the heavily armoured driver's position
with periscopes, instead of direct vision as on the
earlier model. PzKpfw IV type Schürtzen were
usually carried by these vehicles. The last Brumm-
bär produced had a new superstructure with more
vertical sides. Sturmpanzer battalions could de-
ploy up to 45 of these powerful assault howitzers

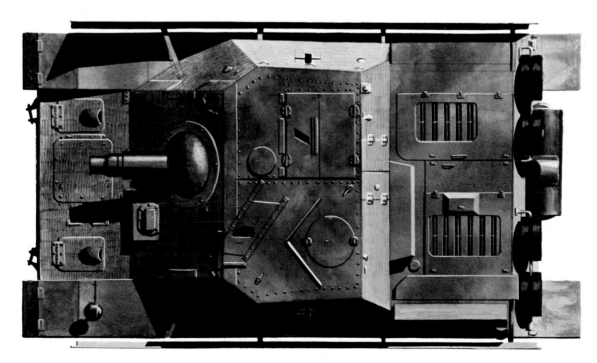

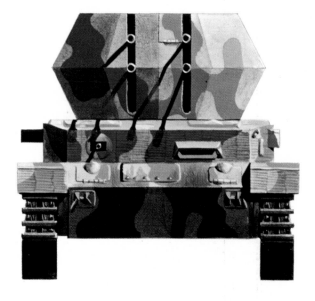

37-mm *FlaK* 43 or the quadruple 20-mm *Flakvierling* 38 was mounted in a high open 10-mm protected superstructure, the sides of which could drop to give all round traverse – if little protection to the gun crew who were behind a small open shield. However, they did provide some degree of extra mobility for the anti-aircraft platoons of tank regiments and 211 of these high, box-shaped *'Mobelwagen'* (furniture vans) were converted from *Ausf* H and J chassis.

A much better vehicle appeared in December 1943 which put the *Flakvierling* weapon in a 16-mm armoured revolving turret. This was known as *Wirbelwind* (Whirlwind) and was built by Ostbau using an *Ausf* J chassis. It was supplemented from March 1944 by the *Ostwind* (East Wind), built by Deutsche Eisenwerke, which put the 37-mm *FlaK* 43 in a slightly better protected 25-mm turret. The rates of fire of these weapons were respectively 800 to 1,800 rounds per minute and 80 to 160 rounds. Some 140 *Wirbelwind* and 40 *Ostwind* vehicles were built and some saw service but they could not do a great deal to mitigate the effects of Allied air power. However, even these vehicles were only considered as interim designs due to their open-topped turrets. A more permanent *leichte Flakpanzer* IV *Kugelblitz* (Fireball) was developed and built by Deutsche Eisenwerke with twin 30-mm *FlaK* 103/38 guns, developed from aircraft cannon, mounted in a fully rotating turret – together these could deliver up to 900 rounds per minute. Only five or six vehicles were completed and on troop trials when the war ended.

Over 10,500 vehicles were produced on the *PzKpfw* IV chassis and its derivatives including over 7,000 tanks. Except on the Eastern Front during 1941 and 1942, before up-gunning, the IV could usually perform adequately on the battlefield; although in the terms of 1944 and 1945 it was hardly up to the highest contemporary standards in protection or gun-power. Its capacity for constant improvement, however, bore witness to the foresight of its original designers. The IV enabled the Germans to keep a satisfactory vehicle coming off the production lines while developments of better tanks were completed, and Guderian was right to insist on its continued production. The 'Mark IV' was less famous than its later named compatriots but it was never replaced by the *Panther* and fought right up to the end of the war.

Flakpanzer IV Wirbelwind (Whirlwind)
Armament four 20-mm Flakvierling 38s with 3,200 rounds, one hull machine-gun with 1,350 rounds
Armour hull nose and driver's plate 80 mm, sides 30 mm; turret sides 16 mm.
Other details as the PzKpfw IV Ausf D

Left: A total of three or four of these quadruple 20-mm anti-aircraft vehicles the Flakpanzer IV Wirbelwind (Whirlwind) were deployed with the HQ companies of individual Panzer battalions from 1944. In all 3,200 rounds of 20-mm ammunition were carried, enough for 40 minutes at minimum firing rate; 1,350 rounds were carried for the hull machine-gun. Problems were faced with the relatively slow speed of traverse of the turret which was armoured to 16 mm. Hull armour was as in the Ausf J with 80 mm on the nose and driver's plate and 30 mm on the sides

PzKpfw 35(t) and 38(t)

When Germany finally dismembered Czechoslovakia in 1939 she inherited a long-established armaments industry that was already a noted producer of armoured fighting vehicles. The main manufacturers were Škoda and Českomoravská Kolben Daněk (ČKD) with Praga, who in 1935 had combined their research to develop a 10½-ton light tank. Based on Škoda's S II, the S IIa had a similar rear-mounted six-cylinder engine of 120-hp, driving through the rear sprockets to leave the fighting compartment uncluttered by the transmission. Both steering and gear change were pneumatically assisted to ease the strain on the driver, and an improved leaf-spring suspension was fitted with two sets of double bogie wheel pairs each side which equalized wear and gave long track life. Frontal armour protection was 35-mm to 28-mm and the gun remained the Škoda A3 with a prominent hydraulic buffer. A weakness of the design was the large-scale use of rivets in the hull construction: when hit by hostile fire these tended to fly off inside the tank with potentially disastrous results for the crew. It was accepted for Czech service in 1936 as the *LT 35* and it went into production at both plants; the ČKD vehicles had small differences from those of Škoda.

Some 298 *LT 35s* were in service with the Czechs by 1938, in which year they were used against the Sudeten Nazi *Freikorps* units during the period of tension leading up to the Munich Agreement. In 1939 some passed to Slovakia while others were taken over by the *Wehrmacht*, who kept the *LT 35* in production as the *PzKpfw 35(t)* (*t* for *tschechisch* – Czech). Some were used during the invasion of Poland and 106 were on hand with the Sixth *Panzer* Division when France was invaded, in May 1940. They were adequate substitutes for *PzKpfw IIIs*, more or less similarly protected – except for the rivets – but with guns of higher velocity (2,620 fps against 2,500 – 789 m/s against 762 m/s). The crew distribution of the 35(*t*) was not quite so lavish, commander, driver, gunner and loader/radio operator, but the advanced and now reliable transmission made it easy to keep up high average speeds over long distances and exploit the robustness of the suspension.

These attributes were also useful during the invasion of Russia, by which time 190 *PzKpfw 35(t)* tanks were available. However, the new Soviet tanks finally made the 35(*t*) obsolete although some chassis were converted for use as tractors and self-propelled 80-mm mortar carriages. A few were also kept by the Germans for second line policing duties.

The major Czech tank used by German forces was the ČKD/Praga *TNHP* which they redesignated *PzKpfw 38(t)*. This model had an

Above: This picture depicts a Czech LT-35 in pre-occupation yellow, green and brown camouflage. These vehicles formed a significant part of the Panzer forces during their opening victories. Originally very unreliable due to their mechanical complexity these problems were largely solved by the time the tanks went into action

Below: A PzKpfw 38(t) Ausf B dismounts from an armoured train. Armoured train units formed the least remembered part of the Panzerwaffe

improved suspension based on four elliptically-sprung large rubber-tyred road wheels. Two light tanks were initially produced with these features, a small four ton *AH* IV with two machine-guns and single return roller and a larger eight ton *TNH* with 100 hp engine, turret mounted 20-mm gun (in the prototype) and two return rollers. The large wheels may have been designed with the Middle East terrain in mind as Iran was the first customer for both, ordering 50 of each in 1935. They were delivered by 1937, the bigger vehicles with 37-mm guns as the *TNHP* (*P* for Persia). After competitive trials the *TNHP* was chosen for the Czech army as the *LT* 38 with a 125-hp Praga petrol engine and a Škoda turret armed with a 47·8-calibre A7 37·2-mm gun.

Only about 80 of these tanks were in service by March 1939 but production continued after the German occupation as the *PzKpfw* 38(*t*). They were used to equip Seventh and Eighth *Panzer* Divisions, who fielded 228 for the invasion of France in May 1940. With 25-mm armour they were only slightly less well-protected than the *PzKpfw* IIIs and *PzKpfw* IVs but their more powerful guns made up for this, and despite the weakness of a riveted hull the 38(*t*) soon made a

name for itself as a good and reliable tank. By the end of the year, 432 were on strength and by the time of the invasion of Russia over 750. At this period, in fact, the 38(*t*) formed a good 25 per cent of Germany's entire tank force.

ČKD, which became the Böhmisch Mährische Maschinenfabrik A G in 1940, produced some 1,168 *PzKpfw* 38(*t*)s before production of the tanks ceased in 1942. There were eight marks from *Ausf* A (the original 150 Czech vehicles) to G, while a number ordered by Sweden, but seized by the Germans before delivery, became *Ausf* S. There were only small differences between marks but later tanks had an extra 25-mm of armour attached to the nose and frontal plate. There were the usual command versions of all marks with extra radio equipment.

It was only the advent of the *T*-34 and KV series that forced the tank's obsolescence for the chassis was too light for up-gunning with a 75-mm *L*/48 and the entire *PzKpfw* IV turret. A light reconnaissance vehicle, the *Aufklärungspanzer* 38(*t*) (*SdKfz* 140/1), on the standard chassis, did appear in limited quantities in 1943 and 70 were in action the next year. Old 38(*t*) tanks lost their turrets to be used as tractors and ammunition carriers while a few were fitted as

smoke-screen layers, in which role they were known as *PzKpfw* 38(*t*) *mit Nebel Ausrüstung*.

Reliable and easy to maintain the *TNH* chassis was too valuable to lose and for the rest of the war its production continued as a self-propelled gun carriage. With the appearance of the latest Soviet tanks great stress had been put on the need for adequate anti-tank protection for the German forces and, just as the *PzKpfw* II chassis was pressed into service as a *Panzerjäger* anti-tank gun carrier, so the *TNH* seemed to offer an immediate solution to the problem of mobile anti-tank protection.

From March 1942 production began of a simple conversion which placed the Russian 54·8-calibre Model 36 76·2-mm field gun (the only guns capable of adequately penetrating Russian armour) on the 38(*t*) chassis. Captured examples of these guns were modified to take the longer German cartridge case and fitted with muzzle brakes as the 7·62-cm *PaK* 36(*r*). The gun had a muzzle velocity of 2,430 fps (740 m/s) or 3,249 fps (990 m/s) with *PzGr* 40 and could penetrate 83 mm of 30 degree armour at 500 yards (457 m) or 118 mm with *PzGr* 40. It was mounted centrally on the turretless 38(*t*) *Ausf* G chassis in a low, armoured superstructure

Left: This PzKpfw 38(t) artwork represents a typical vehicle of the 7th and 8th Panzer divisions in May 1940. Both these units played important parts in the German victory in the west. The turret markings show this particular tank to be the first tank of the third platoon of the sixth company of its regiment. The tank is finished in the standard 'Panzer Grey'

PzKpfw 38(t) Ausf D
Weight 8.4 tons (8.5 tonnes)
Crew four
Armament one 37.2-mm Škoda A7 (L/47.8) gun with 90 rounds and two 7.92-mm MG 37(*t*) (Model 37) machine-guns with 2,550 rounds
Armour hull nose, glacis and driver's plate 25 mm, sides 15–19 mm, decking 10 mm, belly 8 mm, tail 12 mm; turret front and sides 25 mm, top 10 mm, rear 15 mm
Engine one Praga EPA Model I inline six-cylinder, liquid-cooled petrol, 125-hp
Speed 35 mph (56 km/h)
Range 125 miles (200 km)
Trench crossing 6 feet 1 inch (1.85 m)
Vertical step 2 feet 7½ inches (80 cm)
Fording 3 feet (90 cm)
Overall length 15 feet 2 inches (4.62 m)
Width 6 feet 9 inches (2.06 m)
Height 7 feet 11 inches (2.41 m)

Above: *This first version of the Marder III Panzerjäger mounting the re-chambered Soviet M-36 76.2-mm gun was a modification of the PzKpfw 38(t) Ausf G chassis, note the 'straight' up-armoured driver's plate compared with the earlier artwork. The modifications to the basic tank were kept to a minimum to speed entry into service. Although very much an expedient this first 38(t) based tank destroyer proved most useful in both North Africa and Russia. The use of a captured Russian gun on a foreign chassis illustrates well the forced resourcefulness of German weapons procurement. The camouflage is a standard green on sand pattern typical of those used in both the Marder III's combat theatres*

Marder III

Weight 10.5 tons (10.7 tonnes)
Crew four
Armament one 76.2-mm PaK 36(r) (L/54.8) gun with 30 rounds and one 7.92-mm MG 37(t) machine-gun with 1,500 rounds
Armour hull nose and driver's plate 25 + 25 mm, sides and rear 15 mm, superstructure front and sides 16 mm, gun shield 11 mm
Engine one Praga EPA Model III, 125 hp
Speed 26 mph (42 km/h)
Range 115 miles (185 km)
Overall length 21 feet 1 inch (6.43 m)
Height 8 feet 2½ inches (2.5 m)
Other details as PzKpfw 38(t) Ausf D

with a three-sided shield around the gun itself to protect the two-man crew. The driver and radio operator remained in the hull front, the latter still working his *MG* 37(t) machine-gun. The full designation was *Panzerjäger 38 für 7·62 cm PaK 36 (SdKfz 139)*, but the name soon adopted was *Marder* (Marten) III.

By May 1942 some 120 had been built and all but three of these appear to have been sent to North Africa to deal with the Matilda – the Commonwealth forces were so impressed with the performance of the re-chambered German gun that they thought they were facing mobile 88-mm weapons! The remainder of the 344 vehicles produced in 1942 went to Russia, as originally intended, where allocated to the tank destroyer units of infantry and *Panzer* divisions they provided much needed support.

In May it was decided to supplement, and eventually replace, these stop-gap vehicles with a *Panzerjäger* mounting the new German 46-calibre 75-mm *PaK* 40/3 of similar performance to the Russian weapon and from June the new *Marder* III (*SdKfz* 138) began to appear. It was somewhat different to the *SdKfz* 139 with the gun's standard shield extended round the front and sides to give better protection to the gun crew. Some 400 were built in all; during production the Praga engine was up-rated to 150 hp and the de-

signation changed to *Ausf* H. This chassis was also used to provide a mobile mount for the 150-mm *sIG* 33 heavy infantry gun in the front of a large open superstructure. Designated *SdKfz* 138/1, production began in 1943 and the vehicle soon acquired the name *Bison*. It was issued to the infantry gun companies of *Panzergrenadier* regiments to provide their basic direct-fire heavy-support weapon with mobility.

However, all these vehicles were in the nature of improvisations on what was still basically a tank chassis and considerable re-design took place at BMM to specialize the chassis for the self-propelled gun role. The engine was moved from the rear to a central position with a new sloping front plate from which the machine-gun was deleted. The new fighting compartment was moved to the rear. This much better balanced layout, was designated *Ausf* M and had only a single return roller instead of the previous two. BMM produced both *Marder* IIIs and *Bison* on the new chassis with slightly differently shaped superstructures. This brought the totals of both types to 1,217 and 360 respectively by the time production ceased in May 1944, to concentrate all BMMs production on the *Hetzer*.

This *Jagdpanzer* 38(t) had been developed as a specialized light assault gun for the anti-tank battalions of the infantry divisions. The

Jagdpanzer 38(t) Hetzer
Weight 15.7 tons (16 tonnes)
Crew four
Armament one 75-mm PaK 39 (L/48) gun with 41 rounds and one 7.92-mm MG 34 machine-gun with 600 rounds
Armour front 60 mm, sides 20 mm, decking and tail 8 mm
Engine one Prage EPA/AC Model IV, inline six cylinder 150 hp
Speed 26 mph (42 km/h)
Range 112 miles (180 km)
Trench crossing 4 feet 3 inches (1.3 m)
Vertical step 25 inches (64 cm)
Fording 3 feet (90 cm)
Overall length 20 feet 7 inches (6.27 m)
Width 8 feet 8 inches (2.63 m)
Height 6 feet 11 inches (2.1 m)
Other details as PzKpfw 38(t) Ausf D

Above: *The Hetzer was a useful little tank destroyer although design weaknesses made it unpopular with its crews. The roof-mounted machine-gun could be traversed and fired from inside. The concept of this vehicle fitted Guderian's idea of a Jagdpanzer to defend the infantry from armour much better than the more impressive larger vehicles*

reliable 38(t) chassis was widened to accept a modified version of the PzKpfw IVs L/48 gun, designated PaK 39 L/48, without muzzle brake, in the front plate of a low, heavily-sloped super-structure. The tracks were also strengthened and widened slightly to improve mobility. A remotely controlled machine-gun was fitted to the superstructure to defend from hostile infantry. The prototype appeared in 1943 and from May the next year Hetzer (Baiter) began to enter service. At first only BMM produced the vehicle but from September 1944 Skoda also joined the programme. The Saukopf mantlet was enlarged to increase protection from bullet splash at maximum traverse and as production continued simplified wheels and idlers were adopted. A total of 1,577 were built.

Although Hetzer was a well-designed vehicle externally, it had many drawbacks. The traverse of the gun was the least of any German Jagd-panzer – 11 degrees to the right and 5 degrees to the left – which meant that the whole Hetzer usually had to be slewed to cover a target moving across the front thus exposing the limited side armour to the enemy. The crew layout was also poor with the loader and gunner on the left-hand side of a gun designed for right-handed operation; they were also isolated from the ammunition supply. The commander was remote in the right-hand rear of the vehicle with inadequate means of observation – and he could hardly co-operate with the gunner and driver in order to engage targets. Nevertheless, the Hetzer provided a real improvement in terms of armour over the more improvised Panzer-jäger it replaced and it went into service in both East and West. A number used in the Ardennes offensive were built with flame-throwers as Flammpanzer 38(t). A flame gun replaced the PaK 39 with a tube mounted over it to disguise

Below: *Despite its popularity among modern modellers, the Hetzer only saw service in the last year of war. The Czechs kept the vehicle in production after 1945 and Switzerland purchased a number for service with her Army. The wavy multi-coloured camouflage scheme applied to the vehicle in the photograph was often used on the Hetzer*

Flakpanzer 38(t)
Weight 9.6 tons (9.8 tonnes)
Crew five
Armament one 20-mm Flak 38 automatic AA gun
Overall length 15 feet 1 inch (4.6 m)
Width 7 feet 1 inch (2.15 m)
Height 7 feet 5 inches (2.25 m)
Other details as PzKpfw 38(t)

Right: Another vehicle on the front-engined 38(t) Ausf M self-propelled carriage was the Flakpanzer 38(t) (2 cm) (SdKfz 140). This was an improvisation necessitated by the growing need to defend Panzer formations from allied air superiority, an established fact on all fronts by 1943–4. The 9.6 ton (9.8 tonne) five-man vehicle mounted a single 20-mm FlaK 38 automatic AA gun. Despite a practical rate of fire of 220 rounds per minute this was hardly a very heavy armament for such a large chassis. Protection for the crew in action was minimal as the lightly armoured superstructure had to swing down to give all round traverse. Some were issued to the AA platoons of tank battalions but only 162 had been built by the time production of the Ausf M chassis ceased in 1944

Opposite page, top: The ubiquitous PzKpfw 38(t) was also used to provide mobility for the 150-mm sIG 33 infantry gun for the support of Panzergrenadiers. The first 'Bison' was as usual something of a makeshift utilizing the basic tank chassis but nevertheless these vehicles proved very useful in the direct infantry support role and saw widespread use

Opposite page, bottom: The new front-engined Ausf M version of the PzKpfw 38(t) chassis provided a much better balanced Marder III as this rear view shows. Almost 800 of this later type were built compared with about half that number of the earlier rear engined 75-mm Panzerjäger 38(t)

the fitting; 154 gallons of fuel were carried and the projector had a range of 66 yards (60·35 m). Several others were completed with a winch replacing the gun as *Bergepanzer* 38(*t*).

In 1944 a programme to adopt the basic rugged Czech chassis as a standard German type was drawn up; all factories that had been producing the *PzKpfw* IV were to be switched to the production of a new 38(*d*) (*deutsche* – German) chassis to provide a whole family of vehicles using the Tatra engine. Although with Germany's defeat these ambitious plans came to nothing, it was a tribute to the original Czech design that Germany planned to base virtually its entire specialized AFV production on it.

Czech tanks also formed the armoured forces of most of Germany's satellites and the cosmopolitan career of the ČKD/Praga *TNH* continued long after 1945. Czechoslovakia kept the *Hetzer* in production and service and sold 158 to Switzerland as the *PzJg* G13 between 1947 and 1952 and these were in service until 1970. Peru kept *LTP* tanks well into the 1950s. The chassis continued to be used in Sweden as an armoured personnel carrier until 1971, the last in the line of what was one of the most useful designs of armoured fighting vehicle history.

PzKpfw Tiger

Undoubtedly the most famous German tank of the war, the *Tiger,* became to the Allies the symbol of German technological superiority in armoured fighting vehicles. Although by no means invulnerable it was, at the time of its introduction, the most powerfully armed and well-protected tank in the world. To the Allied soldier every German tank became a Tiger, endowed with its offensive and defensive potency and a rather distorted view of German capabilities resulted, as Allied tactical and doctrinal shortcomings could be easily blamed on bigger enemy guns and thicker enemy armour.

The tank which fostered this legend dated back to a 1937 requirement for a 30-ton *Durchbruchswagen* or break-through vehicle. Various designs emerged as ideas changed and finally in May 1941, a month before the invasion of Russia, Hitler demanded a still more powerful tank superior to such heavily armoured vehicles as the French *Char* B and the British Matilda already encountered in the West. The existing plans were enlarged and a year later Henschel and Porsche demonstrated their prototypes.

Trials showed that the Henschel *VK 4501* design was superior and it was accepted into service as the *PzKpfw* VI *Tiger Ausf* H (*SdKfz* 181). The tank was renamed *PzKpfw Tiger Ausf* E in 1944. It was a relatively conventional vehicle with eight torsion bar suspended interleaved rubber-tyred road wheels each side. This suspension was designed to distribute the heavy weight of the tank as evenly as possible and it gave a very smooth and steady ride

to the tank. Reliability was, however, a problem and from early 1944 new all-steel resilient wheels were introduced which allowed the outside wheels to be deleted. The transmission was an advanced design to cope with the tank's 52-ton weight and a pre-selector gear box was fitted. As the Tiger was too heavy for the normal clutch and brake steering a hydraulic fully regenerative system operated by a driver's wheel was adopted which gave two turning radii in each gear. Control was very light but a price was paid in complexity of maintenance and construction.

The construction of the hull was relatively simple with a single unit welded superstructure in turn welded to the hull. As the tank had been designed before the full lessons of the *T-34* had been learnt, the superstructure armour was not sloped but it made up for this in thickness of protection. The turret, originally developed for the Porsche tank, was also simple and well protected, the sides and rear being formed from a single bent piece of 80-mm armour. It mounted in a heavy mantlet a 56-calibre *KwK* 36 88-mm gun which could penetrate 112 mm of 30 degree armour at 500 yards (457 m) using conventional armour-piercing shot. A machine-gun was fitted co-axially in the mantlet fired by a pedal operated by the gunner. There was another in the right hull-front operated by the radio operator/gunner. The other members of the crew were the driver in the left hull-front and the loader and commander who occupied the turret together with the gunner.

Given its weight the Tiger was a relatively

compact vehicle but its heaviness had disadvantages and both range and speed were very limited. The turret traverse was very low-geared and the gun could only be revolved slowly. Power tranverse was fitted but if this failed it took no less than 720 turns of the traversing wheel to get the gun round 360 degrees; this allowed well-handled Allied tanks to put shots into the more vulnerable sides and rear. Wide (725-mm) tracks were fitted to spread the weight although special narrow (520-mm) tracks had to be used for transport by rail to get the tank within the loading gauge. Even with its wide tracks the *Tiger* was too heavy for normal bridges and the first production vehicles were fitted to wade rivers.

Tiger tanks were intended for use in independent three company battalions of 30 tanks allocated to higher Army or Corps HQ for issue in the support role to stiffen various units. This remained the case despite Guderian's intention to make a *Tiger* battalion organic to each Panzer division. This occurred in few

Below: *One of the initial designs that led to the Tiger was the VK 3001(H) sometimes known as 'Leopard'. When made obsolete by changing requirements two of the four prototypes were lengthened and converted into tank destroyers mounting large 128-mm K 40 guns*

Opposite page, bottom: *This clear rear view of a 1942–3 production Tiger shows off the Feifel air pre-cleaners fitted for the dusty conditions in both Russia and North Africa*

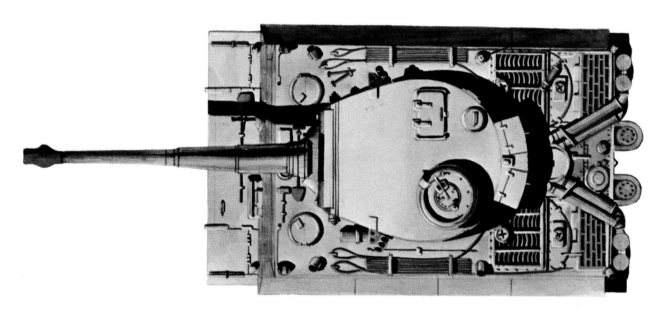

PzKpfw Tiger Ausf E
Weight 54.1 tons (55 tonnes)
Crew five
Armament one 88-mm KwK 36 (L/56) gun with
92 rounds and two 7.92-mm MG 34 machine-
guns with 5,700 rounds
Armour hull nose 100 mm, glacis 60 mm, driver's
plate 100 mm, sides 60–80 mm, decking and belly
26 mm, tail 82 mm; turret mantlet 110 mm,
front 100 mm, sides and rear 80 mm, top 26 mm
Engine one Maybach HL 230 P 45 water-cooled
petrol, 694-hp
Speed 23 mph (37 km/h)
Range 62 miles (100 km)
Trench crossing 7 feet 6 inches (2.29 m)
Vertical step 2 feet 7 inches (79 cm)
Fording 4 feet (1.22 m) or with special equipment
13 feet (3.96 m)
Overall length 27 feet 9 inches (8.46 m)
Width wide tracks: 12 feet 3 inches (3.73 m),
narrow tracks: 10 feet 4 inches (3.15 m)
Height 9 feet 6 inches (2.9 m)

Above: *A middle production PzKpfw VI Tiger
Ausf H, as the tank was originally designated.
Note the Feifel air cleaners and the cup like grenade
dischargers*

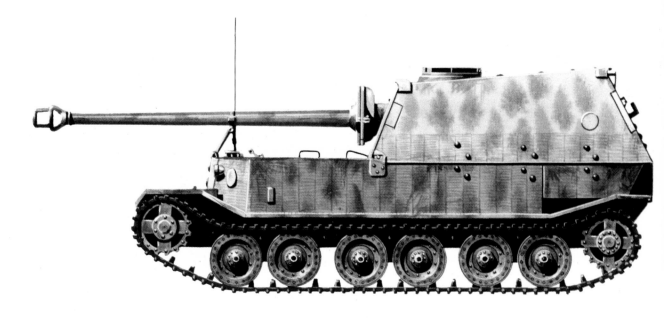

Panzerjager Tiger (P), Elefant
Weight 66.9 tons (68 tonnes)
Crew six
Armament one 88-mm StuK 43/2 (L/71) gun
with 50 rounds
Armour hull nose and driver's plate 100 + 100 mm,
sides 80 mm, decking 30 mm, belly 20 + 30 mm,
tail 80 mm; superstructure front 200 mm, sides
and rear 80 mm, top 30 mm
Engines two Maybach HL 120 TRM V-12 liquid
cooled petrol, 530-hp
Speed 12.5 mph (20 km/h)
Range 95 miles (153 km)
Trench crossing 10 feet 6 inches (3.20 m)
Vertical step 31 inches (78 cm)
Fording 4 feet (1.22 m)
Overall length 26 feet 8 inches (8.13 m)
Width 11 feet 1 inch (3.38 m)
Height 9 feet 10 inches (3.00 m)

Above: *The ill-fated Elefant tank destroyer. One
of the type's crucial weaknesses is clearly visible,
the lack of a hull machine-gun deleted in up-
armouring. As can be seen, vision to the rear and
sides was very limited and the 88-mm gun had a
traverse of only 14° in elevation, 8° in depression
and 14° either side. The extra protection was
added to the mantlet after the appearance of the
initial production vehicles*

Army units, the politically influential *Waffen SS* getting priority. *Tiger* tanks were also used with remote control demolition tanks in *Panzer Funklenk Abteilungen* (Radio Controlled Tank Battalions) in the assault role.

With a gun that could defeat the best Allied tank of its time, and frontal armour that could deflect any available Allied anti-tank projectile, the success of the *Tiger* seemed assured. Unfortunately Hitler's desire to see them in action as soon as possible led to fiasco: badly deployed in small quantities in unsuitable terrain, they were overwhelmed in their first offensive action near Leningrad in the autumn of 1942. Misused at Kursk, in July 1943, as a battering ram against mile upon mile of alerted *Pakfront* defences, defeat was on a larger scale. But in defence the *Tiger* showed its great strength and the real legend grew. When firing from camouflaged positions, using tracked mobility to move from one to the other and supported by other tanks or small groups of infantry the *Tiger* took a great deal of stalking and absorbed a disproportionate amount of Allied strength. On one famous occasion, in July 1944, a single *Tiger* of the 501 *Waffen SS* Heavy Tank Battalion held up the British Seventh Armoured Division, the Desert Rats, knocking out 25 armoured vehicles.

However, as time went on the *Tiger*'s superiority began to be eroded by new Allied tank

Above: *After the Kursk disaster several Elefant tank destroyers fell into Russian hands like this example here. The burnt superstructure is evidence of attack with flame-thrower or 'Molotov cocktail' petrol bombs. In action a wooden plank was wired to the rear on which German infantrymen could ride though at considerable risk*

Below: *The Tiger tanks of the 501st Heavy Tank Battalion were sent to Tunisia in January 1943 to reinforce the Axis position there. Although providing much useful support they did not prove completely invulnerable as shown by this example which has been blown on its side, probably by an Allied bomb or mine*

Sturmpanzer VI, Sturmtiger
Weight 66.9 tons (68 tonnes)
Crew five or six
Armament one 380-mm Raketenwerfer 61 with
12 rounds and one 7.92-mm MG 34 machine-gun
Armour superstructure front 150 mm, sides and
rear 84 mm, top 40 mm
Overall length 20 feet 8½ inches (6.30 m)
Height (with crane) 11 feet 4 inches (3.45 m)
Other details as PzKpfw IV Tiger Ausf E tank

Right: *This is one of the ten production Sturm-
tigers built on a 1944 production Ausf E tank
chassis with the later type wheel arrangement.
The prototype Sturmtiger had a similar suspension
to that of the tank previously illustrated. The
new arrangement placed a lower strain on the
wheel bearings and was less prone to packing
with mud or ice. The crane was to assist in loading
the 761-lb (345-kg) 380-mm rocket projectiles.
Their maximum range was over 6,000 yards
(5,500 m) but accuracy was not very great and
the Sturmtiger was meant to be used at closer
distances*

guns which had sufficient performance to penetrate the *Tiger*'s armour at average combat ranges (500 to 1,000 yards or 457 m to 914 m). Production was gradually phased out, and finally ceased in August 1944. In all 1,355 had been built, surprisingly few considering their tremendous reputation.

Although not selected for quantity production the *Tiger* offered by Dr Ferdinand Porsche, the *VK 4501* (P), saw limited service as a heavy assault gun chassis with the long (70-calibre) 88-mm *PaK 43/2* – a more powerful gun than that of the Tiger tank. Eighty-five chassis were converted by Alkett and they emerged as the *Panzerjäger Tiger* (P) (*SdKfz* 184); originally called *Ferdinand* after their designer they later received the official name *Elefant*. To make it more suitable for its task the chassis was changed in layout. The driver and radio operator remained in the front, the former fighting compartment now contained the engines – two standard Maybach 120 TR units – and a large fighting compartment was rear-mounted to minimize the long gun's overhang. The suspension remained on the Porsche principle with six large, steel-rimmed road wheels each side, in pairs mounted on three horizontal torsion bars. Drive was transmitted to rear sprockets via a Siemens Schuckert electric generator and two electric drive motors; steering was hydro-pneumatically assisted. Armour was increased to an extraordinary level, an extra 100-mm armour plate being bolted to the hull front, already armoured to this thickness. The superstructure received 200-mm armour at the front, the rest being armoured to 80 mm.

The *Elefant* was a formidable, if specialized, tank destroyer. Great things were expected of it and two army Tank Destroyer Battalions, 653 and 654 were re-equipped each with three companies of twelve *Elefant* with an HQ Company of two extra vehicles and a *PzKpfw* III. But its first major offensive role at Kursk was a disaster. Employed as an assault vehicle, to lead the infantry through the Soviet defences, its lack of flexibility or close-in defence capability was fatal. The *Elefant* is usually remembered for this failure but this was as much a product of misuse as intrinsic defects. As a long range tank killer it was supreme for its day, totally impervious frontally to enemy fire and capable of knocking out a *T-34* at three miles (4·83 km) in open country. The lessons of Kursk were learnt and those which were salvaged from the battlefield were fitted with machine-guns in the right hull-front. The two battalions served later in Russia and Italy, where they were used more prudently as mobile anti-tank pillboxes. Nevertheless, they remained awkward machines to operate, proving too heavy to be very mobile especially on Italian roads in bad weather; reliability and spare parts remained a problem and many had to be destroyed to escape capture.

The spectacular *Sturmtiger* assault howitzer originated from a requirement for a 210-mm assault howitzer to destroy heavy buildings which the Russians had converted into fortresses; no suitable weapon was available and a 380-mm heavy rocket launcher, developed as an anti-submarine weapon for the German Navy, was mounted in a Henschel *Tiger* chassis. A prototype was built in October 1943 but production only began at Alkett in August 1944 when ten standard chassis could be spared for re-working.

Sturmtiger was a clumsy vehicle, almost as heavy and certainly as specialized as *Elefant* and by the time it came into service there was little real function for a mobile assault rocket launcher as Germany's armies were on the defensive, not storming through Russian cities. Its fuel consumption, two gallons per mile, was even higher than the *Tiger* tanks, not very suitable for a country short of fuel with its synthetic oil plants coming under increasing air attack. *Sturmtiger* assault howitzers were committed to battle individually but were soon knocked out or captured.

Not many *Tiger* tanks were exported but Italy received 36 which were repossessed when she changed sides. Spain also managed to acquire a few as part of arms deals with Germany.

Below: *A captured Sturmtiger with an example of its ammunition in front of it. The spin-stabilized 761-lb (345-kg) rocket came in two versions, a normal high explosive and a hollow charge*

PzKpfw Panther

In early October 1941 the Fourth *Panzer* Division, part of Guderian's recently renamed Second *Panzer* Army was severely mauled by the new Soviet *T-34* tanks, encountered in significant numbers for the first time, near Mzensk. Tank losses were heavy and Guderian asked for a commission of representatives from all sides of German tank development to be sent to the front to report on the situation. Ideas of building a simple copy of the *T-34* were soon dismissed due to difficulties in copying the Soviet aluminium diesel engine and other problems with materials. Daimler Benz and MAN were therefore contracted to produce a new German *VK 3002* design to regain technological superiority.

Detailed specifications were issued in January 1942 with the following parameters: weight 35 tons, armament a 75-mm gun and co-axial machine-gun, maximum hull armour 60 mm and turret armour 100 mm and speed 37 mph (60 km/h). The design was also to include all the features of the *T-34* that made it such a formidable opponent: sloped armour which increased the effective thickness of any given plate, large road wheels to improve the ride and a long powerful gun overhanging the chassis, a feature which German designers had been wary of.

In April designs were submitted by Daimler Benz and MAN. Hitler preferred the former's but a special committee of the OKH's Army Weapons Department, set up to deal with the problem, came down in favour of the more conventional MAN design with a petrol engine, front drive sprockets. interleaved suspension and a turret set back to minimize the overhang problem. The hull was a single welded unit with

strengthened edges and well-sloped 55 degree 60-mm glacis armour. It was hoped that 250 *PzKpfw* V *Panther* (*SdKfz* 171) would be in service by May 1943; in September, the month that the first two pilot models appeared, Hitler raised this target to 600.

Tests showed that the design was overweight and underpowered but the first 20 vehicles designated *Ausf* A (but not to be confused with the later *Ausf* A mass produced after the battle of Kursk) were built to the prototype design in order to get production under way. To increase power a new HL 230 engine was fitted to subsequent production vehicles (*Ausf* D) together with a specially designed AK7 200 synchromesh gearbox and regenerative steering system to cope with the extra weight. Armour thickness was increased, in accordance with Hitler's order of June 1942, to 80 mm and the turret cupola was moved over to the right to simplify production. A new double-baffle gun muzzle brake began to be fitted.

In January the first production *Panther* appeared from both MAN and Daimler Benz – the latter having been brought in to meet the ambitious production schedule. By February MNH were also in the programme and Henschel and Demag joined later. In early 1943 *Ausf* A vehicles were officially reclassified D1 and production vehicles D2 while from May *Schürtzen* began to be fitted to guard the gap between the track top and the superstructure side. By that month 324 *Panther* tanks were in service.

The modifications to the *Panther Ausf* D2 were far from sufficient to solve its mechanical difficulties: the HL 230 engine was prone to

overheating and catching fire; the final drive was also a particular weakness, closely followed by the rest of the transmission and the steering. The increased weight (44 tons) also put extra stress on the rim bolts holding on the tyres which often necessitated much time consuming wheel removal to get at the offending failure. All this reflected insufficient development time but, despite Guderian's doubts, Hitler insisted that the *Panther* should be put into service as soon as possible, notably in time for the big armoured offensive at Kursk, Operation *Zitadelle*, which was delayed until July 1943 so that the new tanks could be used. Not surprisingly their *début* was inauspicious. Of the 200 *Panther* tanks in Hoth's Fourth *Panzer* Army, 160 were out of action by the end of the first day, and, nine days later, only 43 were in German hands. Many had broken down between the railheads and the front, others on the battlefield where, as they could not be easily towed, they had had to be left.

By the time the Kursk offensive was abandoned a new *Panther* model, rather confusingly called the *Ausf* A was in production, with a proper ball-mounted hull machine-gun and a better protected turret with new cupola. To ease production and in order to help mitigate the effects of the weight problem more tyre bolts were used in the wheels, 24 instead of 16.

Below: *The fate of many a Panther is exemplified by this burnt out Ausf A; neither its extra camouflage nor well-sloped armour has saved it from Allied firepower*
Opposite page, right: *A Panther Ausf G – note the new shape of the superstructure sides*

PzKpfw V Panther Ausf G
Weight 44.8 tons (45.5 tonnes)
Crew five
Armament one 75-mm KwK 42 (L/70) gun with 79 rounds and two 7.92-mm MG 34 machine-guns with 4,500 rounds
Armour hull front 80 mm, sides 50 mm, tail 40 mm, decking 15 mm, belly 20+13 mm; turret front 120–110 mm, sides and rear 45 mm, top 15 mm
Engine one Maybach HL 230 P 30 V-12 liquid-cooled petrol, 690-hp
Speed 34 mph (55 km/h)
Range 110 miles (177 km)
Trench crossing 6 feet 3 inches (1.9 m)
Vertical step 3 feet (90 cm)
Fording 4 feet 7 inches (1.4 m)
Overall length 29 feet 1 inch (8.86 m)
Width 10 feet 10 inches (3.30 m)
Height 9 feet 8 inches (2.95 m)

Below: This Ausf G Panther is identified as such by its new-style upward hinging hatches and the deletion of the driver's vision visor. A brown camouflage scheme has been applied over the basic sand yellow which was the standard finish for tanks leaving the factories in 1943–4

Jagdpanther
Weight 44.8 tons (45.5 tonnes)
Crew six
Armament one 88-mm PaK 43/3 (L/71) with
60 rounds and one 7.92-mm MG 34 machine-gun
with 600 rounds
Armour front 80 mm, mantlet 120 mm, sides
40–50 mm, decking 17 mm, belly 20 + 13 mm,
tail 40 mm
Speed 28.5 mph (46 km/h)
Range 100 miles (160 km)
Overall length 33 feet 3 inches (10.m)
Height 8 feet 11 inches (2.72 m)
Other details as PzKpfw V Panther Ausf G tank

Left: *A late model Jagdpanther with two-piece
gun barrel and simplified heavy bolted-on mantlet
collar. Schürtzen are fitted and the excellent
ballistic shape of the vehicle's armour can be seen.
Grey camouflage schemes became increasingly
common once more from late 1944. Jagdpanther
was a formidable vehicle; on July 30th 1944 three
from the 654 heavy AT battalion knocked out over
half a squadron of 15 British Churchills in a little
over a minute*

Ausf Ds were modified with extra bolts put in between the existing 16, making 32 in all. Although the engine became a little more reliable with extra cooling fans, improved bearings and other modifications, transmission failures remained endemic. New *Ausf* A turrets were fitted to *Ausf* D hulls by Henschel who kept the older chassis in production until November 1943. Altogether 1,768 *Panthers* were produced in 1943. Further modifications were planned to produce the *Panther* II *Ausf* F to simplify production and improve reliability but production was not quite under way when the war ended.

The need in 1944 was for as many tanks as possible of existing design in the front-line and some of the innovations of the proposed *Panther* II were added to the standard *Panther* in early 1944 to produce the *PzKpfw Panther Ausf* G. (The term *PzKpfw* V was now dropped.) To simplify production further the design of the sides of the tank were modified to make the rear stowage areas integral with the hull. The hull sides were also increased to 50-mm armour and the driver acquired a rotating periscope. Late production vehicles had a modified mantlet with thicker bottom to prevent the deflection of enemy rounds into the thin deck armour. In the last vehicles constructed all-steel resilient wheels were fitted which finally solved one dimension of the weight problem and the improved AK7-400 gearbox was also adopted. A progressive

Below: A knocked out Jagdpanther being inspected by an American soldier. This vehicle has the 'clean' gun barrel but the later style mantlet collar. Note the penetration made through the wheels. Jagdpanthers were vulnerable to such flanking shots and also to track damage caused by high-explosive fire

feature introduced in action just before the end of the war was the use of infra-red night fighting equipment which enabled the crews to engage targets at night up to 547 yards (500 m) away.

During 1944 and 1945 over 3,740 *Panther* tanks were produced, more than any other single type of German tank in this period. It provided a numerous and powerful supplement to the *PzKpfw* IV as the major battle tank of the *Panzer* divisions. Each division was supposed to contain one battalion of *Panther* tanks together with one of *PzKpfw* IV but as usual the *élite Waffen SS* tended to get priority.

Ausf A and G vehicles played a prominent part in the large-scale defensive tank battles in Normandy. Here mobility was less important than their formidable frontal protection and 3,068 fps (935 m/s) gun that could penetrate over 120 mm of 30-degree plate at 1,000 yards (914 m). Only crushing Allied air and numerical superiority prevented this technological advantage becoming decisive strategically.

The *Panther* had a small number of special versions, the most famous was the *Jagdpanther* (Hunting Panther) tank destroyer. This was developed in 1943 as a well-protected mobile mount for the formidable *PaK* 43 88-mm gun with its 3,708 fps (1,130 m/s) muzzle velocity and which could penetrate 226 mm of 30 degree armour at 500 yards (457 m). *Nashorn* was too lightly protected and *Elefant* too expensive, complex and vulnerable for the task, so it was decided to use the *Panther* chassis with a low sloped front superstructure. The gun was fitted in the frontal plate with 11-degree traverse to each side, 8-degree elevation and 14-degree depression and a machine-gun was fitted in the right hull front to prevent a repetition of the Kursk *débâcle*. A crew of six was needed: commander,

gunner, wireless operator/machine-gunner, driver and two loaders for the heavy, clumsy ammunition. First called *Panzerjäger Panther* (*SfKfz* 173) it received from Hitler the designation *Jagdpanther* in 1944.

Production began in December 1943 and MIAG had it well under way by May using *Ausf* G chassis with an improved AK7-400 gearbox to take the extra weight. The vehicles were issued to special tank destroyer battalions composed of 30 *Jagdpanther* which were kept under central army control. It was intended to build 150 *Jagdpanther* a month but an increasingly bombed and starved German industry could not keep up and only 382 were eventually completed. Several other *Panther*-based vehicles saw service: the demand for heavy recovery vehicles after Kursk resulted in the *Bergepanzer Panther* or *Bergepanther* recovery vehicle (*SdKfz* 179); *Ausf* D, A and G vehicles were converted to *Befehlspanzer* (command tanks) and there was also an artillery observation post vehicle or *Beobachtungspanzer* (*SdKfz* 172).

Some 5,508 examples of the *Panther* tank were built in all. Although considered excessively large by the Ministry of Armaments and retaining mechanical problems which were never entirely ironed out, it was probably the best all round German tank of the war, not too heavy but well-armoured and armed. Its complexity hindered mass production but two could be built in as many man-hours as one *Tiger* and, in the 1944 rationalization plan, it was hoped to concentrate on it and the *Panther* II as the main battle tanks of the 1945 German Army. A total of 400 a month was planned but this was far beyond the capacity of German industry, even though 132 *Ausf* Gs were still produced as late as February 1945.

PzKpfw Tiger Ausf B

In August 1942 specifications were issued for a modified *Tiger* tank incorporating the latest sloped armour of the *T-34* and *Panther*, increased protection and the longer 71-calibre 88-mm gun. It was hoped that this would keep German tanks ahead of any future Soviet designs in the gun/armour race. Both Porsche and Henschel were again asked to tender and the former produced modified *VK* 4502 (P) versions of his earlier *Tiger* (P). Interest was shown in a version with electric drive and rear mounted 88-mm gun, and, with Porsche this time sure of a production order, construction of turrets was begun. But the need for copper, a scarce commodity in blockaded Germany, for the electric transmission resulted in the Henschel *VK* 4503 (H) design being chosen for service.

Ordered in January 1943 the first *PzKpfw* VI *Tiger* II or *Ausf* B (*SdKfz* 182) did not appear until the end of the year due to the need for close liaison with MAN in order to standardize as many components as possible with the proposed *Panther* II – the *Tiger* II, for example used the same engine as late model *Panther* tanks. Suspension was on the classic German principle with conventional torsion bars but the arrangement of wheels was slightly altered compared with the earlier *Tiger*; the interleaved system was abandoned due to the difficulty of access to the inner wheels and the tendency of these arrangements to freeze or jam and the nine sets of double bogie wheels were set merely to overlap. Resilient steel wheels were also employed to improve reliability. As with the older

Tiger two sets of tracks were provided: one for action and the other for transport to minimize the vehicle's width.

Production was under way by February 1944 when the first eight vehicles were produced by Henschel side by side with 95 standard *Tiger Ausf* Es. It was the intention to produce 145 *Tiger* II *Ausf* Bs per month by 1945 but this proved impossible and the total production run was only 484. The first 50 vehicles carried the turret designed for the Porsche tank, the others had the proper Henschel turret with its heavier armour and squared-off front which prevented shots being deflected down into the hull. Some Porsche turreted vehicles and all the Henschel turreted tanks had a two-piece gun barrel which allowed differential wear to be exploited in replacement of parts.

Tiger Ausf B, known to its own side as *Königstiger* and to the English-speaking world as Royal or King Tiger, was a formidable and huge vehicle. It was at once the heaviest, most thickly protected and most powerfully armed battle tank to see service in any numbers during the war. Its armour would do justice to a modern main battle tank and its gun had a muzzle velocity of 3,220 fps (981 m/s) and could penetrate 182 mm of 30-degree armour at 500 yards (457 m). This was more than enough to deal with the heaviest Soviet JS IIs. But a price had to be paid in size, weight and reliability. Hull length was 23 feet 8½ inches (7·22 m) and height was also greater. Most important, weight was also increased, by over ten tons. Although, sur-

prisingly, this did not affect performance 'on paper', speed and radius of action actually being slightly increased, power/weight ratio, manoeuvrability and ground pressure all suffered. Also, inevitably, reliability was a problem with a highly stressed engine and transmission.

These drawbacks did not matter too much in defensive battles but it was a significant drawback in, for example, the Ardennes offensive. Indeed, although *Tiger* IIs were available to Obersturmführer (Lieutenant-Colonel) Jochen Peiper he chose *PzKpfw* IVs and *Panther* tanks to lead his *Kampfgruppe* that spearheaded the advance of First *SS Panzer* Division. The *Tiger* II had made its combat *début* on the Eastern Front in May 1944 and was in service in France by August of the same year. It was allocated in the same way as the *Tiger* I being either kept in independent battalions or being formed into the tank regiments of privileged *Panzer* divisions. With such a small production run the *Tiger* II was never a common tank and, although the previously mentioned Ardennes offensive is usually associated with it, there were comparatively few in action.

Opposite page, right: *A Tiger Ausf B with standard Henschel turret. These vehicles were used, to a limited extent, in the closing months of the war only being employed in any numbers in the Ardennes and in the defence of Budapest in late 1944 and early 1945*
Below: *One of the first 50 Royal Tiger tanks with Porsche turret, knocked out in Normandy*

PzKpfw Tiger Ausf B
Weight 68.7 tons (69.4 tonnes)
Crew five
Armament one 88-mm KwK 43 (L/71) gun with
80 rounds and two 7.92-mm MG 34 machine-
guns with 5,850 rounds
Armour hull nose 100 mm, glacis 150 mm, sides
and tail 80 mm, decking 40 mm; turret front
185 mm, sides and rear 80 mm, top 44 mm
Engine one Maybach HL 230 P 30 V-12 liquid-
cooled petrol, 600-hp
Speed 23.6 mph (38 km/h)
Range 68.4 miles (110 km)
Trench crossing 8 feet 2 inches (2.5 m)
Vertical step 2 feet 9½ inches (85 cm)
Fording 5 feet 3 inches (1.6 m)
Overall length 33 feet 8 inches (10.26 m)
Width wide tracks: 12 feet 3½ inches (4.72 m),
narrow tracks: 10 feet 8¾ inches (3.27 m)
Height 10 feet 1½ inches (3.08 m)

If the Royal Tiger was the most powerful tank of the war then its tank destroyer derivative *Jagdtiger* (*SdKfz* 186) was the most powerful armoured vehicle. It was German policy to build a limited-traverse mounting of the 'next size gun up' on any given tank chassis and the Royal Tiger was no exception. A lengthened hull was used with a large fixed central superstructure armoured to the extraordinary frontal thickness of 250 mm and mounting a 55-calibre 128-mm *PaK* 80 – a weapon which could out-range any other tank gun and penetrate any other AFV. Earlier models mounted the shorter 128-mm *PaK* 44 and some had to make do with the *Jagdpanther*'s 88-mm *PaK* 43/3. The tank's machine-gun in the hull front was retained and a grenade launcher was also fitted, as in the tank, to deter stalkers.

The first mock-up appeared in October 1943; 150 were ordered but only 70 were completed by the end of the war. The close connection between the plant – Neibelüngenwerke – and the designer enabled Dr Porsche to tinker with the design. One *Jagdtiger* was fitted with a Porsche type suspension with eight overlapping wheels instead of nine; this vehicle may also have been the *Jagdtiger* experimentally fitted with a Porsche *SLa* 16 (Type 212) 700-hp diesel engine. Neither of these developments went further due to the need to concentrate on existing designs if any vehicles were to be built at all. A more powerful engine would at least have alleviated the *Jagdtiger*'s greatest drawback – its extra-ordinary weight of over 70½ tons, more than any other AFV that has ever seen widespread service in any army. This created severe tactical problems as the *Jagdtiger* was impossible to operate on anything but strong roads and the hardest ground and its practical maximum road speed was also very slow, no more than seven to nine mph (11 to 14 km/h).

The *Jagdtiger* equipped independent tank destroyer battalions, usually those of the *Waffen SS*. They were used as infantry support vehicles and as stiffeners in the *Panzer* forces used in the Ardennes offensive but their lack of mobility was a severe drawback and they were most suitable for the final last ditch stands against the Allied forces closing into Germany. Impenetrable to Allied fire, the *Jagdtiger* provided a formidable static anti-tank defence.

There were two other versions of the *Tiger* II *Ausf* B. One, the *Panzerbefehlswagen* command vehicle, was a normal tank with extra radio equipment added and armament stowage decreased in the usual manner; few were produced. The other, the largest of the family of weapons carriers, had *Tiger* II chassis with two extra bogie wheels fitted with a large protected rear superstructure to carry a dismountable 170-mm gun or a 210-mm howitzer. A prototype was almost completed when the war ended. After the war some *Tiger* II tanks served with the French army until being expanded as targets.

The massive proportions of the *Tiger* II series reflected Hitler's enthusiasm for large AFVs and there were plans for even larger vehicles. In 1942 he had given personal authorization to Porsche to develop a huge 185-ton *Maus* (Mouse) tank with 200-mm armour and an armament of one 128-mm gun with co-axial 75-mm. This led the Army Weapons Office to look for a slightly less impractical design of 'super tank'. At first it was hoped to build a bigger version of *Tiger* II developed by Krupp as the *VK* 7001 (K) called *Tiger-Maus* or *Löwe* (Lion). A model was built showing a redesigned hull with rear-mounted 128-mm armed turret and steeply-sloped armour. This was eventually cancelled and efforts concentrated on the development of the largest of a planned *E* (*Entwicklung* – development) series of standardized tanks. Adler developed the 140-ton *E*-100 with a suspension based on the *Tiger* II but with helical springs instead of torsion bars, and its main armament was increased to 150-mm calibre. One prototype petrol-engined *Maus* was built and another with a diesel engine.

Although super-tank projects had soon to be downgraded much time and energy were wasted on what had been described by Porsche himself as mere mobile fortifications. Even less rational were plans for a 1,500-ton tank with one 800-mm gun, two 150-mm weapons and 250-mm armour powered by four U-Boat engines! Such a land monitor would have been the final monument to the German failure to understand that practicality and serviceability were of greater importance than mere technological virtue.

Jagdtiger
Weight 70.6 tons (71.7 tonnes)
Crew six
Armament one 128-mm PaK 80 (L/55) gun with 38 rounds and one MG 34 machine-gun with 2,925 rounds
Armour superstructure front 250 mm, sides and rear 80 mm, top 40 mm
Overall length 35 feet (10.66 m)
Height 9 feet 3 inches (2.82 m)
Other details as Tiger Ausf B tank

Opposite page: A battalion of normal production Royal Tigers parade late in 1944. Such pictures made good propaganda but belied Germany's true armoured strength at this time. The two piece gun barrel and 'Zimmerit' anti magnetic-mine paste are clearly visible on the commander's vehicle. Note how deeply the heavy vehicles have sunk into the ground

Left: Not even massive armour and firepower could hold out for ever. This Jagdtiger has been used as a dug in pill box before being overwhelmed by American firepower

Below: The spectacular Jagdtiger, the most powerful service AFV of the war, did not see a great deal of action, only being available in very limited quantities by the end of the war

ITALY

The Italian armoured forces in World War II fought well within the limitations of their inferior and often unreliable equipment and essentially conservative principles. In 1926 a separate *Corpo Carristi* (Armoured Corps) was formed and the next year its 100 Fiat 3000 tanks (machine-gun armed modifications of the Renault FT) were organized into a five-battalion *Reggimento Carri Armati* (Army Tank Regiment). Although 80 more Model 30 3000s were built with 37-mm guns, the small Carden Loyd tankette (later modified and designated the *L* 3) seemed the best means of quickly boosting Italy's armoured reserves, given her limited industrial capacity. From 1933 developed versions were procured in large quantities from Fiat-Ansaldo. They were allocated to cavalry groups and to infantry support battalions, re-organized in 1936 into four administrative infantry tank regiments. This combination of technology and organization proved adequate in Ethiopia in 1934–5, but not in Spain against more sophisticated opposition from anti-tank guns and Soviet-made tanks.

From 1936 the Italians began to toy with the idea of larger armoured formations to maximize the power of the projected, heavier breakthrough tank eventually designated M 11/39. First *Brigata Motomeccanizzata* (Mechanized Brigade) was formed from a two-company tankette battalion, a light infantry (*bersaglieri*) regiment, an artillery battery and engineer platoon. The next year this was enlarged to form two *brigate corazzate* (armoured brigades), each with a new regiment of three to four tankette battalions, a motorized *bersaglieri* regiment, anti-tank and anti-aircraft guns and engineers.

Although the organization of the brigade, like that of the French *DCR*, was essentially traditional and reflected the conservative doctrine of Italian high command, the Italians did eventually begin to take notice of German theories of tank warfare. In 1939, after air-supported mechanized operations in Albania, exercises in guerra di rapido corso were carried out in Italy. In these Second *Brigata Corazzata* took part, expanded with field artillery and extra support units into the 132nd *Ariete* Armoured Division. First Armoured Brigade was re-formed on similar lines as the 131st *Centauro* and by the end of the year the 133rd *Littorio* had been converted from an infantry division.

Italy had about 1,500 tanks available in 1940, of which 100 were new *M* 11/39 mediums. A few were old 3000s and the rest *L* 3 tankettes. The first vehicles to see service were in independent battalions in southern France, East Africa and the Western Desert. In the last-named theatre most armour was eventually formed into two four-battalion Groups and by December 1940 into a Special Armoured Brigade, but the tanks still tended to be deployed piecemeal. Moreover, the general inferiority of most of them to British tanks and armoured cars made the Italians cautious and the Allied victory more certain.

Quantity production of *M* 13/40s, more heavily armed and armoured modern tanks, was only just getting under way, and these were rushed to North Africa in individual battalions. Even when coherent divisions were available, albeit still largely *L* 3 equipped, they were often dispersed in action. *Ariete* was the first to be completely equipped with modern *M* 13/40s and used by Rommel in his first offensive. *Centauro* was used piecemeal during Greece in the unsuccessful invasion in 1940 and again in Yugoslavia with *Littorio*. The latter was part of a mechanized corps with two unmotorized infantry divisions, so the armour soon outran its support. This combination of incompatible units was due to both shortage of equipment, and, one suspects, lack of proper understanding of the true principles of mechanized operations. It was a common Italian failing. Only in August 1941 was a proper Mobile Army Corps (*Corpo d'armata di Manovra*) formed from a union of the *Ariete* with the *Trieste* motorized infantry division,

and an armoured corps reconnaissance unit.

When it was decided to transfer the *Littorio* to Africa at the end of 1941 its establishment was revised to a three-battalion *M* 13/40 regiment, a *bersaglieri* regiment, an artillery regiment (including two groups of the new *Semovente* 75-mm assault guns), two desert patrol units, support elements and extra reconnaissance grouping of a *bersaglieri* battalion and group of *L* 6/40 light tanks. But the units never fought together: the infantry were sunk in transit and other troops were used to reinforce units which had already been in action. The *Ariete* was also re-structured along the new lines at the beginning of 1942 but both divisions were destroyed at Alamein.

The *Centauro*, also organized along the new lines with an armoured grouping of *L* 6/40s and *Semovente* 47/32s, was sent to Africa in confusion in late 1942 and was never re-assembled. Its name was taken by an *ad hoc* grouping of some of its elements with the survivors of other divisions. After combat with Allied forces it was destroyed with the Axis collapse in Tunisia.

The Italian failure seems both administrative and logistical for by 1942 tank production was well under way. Considering Italy's limited industrial capacity it was a considerable achievement to produce over 2,000 medium tanks between 1940 and 1943, as well as light tanks and *Semoventi*. The weakness lay in the quality of the vehicles; Italian tanks fell behind in the technological race. Plans for Italian production of German tanks, first *PzKpfw* III *Ausf* J and then *PzKpfw* IV and *Panther*, came to nothing, although 36 *Tigers* were supplied in 1941 and some German *PzKpfw* IVs fought in Italian hands in Russia. There were also plans to produce a virtual copy of the British Crusader, the *Carro Armato Celere Sahariano*, for desert warfare but this was only a prototype by the time of Axis defeat in North Africa.

The major new Italian tank project, the *P* 26/40, began in 1940 to provide a heavy fourth com-

pany in every *M* 13/40 battalion but was badly delayed. The tank finally emerged as a 26-ton diesel-powered vehicle with 50-mm armour and 34-calibre 75-mm gun. But by September 1943 and Italy's surrender, only 24 had been built out of an order of 1,000 and these were taken and used by the Germans. Production of existing mediums had already stopped in March to concentrate on Semoventi.

In April 1943 a new 135th *Ariete* II Armoured Cavalry Division was formed with an establishment of an armoured regiment of three battalions (one company of *M* 15/42s and two of *Semoventi* 75/18 in each), a motorized cavalry regiment, two regiments of artillery (one completely *Semovente*-equipped) and an SP anti-tank battalion, with *Semovente*-equipped armoured grouping and support echelons. After some brief fighting against the Germans this unit was disbanded, as was the *Centauro* II division formed from two Blackshirt units, the *Legionario* motorized regiment and *Leonessa* armoured group. This was originally grouped with the 131st Tank Regiment (equipped with *L* 3s, *L* 6/40s and French R-35s) artillery and other support as the M Division. The 131st were sent on their own to Sicily and, when Mussolini was overthrown, the Fascist units, whose loyalty was in doubt, were joined by a reliable *bersaglieri* regiment and medium tank battalion. With the surrender, the army units briefly fought the Germans, but *Leonessa* and another Blackshirt armoured group, *Leoncello*, continued to fight the Allies in the Army of the Socialist Italian Republic.

Left: A company of M 13/40 tanks pictured in Cyrenaica during Rommel's final drive on Egypt

L 3 and L 6 Light Tanks

The *L* 3 and *L* 6 Light tanks were developed from four Carden Loyd Mark VI tankettes originally purchased from Britain in 1929. The tankette was re-designated *Carro Veloce* (fast tank) 29, and 21 were completed under licence by Fiat-Ansaldo. The first vehicles were vulnerable, semi-open and armed with a single machine-gun. By 1931 development of a fully-enclosed, more heavily-armoured *CV* 3 was under way and this was accepted for service as the *CV* 33.

The new tankette was designed to operate as a battle tank and weight was almost doubled from the 1.7 tons of the *CV* 29. Construction was of riveted armour plates and the suspension was of an improved Carden Loyd type with, each side, two elliptically sprung, rubber-tyred three-wheel bogie assemblies and a single unsprung wheel at the rear. Drive was from the transverse rear-mounted engine through a gearbox in front of the driver to the front sprockets. Steering was by levers and epicyclic clutch.

The driver sat on the right and the commander/gunner on the left. In the first two prototypes the latter worked a 6.5-mm Revelli Fiat water-cooled machine-gun but from the third prototype this was replaced with a lighter,

similar calibre air-cooled Fiat Type 14 weapon. In 1935 the slightly modified *CV* 33 Series II mounted two 8-mm Fiat Model 14/35 machine guns and the older vehicles were altered to the new standard. The original plans for a 37-mm armed *CV* 33 never materialized.

The tankettes were deployed as *carri d'assalto* in infantry support battalions or as *carri veloci* in cavalry groups with 43 vehicles in each. There were three companies/squadrons each of 13 tankettes, three platoons of four plus a commander. From 1935 the tank battalions included new specialized versions. A flame-thrower tank (*carro lanciafiamme*) was developed to enhance infantry support capabilities. The flame-gun had a range of 50–100 yards (46–92 metres) while its fuel was carried at first in an armoured box over the engine compartment, and later, more safely, in an armoured trailer. One platoon in each tank company was eventually equipped with these. A *carro radio* was also issued to each tank company commander with a large circular type aerial on the left-hand side and battery compartments mounted over the engine. Armament was sometimes deleted in order to fit a map table. Radio tanks were not issued to the Cavalry until

1940 when the *gruppo squadroni* went on to a five-squadron establishment, one a command squadron with five *carri radio*. Machine-gun ammunition trailers, in use by the tank battalions for some time, were then issued to the cavalry.

A spectacular modification, produced only in limited quantities, was the *CV* 33/II *Pasarella* bridgelayer developed by the Engineers. This was a winch-fitted tankette which towed a seven-metre (23 feet) bridge in sections on a trailer. When the battlefield was reached the bridge was assembled and pushed on a wheel assembly to the obstacle on which it was lowered into position. As far as is known this was not used in action. Recovery vehicles fitted with towing equipment (and without armament) were built.

In 1936, after 760 *CV* 33s a new version of the tankette appeared, the *CV* 35. This had a bolted superstructure, improved vision equipment and other modifications. There were both flame-thrower and radio versions. From 1938 new 8-mm Breda Model 38 machine-guns began to be fitted to both new and old vehicles and that same year the tank was redesignated *Carro Armato L* 3/33 and *L* 3/35 (*L* for *leggero* – light; 3 for the tonnage and 33 and 35 for the year of

Below: *An L 3/35 Lf shows off its spectacular capabilities during the siege of Tobruk in 1941. These flame-thrower tankettes were widely used for infantry support*

introduction). Tests the previous year with a *CV* 33 fitted with a new superstructure and turret-mounted 20-mm gun were not followed up and neither were tests with a 47-mm gun tank destroyer on the *L* 3 chassis in 1939–40, but some *L* 3s were fitted with an 8-mm Fiat or Breda machine-gun on an AA mount and saw service thus in small quantities. A final *L* 3/38 variant, with twin large road wheels replacing the previous triple bogie assemblies came into service during 1939.

About 2,500 standard *L* 3s were built. Almost 500 saw service during the conquest of Ethiopia where, against unsophisticated opposition, their terrain-crossing ability stood them in good stead. One battalion, followed later by a second, was sent to support the Italian volunteer division in the Spanish Civil War but here, against anti-tank guns and Soviet-made tanks, the story was different, and success more difficult to attain.

Despite these lessons, when Italy entered World War II the overwhelming majority of her tanks remained *L* 3s, including most of those equipping the armoured regiments of the three armoured divisions. *L* 3s fought with Italian forces on all fronts: in France, North Africa (where the long distances showed up reliability problems), the Balkans and even Russia. Despite attempts to up-gun some with 20-mm Solothurn anti-tank guns *L* 3s were hopelessly outclassed against any real opposition. Some, however, were still in first-line Italian service in 1943 and were used by the Germans after the Italian surrender; while both the Greek Army and the Yugoslav partisans used them against their former owners. The *L* 3 sold widely before the war to Afghanistan, Albania, Austria, Bolivia, Brazil, Bulgaria, China, Hungary, Iraq and Salvador.

The other type of light tank to see service with the Italian Army in World War II was the *L* 6/40. The design dated back to 1936 when a larger and more heavily-armed five-ton, two-man tank was developed by Fiat-Ansaldo as a possible *L* 3 replacement. At first the *L* 3 layout was followed with a 37-mm gun in the hull but the next example also had a turret with twin 8-mm machine-guns and a third prototype had a turret-mounted 37-mm. The suspension was on the torsion bar principle with two sets of double-wheel bogies each side.

The Italian army were, at first, uninterested and the design was improved with exports only in mind, though after tests it was ordered to replace *L* 3s in cavalry formations. The new tank which appeared in 1940 was slightly up in weight (hence the designation *L* 6/40) with an improved suspension. Prototypes had a turret with a 37-mm gun or twin machine-guns, but the production version mounted an automatic Breda 20-mm gun and co-axial machine-gun. The same turret was also mounted on the *Autoblinda* 41 armoured car. Weight of the *L* 6 was actually nearer seven tons, length 12 feet 7 inches (3.84 metres) and width and height 6 feet 1 inch (1.85 metres). A four-cylinder Fiat (SPA) engine of about 70 hp drove the vehicle at 28 mph (45 km/h). In all about 500 were produced; a version with a flame-thrower was not adopted.

The *L* 6/40, which was fitted with radio, first saw action with the reconnaissance group of the *CAM* at the end of 1941 when four were sent for service trials. The first formation to use the tank in quantity was the Third Group of the *Lancieri di Novara* regiment sent to North Africa as the armoured group of *Littorio* Armoured Division in the spring of 1942. Generally *L* 6/40s' were issued to the reconnaissance formations of the Italian Army and saw service in Russia, for anti-partisan work in Yugoslavia (where some were captured and used against the Axis forces) and also in Sicily.

Possibly owing to shortage of turrets and 20-mm guns the later chassis were completed as *Semovente Da* 47/32 *Su Scafo L* 40 – self-propelled anti-tank guns with the weapon mounted in an open-box superstructure. Estimates of numbers of these vary from 100 to 250. There was a radio-equipped platoon commander's vehicle and a company commander's vehicle with dummy guns. These *Semoventi* were perhaps first used in the Western Desert in 1942 but they were certainly later in action in Tunisia. After the Italian surrender the survivors were used by the *Wehrmacht* together with the original tanks. *L* 6/40 light tanks remained in Italian service until well after the war.

Carro Armato L 3/35 Lf
Weight 3.4 tons (3.4 tonnes)
Crew two
Armament one FIAT-OCI flame-thrower with 520 litres fuel in trailer
Armour hull nose and driver's plate 13.5 mm, glacis 8.5 mm, sides and tail 8.5 mm, decking 6 mm, belly 6–13.5 mm.
Engine FIAT-SPA CV 3 four-cylinder inline liquid-cooled petrol, 43-hp
Speed 26 mph (42 km/h)
Range 75 miles (120 km)
Trench crossing 4 feet 10 inches (1.45 m)
Vertical step 2 feet 4 inches (70 cm)
Fording 2 feet 4 inches (70 cm)
Overall length 10 feet 5 inches (3.17 m)
Width 4 feet (1.4 m)
Height 4 feet 3 inches (1.29 cm)

Below: *An L 3/33 Lf and 3/35 Lf flame-thrower pictured without its fuel trailer. The obvious rivets on the superstructure of the top artwork mark this as the later model, the L 3/33 having a 'cleaner' appearance. The standard tankette mounted twin Fiat or Breda machine-guns in place of the long flame-thrower gun in the left of the superstructure front. These small and ineffectual vehicles were the main equipment of Italy's armoured forces in 1940 and reflected the general Italian weakness in mechanized warfare*

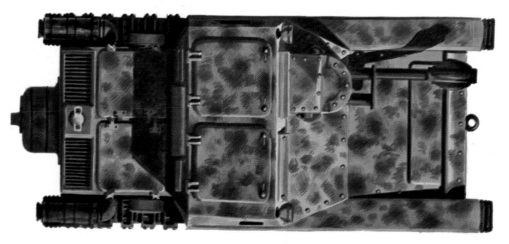

M 11/39 Medium Tank

The *M* 11/39 was a medium, break-through tank developed to complement the light *CV* series. When in 1933 it became clear that the new tankettes were not a complete replacement for the Fiat 3000, Fiat-Ansaldo designed a 12-ton Model 32 assault tank based on a scaled-up version of the tankette chassis. A Fiat 643N commercial diesel engine was fitted and the turretless vehicle mounted a short 45-mm gun in the hull front, with four machine-guns around the superstructure. This vehicle was not put into production but development work continued to a lighter, eight-ton design.

The new tank appeared in 1935 and mounted a 40-calibre Vickers Terni 37-mm gun in the right hull front. The weapon could be traversed 15 degrees left and right and 12 degrees up and down with hydraulic assistance in the horizontal plane. The gunner sat on the right and the driver slightly behind on the left, while there was a ten-sided turret with two 8-mm Breda machine-guns for the commander. The rear-mounted engine, still of commercial type, drove through a crash gearbox and the front sprockets. Steering was by epicyclic clutch and brake.

Trials showed that both the engine and suspension needed modification. Fiat therefore developed a new V8 diesel and Ansaldo a new suspension system utilizing on each side two semi-elliptically sprung assemblies of double-bogie wheel pairs. With the failure of the tankettes in Spain adding impetus to the programme, the eight-tonner was rebuilt to the new specifications in 1937. To ease eventual production a new, more rounded machine-gun turret was also adopted. Still designated *carro di rottura*, or break-through tank, 100 were ordered.

Material shortages delayed production and it was not until 1939 that the tanks, now designated *Carri Armati M* 11/39 (*M* for *medio* – medium), began to be delivered. Weight had gone up during development and the production tanks had small detail modifications and, inexplicably, lacked the prototype's radio. A company of 12 took part in the summer manoeuvres when Italian blitzkrieg ideas were first tested but staff from Ansaldo manned the tanks, owing to lack of time to familiarize army crews. Further trials continued with the Third Tank Regiment and the balance of the order was not completed until well into 1940.

It was intended to use the tank as the main weapon of the armoured divisions. Each battalion would consist of 31 tanks, two companies, each of three four-tank platoons and a command vehicle, with an HQ company composed of a commander's tank and four replacements. The 32nd Tank Regiment of the *Ariete* began conversion, but events intervened and the best tanks available to Italy, 24 *M* 11/39s, were sent out in May 1940 as a *Compagnia Speciale Carri M* to bolster the Italian position in East Africa.

Once war had broken out in June requests soon came from North Africa for a better tank than the *L* 3, whose deficiencies had been shown up in the initial clashes with the British. Seventy *M* 11/39s were therefore put under the command of the Fourth Tank Regiment and arrived at Benghazi in July: First and Second Battalions were thus equipped and a separate company was joined with one of *L* 3s in a mixed battalion allocated to the *Maletti* Group, a typically heterogeneous Italian formation of motorized and unmotorized Libyan units. First and Second Battalions were each allocated to one of the groups of the new Libyan Tank Command when it was set up in August. Each group also contained three *L* 3 battalions.

In their first skirmishes with the British the *M* 11/39s were quite successful, usually used in a relatively dispersed infantry support role during the initial Italian advance into Egypt. Like the smaller *L* 3s, however, they suffered severely from breakdowns. By September, when the armoured groups were reformed the First Battalion was down from 31 to 9 serviceable tanks. Clashes with British armour also began to show up the *M* 11's weaknesses in both armament and protection. The 37-mm gun was an old and weak design and its location in the hull put the tank at a severe tactical disadvantage, while 30-mm frontal armour was no match for the British two-pounder (40-mm) anti-tank and tank gun or 14-mm side armour for the Boys anti-tank rifle.

With the opening of the British offensive in December, disaster struck. Second Battalion, two *M* 11 companies attached to *Maletti* Group, was surprised at Nibeiwa on the first day and all 22 of its tanks overrun. Although First Battalion was part of the new Special Armoured Brigade with an *M* 13 battalion and two more of *L* 3s, it could take little real part in the fighting because most of its tanks were marooned, unserviceable, in Tobruk. During the attack on this stronghold in January 1941 the Sixth Australian Divisional Cavalry Regiment used captured *M* 11/39s against their former owners. There were five of these tanks with large white kangaroos (the divisional sign) painted prominently on the turret, hull front and sides for identification. Together with a later *M* 13/40 they equipped one squadron, Ringo, which operated with two others, Rabbit and Wombat, each of two *M* 13/40 tanks.

The defeat of the Italian Army saw the destruction or capture of almost every *M* 11/39 in the area. The vehicles in East Africa, after a brief moment of triumph in the conquest of British Somaliland in 1940, suffered a similar fate when Ethiopia fell the next year. Only a handful survived in Italy in training roles until 1943.

The *M* 11/39 symbolizes most of the weaknesses of the Italian armoured forces with its poor design, long period of development, production difficulties, unreliability and limited repair facilities. These were all reflections of Italy's limited reserves of raw materials and technological expertise which also discouraged the whole-hearted adoption of a more advanced armoured doctrine. The Italians were unprepared for the British blitzkrieg of December 1940, spearheaded by Matilda and Cruiser tanks far superior to the *M* 11/39. Even if more had been in working order the result could hardly have been different. To use a sporting metaphor: earlier in 1940 the First Division in armoured warfare had beaten the Second. Now the Second had smashed the Third.

Carro Armato M 11/39
Weight 10.8 tons (10.97 tonnes)
Crew three
Armament one 37-mm Vickers-Terni (L/40) gun with 84 rounds and two 8-mm Breda Model 38 machine-guns with 2,800 rounds
Armour hull nose 30 mm, glacis 14 mm, driver's plate 30 mm, sides 14–15 mm, decking 8 mm, belly 10 mm, tail 14 mm; turret front 30 mm, sides and rear 14 mm, top 7 mm
Engine one FIAT-SPA 8T V-8 liquid-cooled diesel, 43-hp
Speed 21 mph (34 km/h)
Range 124 miles (200 km)
Trench crossing 6 feet 6 inches (2 m)
Vertical step 2 feet 7½ inches (80 cm)
Fording 3 feet 3 inches (1 m)
Overall length 15 feet 6½ inches (4.73 m)
Width 7 feet 2 inches (21.8 m)
Height 7 feet 4½ inches (2.25 m)

Top right: *The M 13/40. The M 11/39 was developed into this much superior tank. The similarity in design to the earlier tank is obvious*
Bottom right: *The M 11/39*

Below: *Desolate and abandoned, this vehicle typifies the fate of almost every M 11/39. It is one of the 22 tanks which fell into British hands at Nibeiwa in December 1940. An obsolete design at birth the M 11/39 stood little chance against vastly superior British types such as the Matilda. Unreliability was added to inadequate armour and an armament which was both badly placed and also weak*

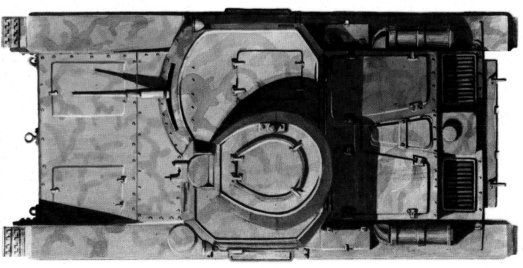

M 13/40 Series

From 1938 the possibilities were explored of mounting a more powerful gun on the M 11/39 chassis and after the invariable delays the first prototype of the M 13/40 appeared in early 1940 and 1,900 were ordered. The gun, a 32-calibre 47-mm weapon of adequate performance (muzzle velocity 2,060 fps or 630 m/s) was mounted in a revolving turret, a major design advance over the M 11/39. There was a co-axial Breda 8-mm machine-gun and another could be mounted in the turret roof for AA purposes, firing through open hatches. Two more machine-guns were mounted in the right hull front. Although maximum hull armour remained unchanged from the M 11/39, all-round general protection was improved. The crew was increased to four: driver, machine-gunner, loader and commander/gunner. The internal layout and the commander's combination of functions was unfortunate as was the design of the turret itself, the slots in the fixed mantlet for the armament being very subject to bullet splash.

The tank was built from armoured plates bolted to a steel frame and it retained the engine, transmission and suspension of its predecessor. With the increase in weight this meant that, although paper performance figures were only slightly reduced, the tank tended to be sluggish, especially when extra appliqué armour and sandbags were added in the field. The armour also had an unfortunate tendency to crack when it was hit, a result of Italy's less advanced metallurgy.

In all, however, the M 13/40 was an adequate tank by the standards of 1940 and almost as good as the German PzKpfw III. Some 250 were built by the end of the year. As with the M 11/39 it was intended to use it as the basic tank of the armoured divisions, with regiments of three battalions each containing three companies of three platoons of five tanks. With command vehicles and replacements this came to 50.

Ariete's 32nd Regiment was the first to begin re-equipment but events forced the pace of deployment. Faced with the need to strengthen the forces in North Africa the 32nd's Third Battalion was sent on its own to Libya, where, although allocated to the Special Tank Brigade, it was kept under central army command. Deployed piecemeal the M 13/40s were rapidly outmanoeuvred in the major British counter-offensive in December 1940. Three more battalions were sent out but they could not retrieve the situation and, cut off by British armour at Beda Fomm, no fewer than 101 were destroyed or captured. A total of 112 fell into British hands in a usable condition during the campaign and they were used to equip the Sixth Royal Tank Regiment. When Rommel began his major offensive on 31st March it was Britain's turn to be outflanked and most of their Italian tanks had to be abandoned. The year 1941 saw M 13/40s in action in Greece (with a battalion of the Centauro) and Yugoslavia. The Ariete also brought more to North Africa and later, with the similarly equipped Littorio, fought with Rommel through his successes and failures of 1941–2.

As production continued the long mudguards were cut back (after about 150 tanks) and radios began to be fitted. After 800 M 13/40s a new version appeared, usually called the M 14/41.

To improve performance a new 125-hp SPA 15T diesel engine was fitted, boosting speed slightly and range to 175 miles (280 km). Better filters were fitted to the air and fuel systems for desert service and most had the long mudguards restored. The M 13/40 continued in production beside the M 14/41 into 1942 and some of the former were re-worked with the new engine and filters. M 14/41s reached the Western Desert by the summer of 1942 and equipped the tank units of the Centauro Division which fought in Tunisia during this period.

By this time the design was beginning to show its age. Although Rommel compared the M 13/40s gun favourably with those of his own PzKpfw IIIs still fitted with short 50-mm weapons (despite the lower velocity), the Italian tank's armour had become thin by contemporary standards. An attempt was made to modernize the design further and an improved M 15/42 was developed. A longer 40-calibre 47-mm gun was fitted and a new 15TB petrol engine to boost power to 192 bhp (in practice 170) and economize on Italy's dwindling reserves of diesel oil. To accommodate the new engine the hull was lengthened and the tank was slightly wider.

Opposite page, right: The Semovente 75/18 assault gun based on the M 14/41 chassis
Below: An M 40 Semovente 75/18 assault gun group in action during the Battle of Alamein. Semoventi provided a cheap and more powerfully armed alternative to available Italian tanks and M 13/40 series chassis were increasingly diverted to their production from 1941

Semovente da 75/18 Su Scafo M 41 (illustrated right)
Weight 13 tons (13.2 tonnes)
Armament one 75-mm Model 34 (L/18) gun
howitzer with 44 rounds
Armour superstructure front 25 + 25 mm, mantlet
50 mm, sides and rear 25 mm, top 9 mm
Engine one FIAT-SPA 15T, 125-hp
Height 6 feet 1 inch (1.85 m)
Other details as M 13/40 tank

Carro Armato M 13/40
Weight 13.5 tons (13.7 tonnes)
Crew four
Armament one 47-mm Model 37 (L/32) gun
with 104 (later 87) rounds and three 8-mm Breda
model 38 machine-guns with 3,048 rounds
Armour hull nose 30 mm, glacis 25 mm, driver's
plate 30 mm, sides 25 mm, decking 14 mm, belly
6 mm, tail 25 mm; turret front 40 mm, sides and
rear 25 mm, top 14 mm
Engine one FIAT-SPA 8T V-8 liquid-cooled diesel,
105-hp
Speed 19 mph (30 km/h)
Range 125 miles (200 km)
Trench crossing 6 feet 11 inches (2.1 m)
Vertical step 2 feet 11½ inches (90 cm)
Fording 3 feet 3 inches (1 m)
Overall length 16 feet 1½ inches (4.91 m)
Width 7 feet 4 inches (2.23 m)
Height 7 feet 10 inches (2.37 m)
(See illustration on page 49)

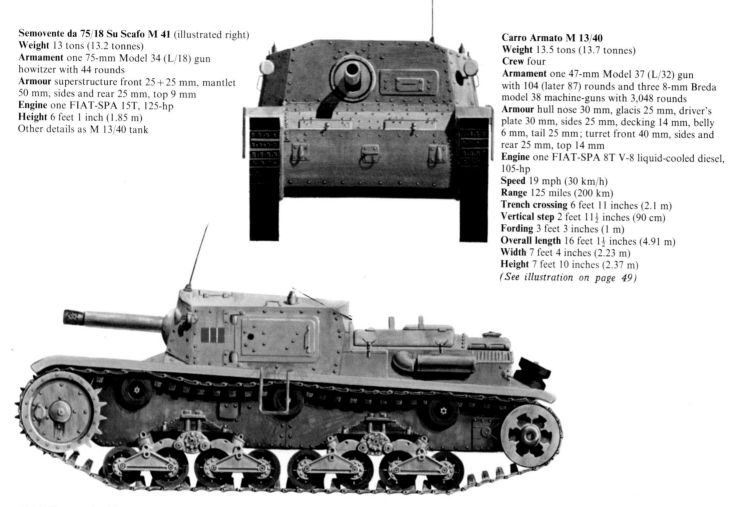

M 15/42s served with *Ariete* II Division in 1943 and continued with the post-war Italian army.

Only 82 were built owing to the decision in March 1943 to concentrate all medium-tank chassis production on *Semovente* assault guns. These had first been built in 1941 on the suggestion of Colonel Borlese of the artillery, basing his ideas on the successful use of German assault guns in the French campaign. Ansaldo demonstrated a mock-up on an *M* 13/40 chassis using the short 18-calibre 75-mm gun howitzer in a ball-mount at the front of a low superstructure armoured similarly to the tank. Thirty were ordered in January 1941 with the designation *Semovente da 75/18 su scafo M 40*. After successful trials with the prototype the order was doubled a month later. The *semovente* concept was simple but sound and well suited to Italian technical capabilities. After the initial orders were fulfilled 120 more were built, most using the new *M* 41 chassis. The tank was manned by a crew of three: driver, loader/radio operator and commander/gunner. These guns were used to equip artillery assault groups of, at first, two batteries of four guns each and later (1943) three batteries of six. *Semoventi* had come into service in North Africa with the *Ariete* the year before and with their powerful armament soon became an important part of Italy's armoured strength.

Each *Semovente* group had a number of command vehicles, usually four. These were developed from a prototype turretless *M* 13/40 converted in 1941. Production vehicles had range-finding equipment and two radios and were armed with twin 8-mm machine-guns with a third for AA use. In 1941 the *Carro Comando M* 41 was developed on the new *M* 14/41 chassis with a 13.2-mm Breda heavy machine-gun. Command vehicles were also eventually built on the *M* 15/42 chassis designated *M* 42 and some of these had longer-range radios for the control of aircraft. There was also an observation post version of the *M* 13/40 tank with dummy gun and rangefinder in the turret.

The *M* 42 chassis began to be used for *Semovente* production about the time that of tanks ceased and the assault guns were allocated to tank units. Initially the usual 75/18 was fitted, bringing numbers of such *Semoventi* to over 200, but two modifications were under development. The first was a new version of the chassis – lower, longer and wider. More heavily-armoured (50-mm) this *Semovente* mounted a version of the standard 105-mm gun howitzer developed by Ansaldo. The prototype appeared in January 1943 and eventually 454 were on order as the *Semovente da 105/25 su scafo M 43*. The first 30 of these impressive vehicles were delivered by the armistice and a group each was allocated to *Ariete* II and *Centauro* II. They were the most powerful Italian AFVs of the war.

The second was based on the normal *M* 42 chassis and involved the fitting of a longer gun. A 32-calibre 75-mm had been mounted experimentally on an early *M* 41 chassis and Ansaldo developed a new 34-calibre version, without

muzzle brake, for the *Semovente*. Despite orders for 500, only one had been delivered by the time of surrender.

Two other self-propelled weapons produced by the Italians were open mountings on the rear of cut-down versions of tracked chassis. The more numerous was the 90-mm AA/AT gun on the *M* 14/41 chassis; 30 were built and saw service in North Africa in 1942–3. There was also a larger 149-mm model 1935 gun-howitzer on the *M* 43 chassis.

Following Italy's armistice with the Allies her armoured units were temporarily disbanded but two Blackshirt armoured groupings continued the battle for the *RSI* with various *M* 13/40 derivatives. *Semoventi* proved very popular with the Germans who adopted them in large numbers. Ansaldo produced for them in addition 55 of the *M* 42 75/18s as *Sturmgeschutz M* 42 *mit* 75/18 (850)(i), 79 of the later type as *Sturmgeschutz M* 42 *mit* 75/34 (851)(i) and 91 of the larger *Sturmgeschutz M* 43 *mit* 105/25 (853)(i).

It had been planned by the Italians to produce a variant of the *M* 43 *Semovente* using the 75-mm AA gun and the Germans continued this, producing a *Sturmgeschutz M* 43 *mit* 75/46 (852)(i). with a modified version of the gun fitted with a prominent counterweight. Thirteen of these were built from 1944 to 1945, together with eleven fitted with the shorter 34-calibre gun of the later *M* 42s, designated *Sturmgeschutz M* 43 *mit* 75/34 (851)(i). *Semoventi* 75/18 were used after the war by Italian forces.

JAPAN

Japanese tanks were first developed for the support of the traditional infantry and cavalry arms: tankettes followed for logistic and communications purposes and, during the 1930s, light tanks for a more independent armoured role. These functions tended to merge as technological developments, operational utility and doctrinal conservatism overtook procurement intentions. Japanese use of armour was also conditioned by her theatres of operations. In the war against North America and Britain, from 1941 to 1945, tanks could usually only be transported and used in small groups. On the Asian mainland against China and Russia larger forces could be exploited in a war of manoeuvre, but the differing sophistication of these two opponents affected Japanese equipment and ideas significantly.

At first Japan used British and French tanks for experiments at the infantry school and in 1925, when modernization of the army began, the first tank company was established. More vehicles were purchased from abroad for both use and experiment, including Renault FTs and later NCIs from France (designated KO-GATA SHENSA and OTSU-GATA SHENSA), Vickers 'Six-Tonners' and a Medium C from Britain. Japan also began development of an indigenous Number 1 Tank of ambitious specification to test her own construction capabilities. The Army Technical Headquarters, which was a moving force behind this project, was to be a constant factor for progress in the development of Japanese armoured forces.

The lessons learned from this tank – which compared well with foreign tanks – were combined with those from the Medium C to produce a smaller vehicle for infantry support purposes. This appeared in 1929, 2589 in the Japanese calendar, hence the designation Type 89. It was the earliest Japanese tank produced in quantity and was used during 1932 in Japan's first major aggression against China. From the next year

tank regiments were formed, allocated to infantry divisions for direct support and these were later grouped into brigades.

It was at this time that the cavalry also acquired armour. Development of a Type 92 Combat Car, or light tank, was begun for the armoured company of each cavalry brigade in 1931. This was a small 3½ ton vehicle with a three-man crew. The armament consisted of two machine-guns, a 6.5-mm or 13.2-mm weapon mounted in the hull and a turret-mounted 6.5-mm. In the prototype the suspension consisted of two elliptically-sprung pairs of bogie wheels each side, but in production versions three pairs of wheels were adopted to improve cross-country mobility. Later still came four larger wheels with modified springing. Large numbers of these vehicles saw service with the cavalry brigades and cavalry scouting squadrons attached to infantry divisions.

With Japanese ambitions centred on the wide open spaces of Mongolia and Northern China a vehicle was needed for command and liaison

Left: A Type 95 light tank – one of the mainstays of Japanese armoured strength in World War II

roles and to keep open the supply lines to the widely-dispersed garrisons and armies. Small armoured tractors seemed to be the solution and the Carden Loyd tankette was purchased as a guide. The design was developed with a new suspension into the Type 94 Tankette, a small front-engined 2.65-ton vehicle with a 6.5-mm machine-gun turret. Although only armoured to 12 mm against small-arms fire it proved adequate against Chinese forces for infantry support and, manufactured in quantity, was allocated on the basis of one company per infantry division. New versions were later developed; a Type 94 modified with improved suspension and the Type 97 with 37-mm gun and rear-mounted diesel engine used for infantry support.

The lighter, air-cooled diesel engine was the major progressive feature of Japanese armour at this period. Water was scarce in Mongolia, Manchuria and North China and the Japanese had been put off petrol by a serious fire in their imported British Medium C during tests. Diesel oil could be obtained in greater quantities than petrol from any given amount of crude oil and there were other advantages of less fuel loss during storage and increased range, all important to a country short of petroleum. A whole series of standardized diesel engines was developed and used in almost all Japanese AFV designs until 1945; they were also noted for the range of fuel grades that could be used.

The first new type of tank to be diesel-engined was the Type 95 designed for the new Independent Mixed Brigade. This progressive formation was first assembled under the influence of Western theory and practice in 1933. It was a combination of three type 89 companies and an infantry regiment, artillery regiment and engineer company, all motorized. The speeds of the various vehicles soon proved incompatible and a requirement was issued for a fast, light tank for the new brigade. The Japanese also began to develop specialized AFVs such as a fully-tracked Type 97 engineer vehicle carrying flame-throwers and a bridge span projected into place by rockets.

The Mixed Brigade was used to spearhead attacks in the full-scale war with China that broke out in 1937, but the lack of serious opposition prevented its potential from becoming apparent and it was eventually disbanded. However, armoured clashes with the Soviet Union, culminating in Zhukov's use of blitzkrieg methods to shatter Japanese forces at Khalkin Gol on the Mongolian/Manchurian border in 1939, emphasized the importance of modern armour and the deficiencies of Japanese technology, organization and ideas. Although Japanese tanks were outnumbered in the battle their performance was shown to be inadequate compared with the Soviet tanks and development of an up-gunned version of the latest Type 97 Medium began. In 1940 this defeat, coupled with the German victories in Europe, also led to the formation of two armoured divisions in Manchukuo around the tank brigades deployed there and the adoption of new battle manuals stressing

concentration and mobility. Each division had on paper a three-regiment tank brigade of Type 97 mediums and Type 95 lights. A third armoured division was later formed by fully mechanizing the cavalry units in Mongolia and, in 1943, this joined the other two in a Tank Army set up the previous year.

Japanese armour began the war successfully against the Allies in the Philippines and Malaya – Third Tank Brigade's vehicles proving particularly successful in the latter campaign in small, mixed combat groups containing ten to fifteen tanks each. It was partly due to the need for dispersed groups of armour in these campaigns, and in Burma and the Pacific Islands, that the tank divisions were rarely up to strength. One or more tank regiment was usually detached for independent use and there were always as many regiments independent as in the divisions. The Japanese, indeed, rarely displayed a full appreciation of the true nature of mechanized operations. One tank division was effectively used in China during the 1944 offensive in Honan but another, the Second, was frittered away uselessly the same year as a series of static pill-boxes during the fighting in the Philippines.

Japanese vehicles were, moreover, usually inferior to their opponents. It was not that new designs were neglected, many appeared – new battle tanks of increasing size, self-propelled guns and amphibious tanks. No fewer than 1,104 armoured personnel carriers were produced, the fully-tracked Type 1 HO-KI, half-tracked Type 1 HO-HA and amphibious KATSU-SHA. Few were deployed, however, as AFV production had to be subordinated to the more pressing air and naval needs of the maritime war of attrition. From 1944, American air raids also began to disrupt production. Spare parts became a real problem and many vehicles were lost for this reason. As for complete tanks, Japan had produced 1,976 tanks of all types during the 1930s, and 4,424 more were completed by 1945. Peak year was 1942 with 1,290 vehicles but production soon slumped to 750 in 1943, 295 in 1944 and 130 in 1945.

The Japanese high command, conditioned by easy victories against a largely unarmoured foe in China, preferred to keep old, standard and obsolete vehicles in production rather than re-equip. This made some sense given Japan's limited industrial capacity but good designs were delayed too long and when they, and new vehicles, became available, production facilities were not. What new vehicles there were, moreover, tended to be kept for home defence and did not see action in the combat theatres. The final *débâcle* came in August 1945 when Soviet forces, equipped with 5,500 modern AFVs, smashed the Japanese armies in Manchuria with their 1,250 obsolete machines. It was one of the most crushing blitzkriegs of the war.

After the war much Japanese armour fell into the hands of the Chinese Communists and the Viet Minh who used them in action in Korea and also in Indo-China.

Type 89 Medium Tank

The design of this infantry support vehicle dated back to the Number 1 Tank project begun in 1925; its specification had stressed good all-round performance as it was essentially a demonstration of technology rather than an answer to an operational requirement. In order to attack strong enemy defences a 57-mm gun with two subsidiary machine-gun turrets was demanded, together with armour to resist contemporary 37-mm anti-tank guns. Specified performance was 15½ mph (25 km/h), that of the standard army truck, to simplify movement problems. Weight was to be around 15 tons.

Despite problems with the production of armour plate and other technical difficulties the vehicle eventually emerged as an unarmoured prototype. Weight had increased to 18 tons and this was felt by the high command to be too extravagant for the infantry support role. A smaller 10-ton, 37-mm armed light tank was, therefore requested similar to the British Vickers Medium C purchased in 1927. The design of Number 1 was scaled down and a new prototype appeared from the Osaka Arsenal in 1929. Development of the heavy tank continued but it never went into production.

The new light tank mounted a similar 57-mm gun to that in the Number 1. A 6.5-mm machine-gun was mounted in the turret rear (a rather idiosyncratic Japanese feature), and in the left hull front. Instead of Number 1's 140-hp V8, a 105-hp Mitsubishi copy of a six-cylinder Daimler engine was fitted driving through the rear sprocket to give similar performance figures to the earlier tank. Steering was on the clutch and brake principle developed for the Number 1 and the suspension was a simplified and scaled-down version of the larger vehicle's. Instead of 19 bogie wheels each side the new tank had nine, two double-sets of leaf-sprung bogie wheel pairs with an independently sprung wheel at the front. Armoured skirting protected the springs.

With the official designation Type 89, from the Japanese year of introduction, the tank was put into production at the new tank arsenal built by Mitsubishi. With a new larger symmetrical turret the weight rose to 11½ tons and the erstwhile light tank became a medium, acquiring the name CHI-RO from the abbreviated form of the Japanese word *chugata*, meaning medium. Together with the new OTSU-GATA SENSHA tanks purchased from France, Type 89 Mediums were used in the Shanghai incident of 1932 as part of the naval landing force. Despite the unsuitable terrain the Japanese tanks with their stouter suspensions, superior mobility and greater reliability proved more popular in supporting the infantry assaults on the Chinese defensive positions. With no powerful anti-tank guns to worry about, the Type 89's inferior armour protection of 17-mm (as opposed to 30-mm) was not unduly important.

In 1933 three infantry support regiments of Type 89s were formed, each of two companies of ten. Two were stationed in Japan and one in Manchukuo at Kungchuling. Here, the next year, three more companies were formed into a Fourth Regiment as part of the Independent Mixed Brigade. Despite its designed role, the 89 had a moderate range and its mechanical robustness lent itself to mobile operations against ill-equipped opponents. This had been shown when a mixed company of Type 89s and Type 92 Combat Cars had led the long-distance campaign into Jehol in 1933.

In 1934 a major modification occurred with the appearance of the Type 89B (89-OTSU) with the new Mitsubishi-designed diesel engine. Petrol-engined tanks now became Type 89A (89-KO). After extensive field trials in Northern Manchukuo the 89B was adopted and produced by Mitsubishi and the other tank factories that Japan was building up both in the home islands and Manchukuo.

As production continued at the various plants, so external modifications took place. The original turret cupola, which hinged open as a unit, was replaced by one with opening hatches, an improved external mantlet for the gun was adopted and the machine-guns were protected by armoured sleeves. The original girder mounting five return rollers was replaced by a new arrangement with four rollers and a new design of armoured skirting. Most vehicles, either with or without the other modifications, had a new sloping frontal plate replacing the original one with its more vulnerable vertical top. With the new arrangement, the driver's and machine-gunner's positions were sometimes reversed. Western intelligence called the sloping front combined with the older features the Type 92 and those with the newer trackwork the Type 94 but these were not Japanese designations. Unditching tails, to improve cross-country performance, and new tracks, to boost speed, were later fitted.

Type 89s, in their various forms, took a prominent part in the battles of Japan's war with China in 1937, again demonstrating their cross-country capacity, for example in the mud along the Peking–Hankow railway. They fought the Russians in 1938 and, although being replaced by the Type 97, formed part of the equipment of the two tank regiments that helped conquer the Philippines during 1941 and 1942. Type 89Bs also played a part in the conquest of Burma.

By this time the tank was obsolete in world terms. Its gun was short, weak (1,148 fps or 350 m/s muzzle velocity) and only had a high explosive capability. Armour was thin, particularly for a primarily infantry support vehicle. The Type 89 could, however, carry out the World War I function of dealing with machine-guns and barbed wire and its robustness stood it in good stead in both the wide open spaces of China and the jungles of the Philippines and Burma. It was a useful infantry support tank – as long as the opposition was badly equipped.

Top right: A late Type 89B with crew. This obsolete tank was still being encountered in the Philippines in 1944

Far right: A Type 89A – note the early cupola, driver's plate and suspension skirting

Right: A late Type 89B advances over a Chinese bridge repaired by engineers. This tinted photograph shows the multi-coloured camouflage typical of Japanese armour. The unditching tail and later cupola are also illustrated

Type 89B CHI-RO
Weight 12.8 tons
Crew four
Armament one 57-mm Type 90 gun with 100 rounds and two 6.5-mm Type 91 machine-guns with 2,745 rounds
Armour hull front, sides and rear 17 mm, decking 10 mm; turret front 17 mm, sides and rear 15 mm, top 10 mm
Engine one Mitsubishi inline six-cylinder air-cooled diesel, 115-hp
Speed 15.5 mph (25 km/h)
Range 100 miles (160 km)
Trench crossing 8 feet 1½ inches (2.5 m)
Vertical step 2 feet 7½ inches (80 cm)
Fording 3 feet 3 inches (1 m)
Overall length 18 feet 10½ inches (5.75 m) with tail
Width 7 feet 2 inches (2.18 m)
Height 8 feet 5 inches (2.56 m)

Type 95 Light Series

The Type 89 Medium was too slow for convenient operation with the wheeled transport of the mechanized brigade and in 1933 development of a new, faster tank was begun. It was to be a light tank of only seven tons and armoured only against small-arms fire as the high command considered this sufficient for the task. The suspension was based on that of the new Type 94 tankette with two pairs of bogie wheels each side-mounted on bell cranks and supported by compressed horizontal, helical springs. This principle was to become standard for most subsequent Japanese tanks. The new diesel engine was fitted in the rear, driving through the front sprockets. Standard clutch and brake steering was employed and the crew consisted of a driver, a machine-gunner working a hull-mounted weapon and a commander/gunner with a turret-mounted 37-mm gun.

Mitsubishi completed the prototype in 1934 and it was sent for trials with both cavalry and infantry. The latter were not impressed by either its armament or protection but, after operational trials with the Independent Mixed Brigade in Manchukuo, a production order was given. A second prototype was constructed in 1935 (with two return rollers instead of one) and the vehicle was adopted as the Type 95 Light Tank, with a widened fighting compartment.

The Type 95 was produced in large quantities for a Japanese tank: 1,164 at the Mitsubishi tank arsenal (who gave it its most widely used name HA-GO) and the rest, out of a total of approximately 1,300, at smaller plants. The cavalry had earlier shown interest in the design as a gun-armed replacement for the Type 92 Combat Car, and the HA-GO was procured for the cavalry brigades and units attached to infantry formations. The Independent Mixed Brigade adopted the HA-GO and used it during the opening offensive in China in 1937. Opposition was not great and neither the formation nor the tank had an opportunity to prove itself. Despite, or perhaps because of, this combat experience, the reluctance of the infantry to adopt the Type 95 was overcome and it was taken into the Tank Regiments, equipping one ten-tank company (three platoons of three with commander), others being attached to HQ vehicles. Unfortunately, and surprisingly, given its armoured brigade role, radio had not been a requirement and few commanders' vehicles were so fitted.

The HA-GO appeared on every front on which Japanese forces were engaged and had some success particularly in Malaya, although where any well-handled anti-tank guns were encountered, the odds were firmly against it. As usual with Japanese armour, the design, conceived when the only opposition was the ill-equipped Chinese Army, had its major strengths in mechanical robustness and mobility (its cross-country speed was as high as 20 mph or 32 km/h), rather than in armour or firepower. Although production vehicles had an improved gun of 2,214 fps (675 m/s) velocity (as against 1,886 fps or 575 m/s this was over 300 fps (91 m/s) less than its American counterpart. Moreover the limited depression of the main armament – which left a dead zone of almost eight

yards' radius around the tank – compounded the commander/gunner's problem of preventing stalking, particularly in close country, while also trying to attend to the guns and command the tank. By the time production ceased in 1943 the HA-GO was obsolete and many finished their days as not particularly effective dug-in pill-boxes on such beaches as Iwo Jima.

Various improvements to the basic Type 95 were carried out. After experiments with the original prototype, units in North Manchukuo had their tanks fitted with a modified suspension with a small extra road wheel between each normal pair, mounted on inverted cranks. This was to improve performance over fields of kao-liang corn, the basic crop of the area. Although the original fitting was combined with modified springing, the improvement could be applied to the standard unit of any tank deployed in the area. Latterly, attempts were made to up-gun the HA-GO, as the Type 3 KE-RI, with a short 57-mm model 97 gun made available by the up-gunning of the CHI-HA Medium. Owing to the confined space in the turret this conversion was not successful and when the larger 47-mm turret of the SHINHOTO CHI-HA became available the entire fitting was applied to the Type 95 to

become the Type 4 KE-NU with a four-man crew. By this stage of the war, however, few could be produced.

Amphibious tanks had been experimented with for some time but the only one to see widespread service was based on the HA-GO. Appearing as the Type 2 KA-MI in 1942 it had a larger hull for greater buoyancy with an extra crew member carried as a mechanic to supervise the power take-offs to the two propellers and bilge pump. Two detachable pontoons were carried fore and aft for flotation, the latter with two rudders for steering in water. Armour was as on the HA-GO but the gun was a later version and a co-axial machine gun was fitted. By the time the KA-MI was deployed with naval and marine units the days of Japan's maritime offensive were largely over, although it was used for small-scale counter-attacks in the Marshalls and Marianas.

An improved light tank with transversely mounted supercharged engine was developed, the Type 98 KE-NI, lighter and faster (31 mph) with 16-mm armour and a new Type 0 37-mm gun (2,493 fps or 760 m/s muzzle velocity). After experiments with a four-wheeled Christie-type suspension, the alternative was adopted – a modified version of the standard system with

three cranked wheel pairs each side. Owing to the high command's policy of standardization, the tank was belatedly put into production in 1942 and only 200 were made. An improved Type 2 KE-TO with roomier turret and Type 1 37-mm gun (2,625 fps or 800 m/s) was delayed until 1944 and produced in still smaller quantities; a completely new Type 5 KE-HO with 20-mm armour and 47-mm gun, although designed in 1942, did not get beyond the prototype stage. Although these designs attest to the energy of the Army Technical Headquarters, the need might well be questioned for new manifestations of what was, by this time, an outdated concept. After the war, China continued to use this series and some may have seen service in Korea.

Right: This HA-GO is pictured in a typical Japanese camouflage scheme. A version of the Japanese flag often appeared as national marking on tanks. The usual Japanese suspension, of bell cranks and horizontal springs, is clearly seen in the side view
Below: The Type 95 CHI-HA saw large-scale service in World War II. Tanks of this type were attached to infantry and cavalry formations as well as forming an important part of tank units

Type 95 HA-GO
Weight 7.5 tons
Crew three
Armament one 37-mm Type 94 gun with 119 rounds and two 7.7-mm Type 97 machine-guns with 2,940 rounds
Armour hull nose 12 mm, glacis 9 mm, driver's plate 12 mm, sides 12 mm, decking and belly 9 mm, tail 6–12 mm; turret front, sides and rear, 12 mm, top 9 mm
Engine one Mitsubishi inline six-cylinder air-cooled diesel, 110-hp
Speed 28 mph (45 km/h)
Range 155 miles (250 km)
Trench crossing 6 feet 7 inches (2 m)
Vertical step 2 feet 8 inches (80 cm)
Fording 3 feet 3 inches (1 m)
Overall length 14 feet 4½ inches (4.38 m)
Width 6 feet 9 inches (2.06 m)
Height 7 feet 10 inches (2.39 m)

Type 97 Medium Series

The stimulus to develop a new medium tank came, as in the case of most other Japanese tanks, from the technical rather than the operational branch of the Japanese Army's command structure. Army Technical Headquarters saw that the Type 89 was increasingly inferior to European tanks being slow, under-gunned and under-armoured. It was also felt that a new, fast medium should be developed for the Independent Mixed Brigade rather than a light tank and two designs were initiated, a 13.5-ton First Plan from Mitsubishi and a 10-ton Second Plan from Osaka Arsenal. Both prototypes appeared in 1937 as the CHI-HA and CHI-NI respectively and, although the Operations Department preferred the latter, which only had a one-man turret and was therefore cheaper, the outbreak of the China incident downgraded considerations of economy, and led to the adoption of the larger design for service use.

Two prototype CHI-HAs appeared, one with interleaved wheels, and the other employing a version of the standard suspension of the Type 94 tankette and Type 95 Light with three pairs of large, double bogie wheels each side connected by middle-mounted bell cranks horizontally sprung against each other. To improve cross-country performance the production vehicles adopted a modification of this suspension for the centre pairs only, the front and back wheels being independently sprung. Construction was by welding and riveting and the armour was well shaped. A small turret was mounted to the right of the hull. Its firepower was disappointing, being a new Type 97 version of the old short 57-mm gun. This did fire an armour-piercing round, but only at 1,378 fps (420 m/s) – half the velocity of the later British six-pounder (57-mm) of similar calibre. Unlike that of the CHI-NI the turret was two-man so the tank commander did not have to double as gunner, and the ring was large enough to allow later up-gunning. Machine-guns in armoured sleeves were in the hull front and turret rear with a third sometimes fitted for AA use. A powerful new engine of standard pattern drove through the front sprockets and steering was by normal clutch and brake.

The CHI-HA compared favourably with its contemporaries in all except gun power and this deficiency became apparent when the Soviet Army showed the Japanese the nature of modern armoured opposition in 1938–9. Development, therefore, began of a larger turret, mounting a high-velocity armament based on the standard 47-mm anti-tank weapon. The new 48-calibre Type 1 tank gun had a muzzle velocity of 2,625 fps (800 m/s) which compared satisfactorily with foreign weapons such as the contemporary *PzKpfw* III's 2,240 fps (684 m/s) 42-calibre 50-mm. The programme was delayed, however, by renewed complacency and the new SHINHOTO (New Turret) CHI-HA only began to enter service in 1942. By this time it was already becoming obsolete particularly in terms of its armour protection which was only slightly improved on the hull sides. Again, the new turret was set towards the right and had a machine-gun in the rear.

By this time the standard CHI-HA had equipped some independent tank regiments and those

in the armoured divisions. It had seen service in China and Malaya where individual tank companies were handled daringly in co-operation with infantry and engineers to break the British defences at Jitra and on the Slim River. They then spearheaded the swift advance down the peninsula which followed.

In a Japanese tank regiment the Type 97 provided the three or four medium companies, each of three platoons of three with a company commander. More were attached to Regimental HQ, one or more of these sometimes being the SHI-KI command vehicle with extra communications and vision equipment and an additional 37-mm or 57-mm gun in place of the machine-gun in the hull front. There was also a commander's SHINHOTO CHI-HA with a dummy gun. Most CHI-HAs had radio fitted to help tactical co-ordination with a prominent curved aerial in the original tanks being mounted around the top of the turret front. There were various specialized variants. In 1942 three self-propelled guns (gun tanks) appeared on the Type 97 chassis, perhaps stimulated by the successful assault gun designs of Japan's Axis allies. The HO-NI I mounted a modern 75-mm high-velocity gun, the HO-NI II, a shorter 105-mm weapon and the HO-RO, an old 150-mm howitzer. These were mounted in open shields, armoured frontally to the same thickness as the tank, and they proved useful in providing extra firepower in the final defensive battles. A few original CHI-HAs were converted to flail mine-

clearers, flamethrower tanks and bridgelayers while some SHINHOTO CHI-HAs became bulldozer tanks. There was also a SE-RI recovery vehicle on the Type 97 chassis with rear crane jib and small machine-gun turret.

The SHINHOTO CHI-HA, to which standard many older vehicles were converted, was the only new tank to see large-scale service in the period after 1942. A 17-ton Type 1 CHI-HE with the 47-mm gun in a revised turret, a slightly better-shaped welded hull armoured to 50-mm, and a 240-hp engine was put into limited production in 1941. A Type 2 HO-I gun tank with a short 75-mm gun in a revolving turret was adopted for its support the next year, but, although some of both these types saw action, few were produced.

The appearance of larger Allied tanks with 75-mm guns led to experiments with the Type 95 75-mm field gun to improve the Japanese medium tank's firepower. Eventually a version of the higher-velocity Type 90 weapon was adopted and fitted in an enlarged turret on the CHI-HE chassis as the Type 3 CHI-NU. The gun was a 38-calibre weapon and had a muzzle velocity of 2,231 fps (680 m/s) which put it in terms of performance between that of the British and American tank guns of similar calibre. The 18.5-ton tank, if something of an improvization, was almost of American Sherman standard, but it suffered from production problems and only saw service in limited numbers from 1944. The same gun was also mounted in an enclosed

Type 97 SHINHOTO CHI-HA
Weight 15.6 tons
Crew five
Armament one 47-mm Type 1 (L/48) gun with 104 rounds and two 7.7-mm Type 97 machine-guns with 2,575 rounds
Armour hull nose 15 mm, glacis 17 mm, driver's plate 25 mm, sides 20–35 mm, decking 10 mm, belly 8 mm, tail 20 mm; turret front 25 mm, mantlet 30 mm, sides and rear 25 mm, top 10 mm
Engine one Mitsubishi V-12 air-cooled diesel, 170-hp
Speed 24 mph (38 km/h)
Range 130.5 miles (210 km)
Trench crossing 8 feet 1½ inches (2.5 m)
Vertical step 3 feet (91 cm)
Fording 3 feet 3 inches (1 m)
Overall length 18 feet 1 inch (5.5 m)
Width 7 feet 8 inches (2.33 m)
Height 7 feet 11 inches (2.38 m)

Right: *The SHINHOTO CHI-HA was the most important Japanese medium tank of the war. Known as the 'Type 97 Special' to the Americans it could barely hold its own against the Sherman, and was totally outclassed by Soviet armour in 1945. Note the machine-gun mounted in the turret rear, and also the lengthened version of the standard Japanese suspension with centre-mounted bell cranks on the middle wheel pairs. The novel camouflage scheme was a Japanese standard*
Below: *An original CHI-HA of the Third Company, Seventh Tank Regiment advances in Bataan during the conquest of the Philippines – the Japanese were adept at using tanks in difficult conditions*

central superstructure on the Type 97 chassis as the HO-NI III gun tank.

A scaled-up 30-ton Type 4 CHI-TO with 75-mm armour retained the same suspension principles as its predecessors but had seven wheels each side as opposed to six and a 400 bhp engine. A new 38-calibre 75-mm gun, based this time on the Type 88 AA weapon, was fitted but its muzzle velocity was little improved at 2,362 fps (703 m/s), less than the German 43-calibre 75-mm tank gun. The six tanks of this type that were produced were left in Japan for home defence.

All these tanks were diesel-powered but the final Japanese design was fitted with a German-designed 550-hp BMW petrol engine in an attempt to bypass shortages of the standard diesel engines and speed production. This 37-ton Type 5 CHI-RI was the final extrapolation of the

Type 97. It had eight bogie wheels each side and the Type 4 gun in a large turret with a Type 1 37-mm in the hull. Armour was the same as the Type 4. However, it appeared only as a prototype.

As with the Type 98, such a plethora of new designs was hardly necessary and only complicated a production system that was already grinding to a halt. Once the Type 3 had been developed, a vehicle of moderate size and adequate firepower, it might well have been standardized without going on to the larger tanks of 30 tons or more that unnecessarily confused the situation.

Experiments went on in other fields too, although few results saw service. Prototype KA-TO and HO-RI heavy self-propelled guns, on the CHI-RI chassis, were produced just before the war's end. Earlier, an amphibious tank had been produced on the CHI-HE chassis and some were used in action. This 26-ton Type 3 KA-CHI (which weighed almost 29 tons with pontoons) had a large box-type superstructure on which was mounted a turret with a Type 1 47-mm gun. A later Type 5 TO-KU was lower and mounted the 47-mm in the hull. A 25-mm automatic cannon was in the turret.

Despite all this activity it was still the SHINHOTO CHI-HA which met the Americans from Saipan to the Philippines and had to fight Soviet armoured forces when they mounted their offensive in August 1945. Its gun could just defeat the American Sherman but 25-mm armour was no protection from even the smallest enemy anti-tank gun. It stood no chance at all against a Soviet T-34/85. After the war the SHINHOTO CHI-HA saw considerable service with the People's Republic of China.

POLAND

Poland's first tanks were 150 French Renault *FT* 17s delivered in 1919–20 for allocation as infantry support on the classic French pattern. In 1930 a separate command structure, the *Brón Pancerna* or Armoured Forces, was formed to take over all tanks, armoured cars and even armoured trains, but this did not presage any immediate changes in strategy and the new organization remained merely an administrative convenience.

After modifications to the Renaults and un-successful attempts to develop a medium tank, it was decided to buy design abroad. In 1929 both Vickers Carden Loyd Mark V1 tankettes and Vickers 'Six-Ton' tanks were obtained for test and eventually adopted in modified form as, respectively, the *TK/TKS* and VAU 33, to triple *Brón Pancerna*'s paper tank strength to nine battalions by 1935. These were not operational units but groupings of tanks for organizational and train-ing purposes and the vehicles were allocated in company units to infantry divisions and cavalry brigades for tactical use.

In 1936, faced with growing mechanized threats to both west and east, Poland was forced to consider rearmament. After debate between doctrinal conservatives and progressives and those realists who recognized Poland's techno-logical and economic weaknesses, an ambitious six-year plan was drawn up. The traditional arms were to be supported by 479 new 4.3-ton, 20-mm armed 4 *TP* light tanks. In addition, eight new operational tank battalions would be set up to be allocated to army group commanders. As

far as Polish industry allowed these would be equipped with the 7 *TP*, the latest modification of the Vickers 'Six-Tonner'.

The most interesting and progressive feature of the plan was its provision for no fewer than four Mechanized Units (*OM*) which would be rather like small versions of the French *DLM*, with two tank battalions, one of 7 *TP* tanks and a mixed formation of 4 *TP* tanks and new 10 *TP* fast mediums. These 37-mm armed vehicles were to be based on the Christie tanks ordered but not accepted in 1931 and have a speed of 46½ mph (75 km/h) on wheels and 31½ mph (50 km/h) on tracks. Armoured to 20 mm, they were to weigh 12.8 tons and have an American La France engine of 210 hp. In addition the *OM* was to contain two motorized cavalry regiments (in fact, battalions of lorried infantry) and a battalion each of artillery, anti-tank guns and engineers. The purpose of the *OM*, as befitted Poland's real strategic position, if not her un-realistic, self-important image, was defensive, being designed to combat enemy armour rather than form the centrepiece of an offensive.

Over 500 7 *TP* and 10 *TP* tanks were to be built, the extra vehicles going to the cavalry. There were even plans for a multi-turreted medium tank but the whole programme soon foundered on Poland's industrial incapacity and economic weakness. Polish industry was not capable of large-scale tank construction and

much material had to be imported. Army pro-curement had to compete with the more pres-tigious, large-scale, naval construction for the country's scarce foreign reserves and as a result neither the 4 *TP* nor 10 *TP* ever went beyond the prototype stage. Design defects in the former delayed production, and the construction of the latter was prevented by the need to concentrate on the 7 *TP*; only one 10 *TP* was built in 1938 and was under test when Germany struck, while an improved 14 *TP* with 50-mm armour was incomplete at the time of the German invasion.

Worried by German rearmament, France offered the Poles a loan to purchase French equipment in 1936. But France's defence indus-tries were already working at full strength to arm her own forces; an order for Somua S-35s had to be refused and although 100 R-35s were ordered in their stead to equip two of the pro-posed Polish battalions, only enough to equip one had arrived by 1 September 1939.

On that date the paper strength of the Polish armoured forces stood at only a third over that before rearmament began: 12 battalions of 693 *TK* and *TKS* tankettes and 169 7 *TP*, 52 VAU 33 and 53 R-35 tanks, as well as 67 World War I Renault *FT* 17s. Though the numbers of vehicles actually mobilized were respectively 440, 130, 30, 49 and 55. Only three of the pro-jected eight operational battalions were formed: First and Second with 49 7 *TP* tanks each and the 21st with a similar number of R-35s, while a third 7 *TP* battalion was in process of assembly. There were 15 *TK/TKS* companies allocated to

infantry divisions and two independent platoons attached to infantry brigades. Eleven *DP* ('armoured divisions') of a squadron (company) each of tankettes and armoured cars were for allocation to cavalry brigades along with two individual platoons of cavalry tankettes. A platoon of tankettes was also allocated to each of the ten armoured train units. Three *FT* companies were in reserve in the East.

Only one *OM* was ready for action, the 10th Cavalry Brigade, with an actual strength of a command and supply company, a VAU 33 company, a *TKS* equipped company and *DP*, two motorized cavalry regiments, a motorized artillery division, an AA battery, a battalion of engineers and a communications squadron. Another, the Warsaw Motorized Armoured Brigade was in the process of formation and, reinforced by a 7 *TP* company from First Battalion and three *TK* companies, saw action in the counter-attack at Tomaszòw Lubelski.

The 10th Cavalry had some success in its designed role, blunting the thrust of Second *Panzer* and Fourth Light Divisions, and individual 7 *TP* battalions also scored limited tactical successes. Indeed in the terms of the previous World War the Polish Army of 30 divisions (2.5 million men) stood some chance of holding the 50 of the *Wehrmacht*. The Germans, however, were fighting a new kind of war, a blitzkrieg, spearheaded by 2,000 tanks in well-trained formations. Most were inferior to the 7 *TP*, VAU 33 and R-35s but there were only 209 of these (albeit more than contemporary British or American strength in new gun tanks) and the tankettes were of little use against enemy armour. The Poles never had time to mobilize fully; outnumbered and outflanked *Bròn Pancerna* could achieve little.

With final defeat much of the Polish Army escaped to Hungary and Romania. By June 1940 10th Motorized Brigade had been resurrected in France as an R-35 equipped battalion with a few motorized cavalry companies and anti-tank guns. Thrown into another losing battle they retreated southwards and were evacuated to Britain via the Bay of Biscay. A Polish infantry tank brigade was formed there on British lines while 10th Cavalry became a brigade of motorized infantry. Re-formed as cruiser tank brigades in 1942 these became the basis of the First Polish Armoured Division which fought in Western Europe in 1944–5 with Shermans and Cromwells. Another Polish armoured brigade was formed in 1943 and, after fighting with Shermans in Italy, became the nucleus of a second armoured division. Both were disbanded after the War. From 1943 Polish armoured troops fought in *T*-34s and other Soviet vehicles beside the Red Army to liberate their homeland and these became the nucleus of the modern Polish Army.

Above: *A novel use for a TKS tankette. When war came in 1939 most of Poland's armoured capital was invested in these little vehicles and the earlier TK. They were mainly used for cavalry duties and, as in the picture, infantry support. With their single machine-gun armament and thin protection they posed little threat to the German light tanks*

TK Series

The *TK/TKS* series was developed from the Mark V1 version of the small 1½-ton Vickers Carden Loyd tankette, designed to give armoured mobility to individual pairs of infantrymen. In 1929 Poland purchased 16 tankettes together with production rights and a Polish-built prototype, designated *TK* 1, appeared the same year. It had the standard air-cooled, Ford Model T 22.5-hp engine and transmission, and virtually the same suspension as the British vehicles: two pairs of rubber-tyred bogie wheels each side connected by leaf springs pivoting on a girder frame. Armour was 3 mm, weight 1.75 tons and armament a single Hotchkiss 7.9-mm machine-gun. Limited quantities of the *TK* 1 were made, along with the improved *TK* 2 tankette which had a new Model A Ford engine of 40 hp, a new transmission and a modified suspension to improve cross-country mobility. After tests of both Model 30 types the State Engineering Institute Research Bureau took over the project and developed an improved Model 31 in 1930, which was put in production the next year at the Ursus truck factory as the Reconnaissance Tank *TK* 3.

Some 300 of the new vehicles, known as the Small Reconnaissance Tank *TK* or just *TK*, were built. Their suspension was a further modification of the *TK* 2 and, with a fully-enclosed body and increased (8-mm) armour protection, weight was up to 2.43 tons. The engine was similar to the *TK* 2's, maximum speed remained 30 mph (48 km/h) but range was increased to 124 miles (200 km) from 93 (150 km). A Hotchkiss rifle calibre machine-gun remained the standard armament mounted normally in the hull; it could also be placed on an external AA mounting outside the tankette to improve protection from the air. To save the *TK*'s tracks on the way to battle, a four-wheeled truck chassis on which the tankette could be driven was built: the front driving sprockets of the *TK* were connected to the wheels and the composite vehicle could be driven along roads by the tankette's driver. However, this novel concept never got beyond the experimental stage.

In 1932 a still further improved tankette appeared, the *TKS*, with better shaped and distributed armour. A new 42-hp Polski Fiat engine took the extra weight (now 2.7 tons), though with some loss in speed and range, and a new type of periscope, the Gundlach (later used by both Soviet and British tanks), was fitted. A new gun mounting was adopted and although most *TKS* carried the Hotchkiss machine-gun the water-cooled, 7.9-mm Browning model 30 could also be used. Altogether 390 *TKS* were built in the next three years; a number were exported to Estonia.

Various modifications of the *TK/TKS* design appeared but none were suitable for production in quantity. A 1932 *TKD* SP gun/tank destroyer mounted the unsuccessful 47-mm model 25 gun in an open mounting and a later 1936 version, the Bofors 37-mm model 36 gun. A turreted *TK*, the *TKW*, appeared in 1934 but only six were built. By 1935 there was also a *TKF* with a 46-hp engine and two machine-guns, one a heavy 9-mm on an AA mounting that could engage

aircraft with the gunner remaining inside the vehicle, but this was killed by the 4 *TP* project.

In 1938 the *TK* chassis came back into production in modified form as the open-bodied *C* 2*P* artillery tractor for light anti-tank and AA guns. The next year, when it became clear that the 4 *TP* was not going to see service before 1940 at the earliest, it was decided to fit 150 normal *TK/TKS* with the 20-mm *FK* gun designed for the new light tank. This would increase the anti-tank potential of both the *OM* and *DP*. Although 44 were ordered for immediate delivery only 20 were in service by 1 September. They were quite effective: for example, on 16 September one of 71 *DP*'s vehicles knocked out three of the four German tanks the division was engaging. Available in such limited numbers, however, they could make little real impression.

The basic *TK/TKS* formation was the company or squadron depending on whether the tankettes were infantry or cavalry. In each was a command vehicle and two platoons of five

tankettes with a maintenance and supply platoon of two tankettes and various trailers for fuel, supplies and radio (which could also be truck-mounted). The cavalry squadrons formed part of a two-squadron 'armoured division' the other half of which was composed of Ursus model 29 or 34 armoured cars. Their task was reconnaissance and security for the horsemen while the infantry tankette companies were apparently allocated to their divisions for general support duties. The two *TKS* companies in the *OM* were half cavalry and half infantry. It was hoped to allocate eight of the 20-mm gun tankettes to the motorized brigades and four to each *DP* but this remained a paper intention.

When the Germans attacked there were, in addition to the *OM* companies, 25 *TK/TKS* companies and squadrons lining Poland's borders, with one in reserve with the Renaults. Two were with the Pomorze Army in the Polish corridor, six with Poznań Army, seven with the Łódź Army and four with the Krakow Army in the

south. Four were with Modlin Army and two with Marew Army guarding the East Prussian border. Spread out and vulnerable to all German tanks except the *PzKpfw* I, with all but the 20 up-gunned versions unable to inflict damage in return, the *TK/TKS* could not achieve much. The weakness of the tankette concept had been proved as far back as 1933 in the *Gran Chaco* War between Bolivia and Paraguay but it had been disregarded. All tankettes gave their infantry crews was lightly protected vulnerability, while they were too small and lightly armoured to be used as real tanks. Armoured power was not to be obtained so cheaply.

After the surrender the Germany Army pressed the Polish tankettes into service for occupation duties.

TKS

Weight 2.7 tons (2.74 tonnes)
Crew two
Armament one 7.9-mm Hotchkiss or Browning machine-gun or 20-mm *FK* gun
Armour hull front, sides and tail 8–10 mm, decking 5 mm, belly 3 mm
Engine one Polski Fiat inline four-cylinder air-cooled petrol, 42-hp
Speed 25 mph (40 km/h)
Range 112 miles (180 km)
Trench crossing 3 feet 3 inches (1 m)
Vertical step 1 foot 6 inches (45 cm)
Fording 1 foot 8 inches (50 cm)
Overall length 8 feet 5 inches (2.56 m)
Width 5 feet 9½ inches (1.76 m)
Height 4 feet 4½ inches (1.33 m)

Left: *The diminutive size of the TKS tankette is shown by this captured example next to a victorious German soldier. Note the sloping armour plates which distinguish this later model from its predecessor, the Reconnaisance Tank TK. Various types of machine-gun could be carried as armament*
Below: *An unarmed TK mounting the four-wheeled truck chassis experimentally developed to transport the tankette along roads. The TK's sprockets were connected to the wheels to drive the combination along roads*

VAU 33 and 7 TP Light Tanks

The Poles recognized that the tankettes ordered in 1929 would not fulfil all their armoured needs and therefore at the same time they purchased 38 Vickers 'Six-Ton' tanks, together with a production licence. This design, which actually weighed slightly over seven tons, was one of the most influential of the inter-war period, combining relative cheapness with adequate speed, mobility, reliability, protection and firepower. There were two versions: alternative A equipped with two machine-gun armed turrets and B with a single turret normally mounting a more effective short 47-mm gun and a co-axial machine-gun. The suspension was composed of two pairs of transverse leaf sprung bogie units each with two pairs of rubber-tyred road wheels. There were four return rollers and the 87-hp four-cylinder Armstrong Siddeley engine drove through the front sprockets.

Poland bought the A, although 22 were soon converted to B standard mounting the co-axial 7.9-mm machine-gun in a prominent armoured sleeve along with the 47-mm. The As originally had one 13.2-mm and one 7.9-mm air-cooled Hotchkiss machine-gun, the former was sometimes replaced by a short Hotchkiss 37-mm gun or second rifle calibre weapon. Browning machine-guns were fitted later. The Poles were dissatisfied with the British engine and a modified Battle Tank 1931 was developed with an improved Polish-built 92-hp Saurer diesel in a modified rear superstructure. It was put into very limited production two years later as the Vickers Armstrong Ursus 33, using parts imported from Britain. The original British vehicles were reconstructed to the new standard but only 52 VAU 33s, both 7.4-ton single (VAU 33 *jw*) and 7.2-ton double-turreted (VAU 33 *dw*) were assembled or rebuilt. Some of the Vickers chassis components went to build a new heavy artillery tractor, the *C 7P* which went into production in 1936 – this was also used as the basis for an armoured recovery vehicle.

A further modification of the Six-Tonner, the *7 TP* also appeared in 1936. This had improved armour (17-mm as against 13-mm) and a more powerful engine, the Saurer VBLD of 110 hp. The rear superstructure was again redesigned, as were the turrets. Owing to the lack of a suitable gun, all 22 of the new design were twin-turreted and designated Light Tank *7 TP dw*. Like the standard VAU 33 *dw* they normally mounted two 7.9-mm water-cooled Browning model 30 machine-guns, although Maxim 7.9-mm, Hotchkiss 7.9-mm or 13.2-mm weapons could be fitted. Six were later converted to the single-turreted *jw* configuration.

Under the 1936 rearmament plan a new single-turret, gun-armed *7 TP* was to be built. The Swedish Bofors 37-mm anti-tank gun was chosen by the Polish Army and the same manufacturer offered to develop a new turret for a tank version of this weapon for the *7 TP*. The first 18 turrets were built in Sweden and in February 1937 the first new *7 TP jw* was tested. Production began the next year: these later tanks had a modified turret with an extended, overhanging rear to accommodate a radio in company and platoon commander's vehicles. Fifty tanks, with

a new lighter CTID diesel, were ordered in 1939 and some may have come into service before 1 September. It was planned to exploit the new engine to increase armour thickness to 40 mm but neither this, nor a similar project which also involved hull redesign and a new Polish designed diesel engine, reached production.

A bridging tank was based on the *7 TP* or *C 7P* and both chassis could also be fitted with a bulldozer attachment. The most interesting variant was a railway wagon upon which either a tank or tractor could be driven and which then powered itself along the track, towing other wagons, if necessary. The *7 TP* wagons provided a dismountable armoured train and the *C 7P* the support and repair units. Some ten tank wagons and several *C 7P* tractors were ordered but their fate is unknown.

The *7 TP* first saw 'action' during the occupation of Teschen, Poland's share of the Munich dismemberment of Czechoslovakia. When she herself was the victim of aggression there were 169 on hand. Of these, 114 were immediately available for action in the two tank battalions and a third was in the process of formation. Sixteen more went into action before the campaign ended. The two complete battalions had an establishment of three companies each of 16 tanks, three five-tank platoons and a commander. There was also a battalion commander's tank and a maintenance and supply company. Third Battalion never got much beyond one company of tanks.

First Battalion was in process of transfer to the Pomorze Army in the Polish Corridor when Germany struck. It was ordered back to Warsaw

7 TP jw
Weight 9.25 tons (9.4 tonnes)
Crew three
Armament one 37-mm Model 37 (L/45) gun with
80 rounds and one 7.9-mm Hotchkiss machine-
gun with 4,000 rounds
Armour hull front and sides 10–17 mm, decking
5 mm, belly 4–10 mm, tail 9 mm; turret 8–15 mm
Engine one Saurer VBLD inline six-cylinder liquid-
cooled diesel, 110-hp
Speed 51½ mph (32 km/h)
Range 99 miles (160 km)
Trench crossing 6 feet (1.8 m)
Vertical step 2 feet 6 inches (76 cm)
Fording 3 feet 3 inches (1 m)
Overall length 15 feet 1 inch (4.6 m)
Width 7 feet 11 inches (2.41 m)
Height 7 feet 2 inches (2.15 m)

and after some small-scale fighting its survivors, reduced to company strength, joined the Warsaw Motorized Armoured Brigade. Second Battalion, fighting further south in Silesia, was more successful: on 4 September it destroyed six German tanks and two armoured cars for the loss of one *TP*, and next day wiped out an entire mechanized column. On the same day, in a major armoured battle eleven German tanks were knocked out for the loss of two *TP* and damage to another five. After this, German flanking advances caused withdrawal and the destruction of much of the Battalion's strength, owing to lack of fuel. Third Battalion fought in the defence of Warsaw and one of its platoons, together with anti-tank guns and a field gun in prepared defensive positions destroyed 40 German tanks in one of the latter's more ill-considered frontal attacks.

Forty VAU 33s were mobilized. Each *OM* had a company and both fought some major operations. After its success against the German Divisions, 10th Cavalry Brigade helped keep the escape routes to the south open. The Warsaw Brigade, reinforced by First Battalion's remaining 7 *TP*, mounted a series of counter-attacks that had some limited success before heavy losses and mounting resistance caused their abandonment.

After the surrender, 7 *TP jw* tanks saw limited service with the *Wehrmacht* as *PzKpfw 7 TP (p)*, and some were later passed to Romania. Both the 7 *TP* and its predecessor were good tanks for their time. Their firepower, at least in the *jw* versions, was still good by 1939 standards, but this could not compensate for numerical inferiority. Overwhelmed, they disappeared into the limbo of defeat.

Above: A late model 7 TP Light Tank, the single-turreted 7 TP jw, in one of the standard 1938–9 Polish camouflage schemes. Other tanks had additional brown patches or remained in plain green. Note the 37-mm tank gun which was developed by Bofors of Sweden
Left: A battalion of production 7 TP Light Tanks on exercise before World War II. Like the earlier VAU 33, the 7 TP was a modified version of the Vickers 'Six-Tonner' and was built to first twin-turreted (dw) and then single-turreted (jw) configurations

GREAT BRITAIN

Britain, the pioneer of armoured warfare, entered World War II with only 79 modern medium tanks. The rest of her tank strength was composed of 65 small, heavily armoured infantry support vehicles, 1,000 machine-gun light tanks and worn-out survivors of the 160 Vickers Mediums built in the 1920s. Apart from safeguarding the British Expeditionary Force's withdrawal, British armour was able to make little contribution to the 1940 campaign that was won by an enemy using ideas that were, ironically, fundamentally British.

In the period between the wars British military analysts, such as J F C Fuller and Basil Liddell Hart, had written of the strategic revolution that armour had wrought: the new mobility that could score decisive victories without the casualties of the previous world conflict. But Britain's commitment to modern land war at this time was at best half-hearted. For after World War I, the British Army reverted to its traditional role of colonial policing. Infantry, cavalry and, at most, a company of armoured cars or light tanks were the means of this style of operation – not the armoured division.

The 1920s were years when official policy was based on the premise that there would be no major war for ten years. Even after this assumption was abandoned in 1932 what rearmament there was tended to be concentrated on air and sea forces. Throughout the inter-war period money was hard to get. The official Tank Design Department was closed down and

Vickers had a virtual monopoly of tank design, producing first the Medium which provided a cheap and reliable new tank for the Royal Tank Corps (RTC) and then a range of tankettes, and light tanks.

During the late twenties and early thirties the British army toyed with progressive armoured doctrines and established the first experimental mechanized force in the world for independent operations. But by 1935 the emphasis had firmly shifted to the mechanization of the traditional arms. The infantry were to be given tracked carriers and heavily armoured tanks for close support. The cavalry were to get light tanks and scout carriers for reconnaissance, for the infantry divisions and mechanized cavalry were also to be grouped with tanks into mobile divisions for the traditional cavalry task of screening and exploitation. By the outbreak of war the British Army was perhaps the most mechanized in the world – but firmly wedded to traditional concepts of operations.

While light tanks continued to be produced in the largest numbers new types of infantry tanks were developed for the infantry support battalions and cruiser tanks for the tank brigades of the mobile divisions. With the infantry tank the emphasis was on protection; the cruiser stressed speed and mobility. So the shape of British tank procurement was set, with vehicles that were either heavily armoured but slow, or fast but thinly protected.

From 1935 the systematic conversion of

cavalry regiments into armoured formations began. By 1939 only four horsed cavalry regiments remained and the 18 regular mechanized cavalry regiments, nine reserve mechanized cavalry regiments, together with the eight regular and seven reserve battalions of the RTC were formed into the Royal Armoured Corps. The RTC units became battalions of the Royal Tank Regiment.

When the First Mobile Division had been formed in 1937, its establishment consisted of two, poorly equipped, light armoured brigades – as the cavalry brigades were now designated – with First Tank Brigade and support troops which included two motorized infantry battalions. Two years later the requirements for armoured forces were raised to two regular and four reserve armoured divisions. The structure was altered and First Armoured Division's establishment became two armoured brigades of three regiments each. There were to be 321 tanks in each division, 213 cruisers and 108 lights. The rest of the division was concentrated in a support group of one motorized infantry battalion and one motorized artillery regiment and engineer company. Early in 1940, a second battalion of motorized infantry was added to the support group together with an anti-aircraft/anti-tank regiment. When the crunch came and the division was actually deployed some 134 of its 284 tanks were still light tanks and it went to France without its infantry and other important services. In all over 700 British tanks, from various units,

were lost in the *débâcle* in France and Belgium.

In Egypt the story was happier, at least at first. Western Desert Force of 31,000 men and 275 tanks (including the Seventh Armoured Division and two infantry divisions with a regiment of infantry tanks in support), smashed the traditionally based Italian forces of 240,000 men which had invaded Egypt, destroying or capturing 380 Italian tanks. But once mature German armoured forces appeared the imperial forces were less successful.

With the example of the French campaign and armoured successes in North Africa, the British pressed ahead with the creation of more armoured divisions. A division now amounted to some 14,000 men with 340 tanks. The infantry component was now three battalions, which improved the balance of the formation, but it still remained too heavily weighted with tanks to the detriment of all arms co-ordination.

In order to provide the vehicles for the new formations, British industry was mobilized for tank production. Motor firms were involved from an early stage in the British tank programme and heavy engineering firms including railway companies were also brought in. By 1939, after a slow start, tank production had already outstripped Germany's; in 1942 8,611 British tanks emerged, more than double Germany's output of 4,198.

Many of the tanks produced, however, proved too unreliable for active service and many which reached the front line had problems with troublesome engines and other components. Nevertheless much of the criticism that has been levelled at the quality of British armour is unjust. In the early years of the war the armour of British cruisers usually equalled that of their opponents and they often had a speed advantage, while British infantry tanks were immune to enemy anti-tank or tank weapons. Later, when total immunity disappeared, British infantry tanks always proved tough opponents and their protection and superior mobility made up for their deficiencies in firepower. The two-pounder (40-mm) gun in service for the early years of the war was the finest tank weapon in the Western world, in terms of armour penetration.

In the unsuccessful desert battles of 1941–2, defeat was usually caused by the futile offering of unsupported tanks as sacrifices to the German anti-tank guns. Such operations showed that tanks needed proper all arms support and the modifications in the structure of the armoured division adopted by General Auchinleck in this theatre became standard. One armoured brigade was replaced by a three battalion infantry brigade and the artillery was increased to four regiments. In 1943 the reconnaissance element was changed to a full scale tank-equipped armoured reconnaissance regiment and as time went on self-propelled equipment began to be allocated to the division's artillery. By 1944 the British armoured division had an establishment of almost 15,000 men and it contained 306 tanks; with four battalions each of tanks and infantry.

British factories were unable to keep up with demand and from 1941 American tanks were adopted in increasing quantities. With their increased reliability and superior armament, they tended to be used in action in preference to British models. The 75-mm armed Grant/Lee series gave British armour a good dual-purpose weapon for the first time which could engage anti-tank guns as well as tanks. And the Sherman, which first appeared in 1942, gave the armoured divisions a better all-round tank than any available from domestic industry; during 1943–5 this became the most numerous type in British service.

Other armour was imported from the USA and Canada, notably self-propelled guns and tank destroyers, but the modification of tank chassis for specialized tasks was a field that the British made their own. The main stimulus was the need to penetrate the German 'Atlantic Wall' and 79th Armoured Division, under Major General Sir Percy Hobart, was formed as a special siege train for this purpose. The range of vehicles developed for this force, based on British, American and Canadian chassis, was bewildering and they proved their worth on many occasions in 1944–5.

In 1944, with the Allies forced to use numbers to defeat an enemy at least their equal, and often their superior, in technology and tactical skill, the accent changed to a slower moving war of attrition. Co-operation between arms was even more at a premium and armoured brigades began to be employed individually, joining the infantry tank brigades as the armoured edge of what had become an entirely mechanized army.

Attrition put a premium on numbers and some 25,115 tanks were produced in Britain during World War II, slightly more than the German 1939–45 total of 23,487. Total British AFV production, including all tracked carriers, came to a massive 85,340. For a declining industrial power such a translation of technological resources into military power was a great achievement.

Left: *A Churchill AVRE on the Normandy beaches; the development of armoured siege vehicles was one of Britain's major contributions to World War II*

Light Tanks Marks I-VIII

The origins of the British Light Tank series go back to the two 1925 tankette designs of Major Martel and Captain Carden. These small two-man vehicles were designed to put the infantry on tracks in response to the ideas of such analysts as J F C Fuller or General Estienne. Both types – the Morris Martel and the Carden Loyd – had tracks and wheels; armament was a single limited-traverse machine-gun.

After the Experimental Mobile Force exercises of 1927–8 it was found that the Carden Loyd vehicles, by now designated light tanks, were more robust, stable and mobile, and development of the latest Mark VI, which dispensed with wheels, continued in two directions. One was as a machine-gun and general carrier for infantry and cavalry (later to be produced in great quantity) and the other a proper light tank for the Royal Tank Corps (RTC). For the latter task, Vickers Armstrong produced a Mark VII with low revolving turret and modified suspension. This was numbered A4E1. The next tank, A4E2, was to a modified Mark VIII design and was accepted by the Army in 1929 as Light Tank Mark I.

Instead of the A4E1's suspension of two, large, solid bogie-wheel pairs each side suspended by leaf springs from a common external girder, A4E2 had two separate leaf-sprung pairs of spoked wheels connected to the hull. A 60-hp Meadows 6 EPT engine was mounted in the right hull front and the driver sat to its left with a commander gunner behind in an off-set turret mounting a single 0.303-inch (7.7-mm) Vickers machine-gun. Drive was through a crash gearbox and front sprockets, and steering by clutch and brake. The tank was of simple bolted construction and armour was 14 mm maximum.

Three more tanks were built followed by five Mark IAs with a better shaped hull. The third Mark IA, A4E8, had Horstmann suspension which utilized coil springs working on large quarter-circle cranks connected to the hull pivot. This was used in the next model, the Rolls Royce engined Mark II, which had a larger turret and was ordered in slightly greater quantities. Sixty-six were produced in three variants, including 21 Mark II Bs which reverted to the Meadows power unit and crash gearbox.

A new, further improved suspension system was tested using modified cranks and twin angled springs on either side of the road wheels. This was adopted on the slightly modified Mark III light tank which entered service in 1933, the new suspension being retro-fitted to earlier vehicles. The Mark III also had the six-cylinder Rolls Royce engine and Wilson transmission of Marks II and IIA.

Vickers tried to simplify the design to aid production and increase protection and speed. Two prototypes appeared in 1933 – A4E19 and A4E20 – both equipped with Meadows engines

Top right: *A Mark IVC captured by the Germans. Note the air-cooled Besa machine-guns*
Bottom right: *The Mark III, one of the earlier members of the Vickers light tank series. Note the earlier-type suspension with separate idler and the single machine-gun in the one-man turret*

Light Tank Mark VIB
Weight 5.2 tons (5.3 tonnes)
Crew three
Armament one 0.5-inch (12.7-mm) Vickers machine-gun with 400 rounds and one 0.303-inch (7.7-mm) Vickers machine-gun with 2,500 rounds
Armour hull nose and glacis 12 mm, sides 14 mm, decking and tail 10 mm, belly 8 mm; turret front and sides 15 mm, rear 12 mm
Engine one Meadows inline six-cylinder water-cooled petrol, 88-hp
Speed 35 mph (56 km/h)
Range 125 miles (201 km)
Trench crossing 5 feet (1.5 m)
Vertical step 2 feet (61 cm)
Fording 2 feet 6 inches (76 cm)
Overall length 13 feet 2 inches (4.01 m)
Width 6 feet 10 inches (2.08 m)
Height 7 feet 5 inches (2.26 m)

The tank illustrated is the Mark VIB, the most numerous version of the Light Tank series. Note the larger turret and Vickers armament

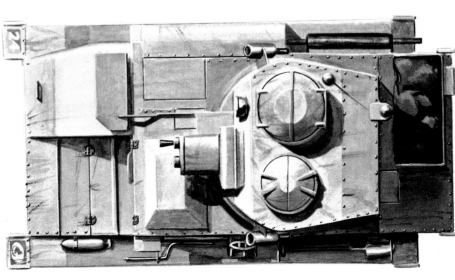

and slightly different versions of a new suspension which dispensed with the return rollers and rear idlers. That of the A4E20, with the addition of a single return roller, was adopted for the next production series, the Mark IV. The Meadows engine was retained with a synchromesh gearbox. Generally speaking the Mark IV proved a disappointing tank with a high superstructure and centre of gravity compounding the cross-country problems of the suspension.

Until now all the light tanks had crews of only two but this put great strains on the commander/gunner, similar to those caused in French tanks with one-man turrets. Vickers, therefore, built two three-man prototypes in 1933, the L3E1 and L3E2, with two-man turrets armed with twin machine-guns – one 0.303-inch (7.7-mm) and one 0.50-inch (12.7-mm). Twelve experimental Mark Vs were built based on these in 1934. The two-man turret was the major new feature with provision for a commander and radio operator/gunner. The 88-hp six-cylinder Meadows ESTL engine was fitted and speed reduced from 37 to 32 mph (60 to 51 km/h). Cross-country performance was superior to that of the Mark IV, but the turret was rather cramped and only ten more were built.

Below: *A Tetrarch, fitted out for action*
Bottom: *A Harry Hopkins*

Further modifications took place to produce the last and most numerous version of this series of light tanks, the Mark VI. The turret was enlarged with provision for a better radio, and armour thickness and weight were both increased. Various small modifications were carried out to produce the Mark VIA and B (the most numerous type), while the Mark VIC had wider tracks, and a new armament of Besa air-cooled machine-guns.

As they became available, light tanks were issued to the Royal Tank Corps battalions and to cavalry regiments. In September 1939 the largest proportion of the 1,300 or so tanks in the Imperial forces were Vickers Lights – about 1,000 of them, with all but 162 being Mark VI variants. An important reason for this preponderance of light tanks was the mere fact that they were a cheap way of providing numerical armoured strength. As far as the RTC was concerned light tanks were better than no tanks, and they were suited to the major operational task of the inter-war period, imperial policing.

When war seemed imminent and progressive armoured doctrines surfaced once more, it was too late. Light tanks were usually the only tanks available, despite being under-gunned and under-armoured little vehicles even by the standards of 1939–40. Cavalry reconnaissance regiments of Mark VIBs formed most of the BEF's armour, and Mark VIB and C light tanks formed a third

of First Armoured Division's strength when it was sent to France in May 1940. Most of the light tanks that served in France never returned. Surviving Vickers light tanks from Mark II onwards retained an important role in Britain for service and training. They also played a significant part in the initial fighting in the Middle East, where Seventh Armoured Division continued to rely on the Mark VI for at least part of its strength until well into 1941.

Commonwealth Mark III light tanks also saw action in Ethiopia, while Mark VI series lights were used in Greece, Crete, Malta, Syria, Java, and Iran. When they ceased to be useful as tanks some were used as armoured observation post vehicles for artillery units in the Western Desert. Others were used as anti-aircraft tanks. Several designs of Vickers light tank were sold abroad in the 1930s to Argentina, Belgium, China, Latvia, Lithuania, the Netherlands, Portugal and Scandinavia.

Vickers light tank development did not stop with the series descended from the Carden Loyd tankette. In 1937 development began of a private-venture, new three-man light tank with a totally new suspension of four, equal-size road wheels each side. An official Mark VII Light Tank specification was written around the design but in 1940 the programme was reconsidered. Lights had been shown to be only useful for reconnaissance purposes and the Army considered armoured cars to be generally sufficient for this role. Only 177 Mark VIIs were actually built. The 7½-ton Tetrarch, as the Mark VII was now known, carried a two-pounder (40-mm) gun and co-axial Besa machine-gun. As a more or less adequately armed light tank it seemed to lend itself for use with airborne formations. The Hamilcar glider was developed for it and in order to increase the tank's utility in a general support role some tanks were fitted with a high explosive shell-firing 3-inch (76.2-mm) howitzer which replaced the original weapon.

Eight Airborne Tetrarchs were deployed on the evening of D-Day to support the troops of Sixth Airborne division at the Orne bridgehead. Despite difficulties, such as one tank falling out of a glider over the Channel and others getting their suspensions entangled with parachute equipment in the dropping zone, they did some useful, if limited, work. Others were used during the Rhine crossing and a troop was retained for a few years after the war for similar use. Tetrarchs were also used operationally by the British in Madagascar and by the Russians.

Vickers persevered with the light tank concept and developed a vehicle with thicker armour (38 as against 16 mm), redesigned turret and hull and power assisted steering. Weight and size were increased making the tank unsuitable for use with the Hamilcar; 102 of the new vehicles were built as the Light Tank Mark VIII – also known as 'Harry Hopkins', after President Franklin Roosevelt's roving ambassador. Armament remained a two-pounder (40-mm) and co-axial Besa machine-gun and, as in the Tetrarch, the Littlejohn Adaptor was sometimes fitted at the end of the muzzle which squeezed the shell to give greater velocity. Enough Stuarts, and later Chaffees, were available for Britain's light tank requirements and no Mark VIIIs were used in action.

Infantry Tanks Marks I and II Matilda

In 1934 the requirement was drawn up for a tank whose task would be to give direct support to infantry. Speed was unimportant and the emphasis was to be on protection. Major General Sir Hugh Elles, Master General of the Ordnance, was a strong supporter of this concept and accepted an offer from Sir John Carden to design a small, cheap infantry tank for around £5,000 to £6,000. The first prototype A11 appeared in September 1936.

Soon dubbed 'Matilda', the new tank was simple to an extreme. It was small, 15 feet 11 inches (4.85 m) long and 6 feet 1½ inches (1.86 m) high, had a narrow, 7 feet 6 inch (2.28 m), riveted hull with small cast turret, and was armoured to 60 mm, more than enough protection from contemporary anti-tank guns. A standard Ford V8 car engine and transmission drove through the rear sprockets; steering was a version of the system used in the Vickers light tank series. Suspension was again of standard Vickers type with two leaf-sprung four wheel bogie assemblies each side to which, in the prototype, the two return rollers were attached.

In the 60 vehicles ordered for production in 1937 as Infantry Tank Mark I the return rollers were repositioned on the hull sides. Another 89 vehicles were ordered before production ceased in August, 1940. This first Matilda weighed 11 tons, was extremely slow (8 mph or 13 km/h), and lightly armed with either a 0.303-inch (7.7-mm) or 0.5-inch (12.7-mm) Vickers machine-gun in an armoured sleeve. These weapons could shoot up enemy infantry and light defences and the 0.5-inch (12.7-mm) had some capability against lightly armoured vehicles.

Several shortcomings were soon apparent, and as early as 1936 a successor was being developed which would be faster (15 mph or 24 km/h), have heavier armament and a much better crew lay-out with a three-man turret. This new tank had very thick 78-mm armour fitted to the hull front and a turret of the same standard of protection. Unlike the A11, the new A12's hull was formed of steel castings, and plates bolted together. The turret was also cast. A new suspension, protected by armoured skirting, was based on that of the Vickers Medium, with five twin bogie assemblies each side mounted on bell cranks coil-sprung against each other with a larger jockey roller at the front. The form of construction and the suspension proved complex to construct and did not lend itself to mass production.

Two rear-mounted AEC diesel engines connected at the front and drove through a Wilson epicyclic pre-selector gearbox via the rear sprockets. Steering was by clutch and brake, and the driver sat in the centre of the hull front. The armament of a standard two-pounder (40-mm) gun and 0.303 inch (7.7-mm) Vickers machine-gun mounted co-axially was concentrated in the hydraulically traversed turret. With its greater protection and firepower the 'Matilda Senior', as it was soon dubbed, was far superior to its predecessor.

In May 1938 orders totalled 165. More soon followed, but only two Infantry Tanks Mark II were in service in September 1939. When First Army Tank Brigade joined the BEF later the same month only one battalion – Fourth Battalion Royal Tank Regiment – of 50 Mark Is was available.

Not until May 1940, days before the German offensive, was Seventh RTR sent over to France with 27 Matildas and 23 new Matilda Seniors. They played a crucial role in the campaign. With the Mark II tanks redistributed among the two battalions and supporting two reinforced infantry battalions the tank brigades struck at the advancing *Panzer* corridor south of Arras. Rommel's Seventh *Panzer* Division and the *Totenkopf SS* Motorized Infantry Division were severely shaken by the sudden onslaught of British armour which proved impervious to the standard German anti-tank weapon, the 37-mm gun. Only hastily deployed 105-mm and 150-mm field howitzers which proved effective against the Matilda Is' unprotected suspension, and 88-mm anti-aircraft guns which were able to penetrate the tanks' armour, saved the day for the Germans. The British attack, delivered with little support, soon ran out of steam, but the

Below: *Matilda II. Note the thick well-shaped armour, the Matilda's main strength. In some tanks from Mark III onwards the two-pounder (40-mm) gun was replaced by a three-inch (76.2-mm) howitzer*

Infantry Tank Mark IIA Matilda III
Weight 26.5 tons (26.9 tonnes)
Crew four
Armament one two-pounder (40-mm) Mark IX or X
(L/50) gun with 93 rounds and one 7.92-mm Besa
machine-gun with 2,925 rounds
Armour nose and front 78 mm, glacis 47 mm, sides
40–70 mm, skirting 25 mm, belly 13–20 mm, deck-
ing 20 mm, tail 55 mm; turret front, sides and
rear 75 mm, top 20 mm
Engine two Leyland E148 and 149 or E164 and
E165 inline six-cylinder liquid-cooled diesel,
190-hp
Speed 15 mph (24 km/h)
Range 150 miles (257.5 km)
Trench crossing 7 feet (2.13 m)
Vertical step 2 feet (61 cm)
Fording 3 feet 6 inches (1.07 m)
Overall length 18 feet 5 inches (5.61 m)
Width 8 feet 6 inches (2.59 m)
Height 8 feet 3 inches (2.51 m)

Above: *Matilda III. Note the distinctive twin
exhaust pipe arrangement of the Leyland engine*
Below: *A Matilda Baron Mark IIIA mine-
clearing flail*

report sent back to German high command confirmed them in their fears that the advanced *Panzer* units were dangerously exposed. Hitler, therefore, stopped short of Dunkirk and the BEF was given time to prepare a strong evacuation bridgehead before the offensive reopened.

After Dunkirk the remaining Infantry Tanks Mark I were relegated to training and the term Matilda became the official designation of the Infantry Tank Mark II. The first vehicles became known as Matilda I; a Matilda II soon appeared (Infantry Tank Mark IIA) with co-axial Besa machine-gun instead of the Vickers. Leyland joined the production programme and produced their own engines for the Matilda III. The Matilda IV had improved E170/1 Leyland diesel engines and the Matilda V an improved gear shift system. In all, some 2,987 A12 Matildas were produced by August 1943.

These later Matildas were modified for desert conditions and in North Africa the type scored its greatest successes. Re-equipped with the latest Matildas, Seventh RTR was sent out to join the Western Desert Force in September 1940. With the Fourth Indian and the Sixth Australian Infantry Divisions, they played a vital part in the Italian defeats at Nibeiwa, Tummar, Bardia and Tobruk. The Matilda's reputation as the 'Queen of the Battlefield' was soon established and their morale value enormous. The Commander of Sixth Australian Division compared the value of each tank to a whole battalion of infantry. The Matilda's

reliability was also demonstrated in East Africa where a squadron of Fourth RTR were sent at the end of 1940 to support Fourth Infantry Division against the Italians in Eritrea. In the absence of proper support facilities, they were able to keep going after suffering such major mechanical defects as damaged suspensions.

With the coming of the Germans to North Africa in 1941 the Matilda met its old opponent of the previous year. Seventh RTR, now joined by the Fourth helped to hold Tobruk, but victory was more elusive. In Operation Battleaxe of June 1941, when the two regiments were joined as the Fourth Armoured Brigade of Seventh Armoured Division, the Matilda was more vulnerable. Matildas could take three 88-mm hits and survive but the operation ended in failure with the loss of 64 tanks. In tank versus tank combat, however, Matildas had proved superior to the German armour: more than 60 per cent of 15th *Panzer* Division's tanks were knocked out in one clash with Seventh RTR at Capuzzo. Back in the infantry support role Matildas also did well during the Crusader offensive.

Yet the era of the Matilda was steadily passing. It lacked the long-range, high-explosive potential that would have enabled it to engage the German anti-tank guns on equal terms. Its two-pounder (40-mm) required a direct hit to destroy the enemy weapon while the Besa machine-gun had a maximum range of 800 yards (731 m), less than the effective range of the German 88-mm or

captured Russian 76.2-mm gun against the Matilda's armour.

First and 32nd Army Tank Brigades had Matildas on strength for the Gazala battle at the end of March 1942, but their counter-attacks were broken up, with heavy losses, by German anti-tank guns. Seventh RTR still had Matildas in the 32nd Brigade at Tobruk and these were lost in the final stand there. Such losses hastened the disappearance of the tank and its replacement by the more easily produced Valentine. Matilda Scorpion mine-sweeping tanks saw service in North Africa while later Baron vehicles were used for training. Matilda CDL (Canal Defence Light) vehicles were produced but never used in action.

As well as fighting in North Africa, standard Matildas served in Malta, Crete, Russia and the Far East. The tank's reliability and mobility made it well suited to the difficult conditions of the Pacific theatre where its armament and firepower were more than able to deal with the Japanese. The Australians turned to the Matilda for infantry support in New Guinea, Bougainville and Borneo. They also produced flame-thrower and bulldozer versions of the Matilda – undoubtedly the finest British tank of the early war years.

Below: *Infantry Tank Mark I Matilda. This light tank series gained its nickname from its appearance in profile which was said to resemble that of a contemporary cartoon duck*

Infantry Tank Mark III Valentine

When they were approached in 1938 with a view to constructing the Infantry Tank Mark II, Vickers decided to produce a comparable vehicle based on their previous A9 and A10 cruiser tanks. The design had certain drawbacks compared with the Matilda Senior, however, and when first offered to the War Office just before St Valentine's Day 1938, it did not gain immediate acceptance. But the deteriorating international situation led to a change in policy and 275 were ordered in 1939. The first tanks, designated Infantry Tank Mark III, were in service by the end of 1940. Soon known as 'Valentine', the designation became official in June 1941.

Construction of the new tank was simple, the hull comprising plates bolted and riveted together. Some castings were used in the construction of the turret. Suspension was on the same simple lines as the A9 and A10, with two three-wheel bogie assemblies each side, each with a single coil spring damped by shock absorbers. The 135-hp AEC A189 petrol engine drove through the rear sprockets. Steering was by clutch and brake. The power-traversed turret mounted a two-pounder (40-mm) gun and co-axial Besa machine-gun. Armour was thick, although not as strong as the Matilda's. Maximum speed was the same, 15 mph (24 km/h), but range disappointing at 70 miles (113 km). This could be extended to 105 miles (169 km) with auxiliary fuel tanks.

Valentine had one significant advantage over Matilda however – ease of construction. It took one-third less man hours to produce and soon other firms were producing the vehicles in addition to Vickers. Arrangements were also made for the construction of Valentines in Canada. Canadian Valentines were to be fitted with GMC diesel engines and it was soon decided to convert the British version to diesel power to increase range, reduce the fire risk and economize on crude oil. After 350 tanks, therefore, the

Valentine I was replaced by the Valentine II (Infantry Mark III Star) which adopted the A190 diesel version of the original AEC engine with slightly reduced power. Some 700 of this version were built before the end of 1941; it was the first type to see combat service, being sent out with Eighth RTR to take part in Operation Crusader as part of First Army Tank Brigade. Valentines were also used by other infantry tank regiments in the Western Desert, Seventh, 42nd and 44th RTR steadily replacing the Matilda tank with them as losses mounted during 1942.

Valentines did not go only to the infantry tank formations for which they had been intended. From the middle of 1941, as readily available and well-protected tanks, they were allocated to the armoured divisions as cruisers: Sixth, Eighth, Eleventh and First Polish Armoured Divisions were so equipped. In the Alamein fighting the Eighth's 23rd Armoured Brigade was thrown into action as an infantry support formation. Despite heavy losses charging anti-tank guns at Ruweisat Ridge unsupported, the Brigade played a vital part in assisting the initial infantry assaults during Second Alamein – the task for which the tank had been designed. Following the break-through, the 23rd's Valentines demonstrated their great mechanical reliability, travelling 3,000 miles (4,828 km) on a set of tracks. Sixth Armoured Division, which landed in North Africa with First Army in November 1942, had mixed squadrons of Crusaders and Valentines in its 26th Armoured Brigade.

By this time, design improvements had been made. Firstly, a three-man turret had been adopted with the gun moved forward and the turret sides extended backwards so that a fourth crew member could be incorporated. Not many of these Valentine IIIs, saw service.

More common was the Valentine IV which adopted the General Motors engine of the

Canadian vehicle in a standard Valentine II. Although range was decreased to 90 miles (145 km) or 165 miles (266 km) with auxiliary fuel tanks compared to the AEC engined version, the twin stroke GM 6-71 Model 604 diesel of 138 hp was quieter and more reliable. The new engine was also fitted to the Valentine III to produce the Valentine V.

Before the end of 1941 development had begun of a Valentine mounting a new six-pounder (57-mm) gun. The three-man turret was used, with its crew reduced to two once more due to the size of the gun. The commander now doubled as loader and the gunner as wireless operator. Side armour was reduced to keep weight within limits at 17.2 tons and the machine-gun was deleted from the turret. The six-pounder (57-mm) had a disappointing high explosive capability, and the first tanks tended to be issued together with two-pounder (40-mm) vehicles (which at least had a machine-gun) as anti-tank support tanks. The AEC engined vehicles were designated Valentine Mark VIII and those with General Motors engines became Valentine Mark IX, some with uprated engines of 165 hp. Some of both marks had the 45-calibre Mark III six-pounder (57-mm) replaced by the longer 52-calibre Mark V. The Valentine X which came into production in 1943 reintroduced the turret machine-gun with the Mark V six-pounder (57-mm). By now the up-rated General Motors engine was standard. Finally came the Mark XI which had the six-pounder (57-mm) replaced by a 75-mm weapon with dual anti-tank/high explosive capability. The XI was the last Valentine mark to appear, as production of the tank ceased in early 1944.

Below: Valentine IVs on manoeuvre in Britain. Valentines were widely used from 1941–3 for training new British armoured divisions as well as the infantry tank battalions for which they had been originally intended

Infantry Tank Mark III Valentine II
Weight 16 tons (16.25 tonnes)
Crew three
Armament one 2-pounder (40-mm) Mark IX or X (L/50) gun with 79 rounds, one 7.92-mm Besa machine-gun with 1,575 rounds and one 0.303-inch (7.7-mm) Bren machine-gun with 600 rounds
Armour hull nose, driver's plate and sides 60 mm, glacis 30 mm, decking 17 mm, belly 7–20 mm, tail 60 mm; turret front 65 mm, sides 60 mm, top 20 mm, rear 65 mm
Engine one AEC type A190 inline six-cylinder liquid-cooled diesel, 131-hp
Speed 15 mph (24 km/h)
Range 110 miles (177 km)
Trench crossing 7 feet 9 inches (2.36 m)
Vertical step 3 feet (91 cm)
Fording 3 feet (91 cm)
Overall length 17 feet 9 inches (5.41 m)
Width 8 feet 7½ inches (2.63 m)
Height 6 feet 7½ inches (2.02 m)

The tank illustrated is a Valentine II as used in North Africa. Note the two-man turret

Valentine tanks remained in first line British Army service as battle tanks until their replacement by Shermans at the end of the North African campaign. A Special Service tank squadron took Valentines to fight the Vichy French in Madagascar, while Free French forces were allocated ex-British vehicles in North Africa in 1942–3. The Valentine also saw service against the Japanese with Indian and New Zealand forces. The Soviet Union were sent 2,690 of the tanks – 1,300 British and almost the entire Canadian production run. The tank proved very popular with the Russians who were the major operational user of up-gunned models. Britain used Valentine XIs as battery commander's tanks for tank destroyer battalions in the North-West Europe campaign of 1944–5. Valentines were also used as artillery observation post tanks.

Two types of self-propelled gun saw service on the Valentine chassis. The first of these mounted the standard 25-pounder (88-mm) field gun. An order for 100 was placed in November, 1941. The Carrier Valentine 25-pounder (88-mm) Gun Mark I placed the gun in a simple box-type, thinly protected superstructure on a normal Valentine II chassis. The weapon, intended primarily as a tank destroyer, had only limited traverse, 15° in elevation and 4° to each side. Only 32 rounds were carried and the vehicle normally towed a normal gun limber, in order to double ammunition capacity. The crew numbered four. By the time the vehicle entered service with the Royal Artillery in 1942 the six-pounder (57-mm) anti-tank gun had become available. The new SP became, therefore, a general purpose self-propelled gun, a role which emphasized its several shortcomings.

With the advent of the 'Priest' self-propelled 105-mm howitzer, the Valentine Carrier became known as the 'Bishop'. The superior American weapon eventually replaced the British gun but not until after Bishops had fought through North Africa into Tunisia, Sicily and the early part of the Italian campaign.

As the Bishop was being phased out of service, a much more successful Valentine-based SP was being put into production mounting the 17-pounder (76.2-mm) anti-tank gun. The gun faced towards the rear of the Valentine chassis; the welded front superstructure (later vehicles had a light steel roof) was armoured to 20 mm and the gun had a wide traverse of 45° to either side with 15½° of elevation and 7½° of depression. Together with the American M10, the SP 17-pounder (76.2-mm) Valentine or 'Archer' as it was usually known, served with the Royal Artillery in Northern Europe and Italy in 1944–5.

Valentines were used in the development of flame weapons and for mine-clearing purposes. Most important were the Valentine Scorpion flails – Valentine IIs and IIIs modified with fixed flail equipment powered by two Ford V8 engines in a protected superstructure (14 mm). Some 150 were built and used for training. The most novel means of dealing with minefields was a Valentine fitted with rockets to jump over the mine-laden area. Unfortunately, the tank usually landed upside down so the idea was abandoned.

Rather more practical were the amphibious Valentines. These were Marks V, IX and XI tanks fitted with Straussler duplex drive system with a propeller and collapsible canvas screen; 625 were produced and used mainly for training. The Valentine saw more extensive service as a bridge-layer. The standard 30-foot (9.14-m) 'scissors bridge', placed on the Valentine chassis, was laid by a hydraulic system without the crew needing to leave the tank. The Valentine bridge-layer was used in Italy, North-West Europe and Burma. There were also Valentine bulldozer and CDL variants.

More Valentine tank chassis were constructed than any other individual British type during the war years, 6,855 being built until production ceased in early 1944. Canadian production boosts the figure to 8,275. Ease of construction coupled with reliability were the Valentine's basic assets, but they could not completely overcome the disadvantages of low speed and poor crew layout and, as time went on, deficient armour and firepower. By 1944 the Valentine was patently inadequate as a battle tank and production plans for a later version, the 'Valiant', were abandoned.

Below: *A Valentine X produced in 1943 which reintroduced the turret machine-gun combined with the six-pounder (57-mm) gun. Earlier six-pounder Valentines had dispensed with secondary armament to simplify production*
Bottom: *The reliable Valentine chassis was used for a variety of specialized purposes such as carrier for the 'scissors bridge'. Each armoured brigade had six of these vehicles and they were used in Italy, North-West Europe and Burma*

Infantry Tank Mark IV Churchill

The last and best of the line of British infantry tanks had its origins in the first month of war when a larger and more heavily armed, armoured and mobile infantry tank was called for to replace the Matilda. Armour was to be 80 mm, the tank would be capable of climbing a five-foot (3.7-metre) obstacle and the engine was to be either a Harland and Wolff diesel or Meadows petrol engine giving a maximum speed of 15 mph (24 km/h). It was decided to mount a Matilda turret and armament with another two-pounder (40-mm) in the hull front and extra Besa machine-guns in the hull sides. Prototypes of this project, designated A20, were ordered, but when the first vehicles appeared the design was shown to be inadequate. The Meadows engine did not give enough power, the new Merritt Brown gear-box gave problems and the extra armament had to be deleted to keep weight down to the specified 37½ tons. In June 1940, Vauxhall were asked to redesign the vehicle as a new A22, a scaled down design that would be produced in large quantities from 1941.

The suspension was based on that of the French *Char* B with the tracks carried around the hull to aid mobility across rough ground. The A20's suspension of 14 small bogie wheels each side was shortened to 11, each independently coil sprung. Drive was through the rear sprockets and the new Merritt Brown gearbox steered the tank by means of the controlled differential principle. This system was similar in effect to that of the later German tanks, but simpler and

more serviceable. Armament consisted of a standard two-pounder (40-mm) in the turret with co-axial Besa machine-gun; a three-inch (76.2-mm) howitzer was located in the hull. The tank therefore possessed three capabilities – anti-tank, high-explosive and anti-personnel. Armoured protection was 101 mm maximum and weight 38½ tons. The 350-hp Bedford twin six-cylinder had a maximum speed of 17 mph (27 km/h) which was adequate for the infantry support role. Although the turret was cast, hull construction was of riveted steel plates to which armour was bolted.

The first 14 production models of the Infantry Tank Mark I were completed in June 1941 and the name 'Churchill' was soon adopted. Some 303 were completed before the Mark II appeared, substituting a machine-gun for the three-inch (76.2-mm) hull howitzer. A few Mark II close support vehicles were completed with the howitzer in the turret and two-pounder (40-mm) guns in the hull. These were 1,127 Mark IIs completed while some Mark Is were converted to II standard.

These early Churchills had many mechanical defects due to the speed of development. Transmission, clutch, steering, suspension and even hull construction all needed modification. Older tanks were modified in a systematic reworking programme that began in May 1942. From then on, tanks were regularly brought up to the latest specifications.

Mechanical refinements were incorporated in the Churchill III, which had the new 43-calibre,

six-pounder (57-mm) gun. This increased theoretical armour penetration to 81 mm of 30° plate at 500 yards (457 m) although high explosive capability was disappointing. A welded turret was adopted for the gun. The first IIIs appeared in March 1942; by the middle of the year 40 tanks per week were coming off the production lines. A total of 675 new Churchill IIIs were built. In the middle of 1942 a further type appeared, the Mark IV, which had a better-shaped cast turret. Some 1,622 were built, a number with the improved 50-calibre Mark V six-pounder (57-mm) and slightly improved muzzle velocity and armour penetration.

The first Churchills to see action were the Mark Is and IIIs of the Canadian Calgary Regiment in the Dieppe raid in August 1942. They were specially fitted for deep wading with extended intakes and exhausts. The operation ran into opposition and, without assault engineer or infantry support, the Churchills could do little to save a doomed operation.

The type's mechanical problems prevented immediate deployment in Africa, but six Mark IIIs were sent out to Egypt in time for the Second Battle of Alamein. The Churchills proved to be tough, with armour able to deflect 50-mm and

Below: *A Churchill III (note the angular welded turret) crosses a trench by means of fascines. This tank lacks the track guards fitted from the middle of 1942 and has non-standard extensions to its later model intakes*

even 75-mm anti-tank rounds – one tank was hit no fewer than 31 times by 50-mm anti-tank shells and still remained intact. In the entire battle the six tanks were hit 105 times but only one was knocked out.

With this experience to go on, two Brigades of Churchills, the 21st and 25th, were sent to North Africa to fight with First Army in Tunisia. The brigades were intended for allocation to infantry divisions in order to provide direct support, but each brigade was attached instead to two infantry brigades to form two of the short-lived 'new model' divisions. At Steamroller Farm, Hunt's Gap, Longstop Hill and elsewhere the techniques of 'all arms' warfare were developed anew. In tank versus tank combat the six-pounder (57-mm) proved extremely effective and the vehicle showed its remarkable mobility. Churchills could go where no German thought possible; at Steamroller Farm the German commander ascribed his defeat to the 'mad tank battalion' that had scaled 'impossible heights'.

A plan to replace the Churchill by the Cromwell, as the main battle tank, was soon shelved and it was decided to improve the Churchill's firepower – its major weakness being high explosive capability. A new close support Mark V appeared, therefore, which substituted a 95-mm howitzer for the six-pounder (57-mm) of the Mark IV. This weapon fired a 25-pounder (95-mm) shell, almost double the weight of the three-inch (76.2-mm) howitzer's projectile. One tenth of all Churchills completed were to mount this new weapon to support more conventionally armed vehicles. Other close support firepower was provided by older Churchills kept in service in the Mediterranean theatre with two 3-inch (76.2-mm) howitzers as armament.

The real need, however, was for a genuine dual purpose armament and in North Africa 120 Churchill IVs and one Churchill III had their six-pounders (57-mm) replaced by the salvaged 75-mm guns and mountings of knocked out Sherman tanks. Known as Churchill NA75s, the tanks served throughout Sicily and the Italian campaign. A co-axial 0.30 inch (7.62-mm) Browning machine-gun was fitted in place of the 7.92-mm Besa.

When it became available the British 75-mm was fitted to new Churchills. The first major 75-mm model was the Churchill VI, production of which began in November 1943. It was only considered an interim type until the appearance of a new, drastically redesigned Churchill with improved protection and gun power.

The new vehicle, which appeared at the end of 1943, had armour increased to a formidable 152-mm maximum and 25-mm minimum. This thicker plate was now used as the basic constructional medium of the hull which became of welded integral construction. The turret had cast sides and a welded roof; a cupola was fitted as standard, a modification made to some earlier marks also. Weight was increased to 40 tons with speed reduced to 13 mph (21 km/h). Adopted as the Churchill VII, those built with the 95-mm howitzer became Mark VIIIs.

Older tanks were brought up to the new standards, with appliqué armour and sometimes new turrets. Modified Mark IIIs and IVs were fitted with new turrets but retained the six-pounder (57-mm) to become Churchill Mark IXs. Those that kept the original turret, became Mark IX LTs (light turret). Older tanks with 75-mm guns, Mark VIs, became Mark Xs or X LTs and similarly reworked Mark Vs became Mark XIs or Mark XI LTs.

Three brigades of Churchills, Mark IVs onwards, were deployed in North-Western Europe with Sixth Guards and 31st and 34th Tank Brigades. Two brigades, 21st and 25th, fought in Italy (still with proportions of older Churchills Is and IIIs), playing a vital part in breaching German lines. At 200 yards (182 m) even dug-in *Panther* turrets used as pillboxes could not withstand the Churchill's six-pounder (57-mm) and 75-mm guns.

In these campaigns of 1944–5 a whole range of specialized armour was unveiled that played a crucial part in operations. The stimulus to

Infantry Tank Mark IV Churchill IV
Weight 39 tons (39.6 tonnes)
Crew five
Armament one six-pounder (57-mm) Mark III (L/43) gun with 84 rounds and two 7.92-mm Besa machine-guns with 4,950 rounds
Armour hull nose 89 mm, glacis 38 mm, driver's plate 101 mm, sides 76 mm, decking 15–19 mm, belly 19 mm, tail 64 mm; turret front and sides 89 mm
Engine one Bedford 'Twin-Six' horizontally opposed 12-cylinder liquid-cooled petrol, 350-hp
Speed 17 mph (27 km/h)
Range 90 miles (144 km)
Trench crossing 12 feet (3.66 m)
Vertical step 4 feet (1.22 m)
Fording 3 feet (91 cm)
Overall length 25 feet 2 inches (7.65 m)
Width 10 feet 8 inches (3.25 m)
Height 8 feet 0.5 inches (2.45 m)

Left: *A Churchill IV as used in Tunisia where two brigades proved very successful*

develop what was in effect a modern mechanized siege train resulted from the Dieppe fiasco. This had shown that armoured protection was imperative for the vast majority of engineer tasks if the invading armies were to gain the beaches of North-West Europe. Major General Sir Percy Hobart of 79th Armoured Division cooperated with research organizations to produce 'funnies', as they were called, in profusion. The Churchill proved the best unit for conversion, being tough, highly mobile and with ample room for extra crew members and equipment.

The most significant 'funny' based on the Churchill was the AVRE, Assault Vehicle Royal Engineers. Some 734 conversion kits were produced for Churchills III and IV and slightly more than 700 tanks were factory converted. The AVRE's main armament was a 290-mm Petard mortar which could fire a 40-lb (88-kg) demolition charge over 80 yards (73 m). A wide range of fittings was designed for use with the vehicle. For example, fascines could be jettisoned into or against an obstacle and a Standard Box Girder Bridge or a large Bailey Bridge could be laid.

The development of the carpet-laying technique, to assist the crossing of soft terrain or barbed wire, acquired impetus when it was learned that the Normandy beaches contained soft patches of clay. An early type of carpet-layer had been used on a Churchill III at Dieppe

and four types were later produced for the AVRE. Carpet-layers (Types C and D) Marks II and III were the most important. Sometimes referred to as Bobbins Marks I and II, the first had a movable bobbin while the Type D consisted of a larger, fixed reel. After laying at two mph (3.3 km/h), both could be jettisoned.

The Petard was intended to clear mines as well as blow up obstacles although other sorts of gear were developed for the former role,

Below: Tank brigades equipped with Churchills were also given the 'Jumbo' Churchill Bridge-layers to assist in crossing small streams
Bottom: The Carpet-layer Type D Mark III (Bobbin Mark II). The large fixed reel unrolled a hessian carpet, reinforced with steel tubes, over soft ground or barbed wire. The AVRE here is a converted Churchill III, note the welded turret. It is fitted for deep-wading with long extensions to the air intakes and exhausts

such as the 'Snake' and two ploughs, the 'Bullshorn' and the 'Jeffries'. The Canadian Indestructable Roller Device was issued for use with 79th Armoured Division's AVREs. Another piece of mine-clearing equipment used in conjunction with the AVRE was the 'Conger', a long piece of hose projected by rocket across a minefield. It was then filled with nitro-glycerine and exploded to clear a narrow path.

Another vital contribution to assault operations was the Churchill Crocodile flame-thrower. The first flame-thrower versions of the Churchill were the Churchill Okes – three early Churchills modified for Dieppe to carry the Canadian Ronson flame-thrower system. Later, a Wasp II was adopted for fitting to the Churchill VII as the Churchill Crocodile. A flame projector was fitted to the hull front, fuelled by a 400 gallon (1,818 l) armoured trailer towed behind the tank. The maximum range of the flame-thrower was about 100 yards (91 m), and 80 one-second bursts were available. Conversion kits totalled 800, and all late production Churchill VIIs were built with conversion in mind.

While the AVRE was often used in a bridging role, other types of bridging vehicles were built on the Churchill chassis. A Bridge-layer (sometimes called Jumbo) was developed which put a hydraulically laid 60-ton capacity bridge on a Churchill III or IV chassis. It was usually used to cross small streams and craters. In order to provide a quick means of crossing such obstacles as sea walls or larger craters a Churchill ARK (Armoured Ramp Carrier) was developed by 79th Armoured Division in late 1943. A turretless tank with ramps that hinged down at either end and trackways across the top, it went into

an obstacle and was then driven over by following vehicles.

Soon after the D-Day landings 79th Armoured Division developed an improved Mark II. Extended ramps were fitted at the front; gaps of 47 feet 6 inches (14.47 m) could now be crossed against the 28 foot (8.53 m) span of the original. In Italy a different version was developed which could cross spans of up to 54 feet 4 inches (16.56 m). Armoured recovery versions of the Churchill included an ARV Mark I based on turretless Churchill Is and IIs and an ARV Mark II used the Churchill III or IV chassis with a fixed dummy gun and turret.

Once its initial problems had been overcome, the Churchill tank was arguably the best British tank available in quantity in the war years, being versatile, mobile, reliable and immensely tough. Its infantry support specification may have reflected limited strategic insight, but from 1942 onwards it was ideally suited to a war of mechanized attrition – particularly in difficult terrain where the sophisticated concepts of armoured warfare and blitzkrieg were irrelevant. The only major drawback was the limited armament due to the narrow turret ring dictated by the need to make the tank transportable within the British railway loading gauge. A wider 'Super Churchill', later renamed 'Black Prince' was developed mounting a 17-pounder (76.2-mm) gun but it was produced too late to take part in the war, and, with the decision to concentrate on one 'universal' tank, was abandoned as the requirement was better met by the new heavily armoured cruiser, Centurion. Nevertheless Churchills remained in service for long after the war and served in Korea where Crocodiles were also used.

Churchill VII
Weight 40 tons (40.6 tonnes)
Armament one L/36.5 75-mm Mark V or VA gun with 84 rounds, one 7.92-mm Besa machine-gun with 4,950 rounds
Armour hull front 140–152 mm, sides 95 mm, tail 50 mm; turret front 152 mm, sides 95 mm
Speed 125 mph (201 km)
Width 11 feet 4 inches (3.45 m)
Other details as Churchill IV

Below: A Churchill VII Crocodile flame-thrower. Note the new turret, redesigned side hatch and replacement of the hull machine-gun by a flame projector. The flame-thrower system was powered by high pressure nitrogen carried in the armoured fuel trailer; the trailer could be jettisoned if hit. Three regiments in 31st Armoured Brigade, part of 79th Armoured Division, were equipped with Crocodiles in North-West Europe. Seventh RTR had nine, three troops of three, one troop in each squadron. The Crocodile needed skill and experience to operate but when used properly it was a formidable weapon against enemy positions

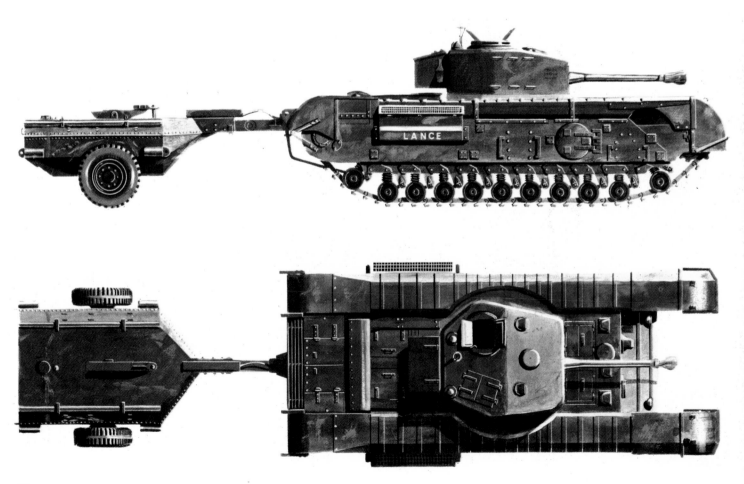

Cruiser Tanks Marks I-V

Work on new designs of British medium tanks continued in the 1920s and '30s, but they proved expensive and remained experimental. With rearmament in 1934, however, Sir John Carden of Vickers was asked to design a new A9 medium that would be smaller, lighter and cheaper, for use in more independent armoured operations. Soon afterwards, to conform with current British Army thinking, a more heavily armoured A10 version was required for direct infantry support. The first A9 prototype appeared in April 1936 but design features were not finally worked out until late 1937. By then British Army doctrine had crystallized around two basic tank types – the infantry tank for close support and the cruiser tank for the projected Mobile Division. With the development of anti-tank guns the armour protection of the A10, enough to protect from heavy machine-gun fire, was deemed to be insufficient for an infantry tank, so A10 and A9 became contenders for the cruiser class of tanks.

The first order was placed for the A9 in August 1937, as Cruiser Tank Mark I, followed the next year by orders for the A10 as an interim 'heavy cruiser' designated Cruiser Tank Mark II. The Mark I was of simple riveted construction, weighed 12½ tons and was armoured to a maximum of 14 mm. Main armament was a turret-mounted two-pounder (40-mm) gun which had replaced the earlier three-pounder (47-mm) as the standard British tank armament. The two-pounder (40-mm) had better muzzle velocity than its predecessor (2,600 as against 1,850 fps or 792 as against 563 m/s) and could penetrate 57 mm of 30° armour plate as against the earlier gun's 27 mm. A 0.303 inch (7.7-mm) Vickers machine-gun was carried with the two-pounder (40-mm) in a hydraulically traversed turret; there were two small subsidiary turrets at the front, each mounting another Vickers gun. A rear-mounted AEC A179 bus engine of 150 hp drove through the rear sprockets and steering was by clutch and brake. Suspension consisted of two three-wheeled assemblies each side, coil sprung with hydraulic shock absorbers. Maximum speed was 25 mph (40 km/h) and range 150 miles (241 km).

The A10 was a similar tank except for its heavier 30-mm armour. Extra plates were bolted to the basic hull and this increased weight to 13¾ tons. Speed was reduced to only 16 mph (26 km/h) and range to 100 miles (161 km). The first 13 vehicles had a Vickers machine-gun co-axial with the two-pounder (40-mm) gun; the rest, designated Cruiser Tank Mark IIA, had a new mantlet with co-axial 7.92-mm Besa machine-gun with another similar weapon in the hull. The earlier vehicles later acquired hull Besas. There was a close support version of both Marks I and IIA with a 3.7-inch (94-mm) howitzer replacing the two-pounder (40-mm) gun.

Despite their various drawbacks, the A9's thin armour and unreliability and the A10's slow speed, both types formed half the available number of cruiser tanks in the early months of the war. Cruisers Marks I and II served in France with First Armoured Division in 1940 and both were in Egypt with Seventh and Second Armoured Divisions in 1940–1. First Armoured Brigade from Second Armoured Division was sent to Greece in 1941 with these cruisers, but by then they had been worn out by many miles of desert running, and breakdowns, particularly track failures, were endemic. More tanks were lost due to unreliability than to enemy action and they were not able to inflict any significant delay on the Germans. A9s continued in use until Operation Battleaxe in June 1941, and the A10 was not phased out of service until the end of that year, 26 still being used by Seventh Armoured Brigade in the Crusader offensive.

Both these types were procured in only limited quantities because of the availability of a better cruiser tank design, the A13. Lieutenant-Colonel Martel was appointed Assistant Director of Mechanization in 1936 and that year visited Russia to report on its army manoeuvres. He was very impressed by the mobility of the Soviet *BT* tanks, obtained from their Christie suspension of large independently coil-sprung road wheels. He saw this as a better cruiser tank than the A9 and tried to get the army to buy one. This was refused, but, via the Morris Commercial Motor Company, approaches were made to J Walter Christie in the United States.

Christie, a brilliant and eccentric man, had fallen out with the United States Army and was in deep financial difficulties. His last remaining

Below: A Cruiser Tank Mark II A with 3.7-inch (94-mm) howitzer. These close support vehicles were designed to give smoke-shell support to sister vehicles equipped with normal high velocity armament

prototype had been seized to pay his debts – a fact which the British only found out after agreeing to pay Christie £8,000 for it. Eventually, together with the designer, it was brought back to Britain, with the hull labelled 'tractor' and the other parts 'grapefruit' in order to circumvent the American Neutrality Act.

This M1932 prototype, which was tested extensively in Britain as the A13E1, was a turretless vehicle, built as narrow and low as possible in order to present the smallest possible target to the enemy. Much of the original Christie conception disappeared in the final British design. Only two fundamental elements of the M1932 were used, the powerful aero engine and the suspension system – but even the latter was modified to such an extent that the vehicle lost the capability of running at very high speeds on roads without tracks. Such a feature was considered a rather pointless extra having little tactical usefulness.

The British wanted a new tank, not a new and impractical concept of armoured operations, and by the end of 1936 Lord Nuffield and the Morris Company had been engaged to develop a usable tank from the Christie design. The Christie suspension was married to a conventional riveted hull with rotating turret mounting a two-pounder (40-mm) gun and co-axial Vickers machine-gun. The crew numbered four as in the A10 and armour was 14 mm as in the A9. The engine was the American Liberty, produced under licence, which drove the new prototype A13E2 at over 35 mph (56 km/h). Conventional drive sprockets and short pitch tracks soon replaced the original Christie type in order to prolong track life. Tests with this and a modified A13E3 also revealed the need to strengthen the trans-

Below: A Cruiser Tank Mark I. Note the distinctive auxiliary turrets

mission and clutch and brake steering, and for the redesign of other mechanical components. Speed would need to be limited to 30 mph (48 km/h), if reliability was to be obtained.

In September 1937 a new company, the Nuffield Mechanization and Aero Company, was set up to put the tank into production. The first production A13 was delivered by the end of 1938 – remarkable progress considering the project was only two years old. It became Cruiser A13 Mark I then Cruiser Tank Mark III, despite the fact that it beat its two Vickers-designed contemporaries into service.

The A13 soon proved a fast and popular tank and at least as reliable as the Vickers. But its thin armour gave cause for concern, so a new A13 Mark II was developed with 30-mm armour on the hull and turret front. The sides of the turret were also extended with extra 14-mm plates as spaced armour. The new up-armoured vehicles became Cruiser Tank Mark IV; the later Mark IVA had a new mantlet and co-axial Besa machine-gun. Older A13s were reworked to various approximations of the Mark IV standard. Some 65 production Cruisers Mark III were built by Nuffield in addition to the prototypes. They also constructed 99 Mark IVs and 141 Mark IVAs. The London Midland and Scottish Railway Company (LMS) produced 34 Mark IVs and 34 Mark IVAs. A few mark IVs were converted to Mark IVA CS standard with the 3.7-inch (94-mm) howitzer in place of the two-pounder (40-mm).

Both the Marks III and IV served in France and North Africa. After successful use in wide flanking movements against the Italians, A13s fought the Germans throughout 1941. They suffered to some extent from breakdowns but had a speed advantage over their Axis counterparts. Although vulnerable to German anti-tank fire the Mark IV was the equal in armour and

firepower of its major German tank opponent, the *PzKpfw* III Ausf G, though with the appearance of more thickly armoured German tanks the tide began to turn. The A13 was still in use during the Crusader offensive of November 1941, but this was its last battle. The following year it disappeared from North Africa too.

The final tank of this series, the A13 Mark III, which became known as 'Covenanter', originated in an attempt to develop a new 'heavy cruiser'. The prototype A14E1 chassis built by LMS proved slow, noisy and complicated and was abandoned. They were, therefore, instructed to develop an improved version of the existing A13 with better armour, low height and improved shape. A specially designed tank engine was to be used with a new epicyclic gearbox to provide steering that was less wasteful of power. Maximum armour thickness of the new tank was 40 mm and the armament was one two-pounder (40-mm) with co-axial Besa machine-gun. The first Cruiser Tanks Mark V, which appeared in 1940, had severe engine problems, the 300-hp Meadows flat-12 suffering from overheating. Although the overheating problems were eventually solved, by that time, 1942, better tanks such as the Grant and the up-gunned Crusader were available for service. The Covenanter never saw action although 1,771 were produced.

A number of specialized Covenanter variants appeared, a close support version for all Marks with three-inch (76.2-mm) howitzer replacing the two-pounder (40-mm), artillery observation post vehicles, command tanks and armoured recovery vehicles. Experiments were carried out with an anti-mine roller attachment in 1942 and a bridge-laying version was developed with a 30 foot (9.8 m) 'scissors' bridge. The latter were the only Covenanters to see action, being used against the Japanese by the Australians on Bougainville in 1945.

Cruiser Tank Mark IVA
Weight 14.75 tons (15 tonnes)
Crew four
Armament one 2-pounder (40-mm) Mark IX or X (L/50) gun with 87 rounds and one 7.92-mm Besa machine-gun with 3,750 rounds
Armour hull nose 14–30 mm, glacis driver's plate and sides 14 mm, belly 6 mm; turret front 30 mm, sides and rear 14 + 14 mm
Engine one Nuffield Liberty Mark I or II V-12 liquid-cooled petrol, 340-hp
Speed 30 mph (48 km/h)
Range 100 miles (161 km)
Trench crossing 7 feet 6 inches (2.29 m)
Vertical step 2 feet 6 inches (76 cm)
Fording 3 feet (91 cm)
Overall length 19 feet 9 inches (6.02 m)
Width 8 feet 4 inches (2.54 m)
Height 8 feet 6 inches (2.59 m)

The vehicle illustrated is a Cruiser Tank Mark IVA. Note the Christie suspension, Besa machine-gun and extended turret side armour. The tank is in a variant of desert camouflage

Cruiser Tank Mark VI Crusader

When Major Martel went to Russia in 1936 it was not only the Christie *BT* which impressed him but also the larger *T-28* medium tank. A specification was therefore drawn up for an improved 'heavy cruiser' with 30-mm armour. Two projects were begun, an LMS A14 and a Nuffield A16. Both proved unduly complex and in 1939 the A14 was replaced by the smaller A13 Mark III project while Nuffield designed a simple enlargement of this type, the A15, which was ordered into production.

The tank was of riveted and bolted construction and the turret mounted a two-pounder (40-mm) gun with co-axial Besa machine-gun. Two further machine-guns were mounted in the hull one in an auxiliary turret. The rear mounted Liberty engine drove through the rear sprockets and steering was by levers and a pneumatically assisted Wilson epicyclic system.

Various problems soon became apparent such as the difficulty of operating the hull machine-guns, one of which was soon deleted as a result, and poor ventilation. The transmission also proved troublesome and difficulties with the engine were never entirely overcome. This Cruiser Tank Mark VI was soon dubbed 'Crusader'. The next model, Crusader II, also deleted the auxiliary turret. The new type had armour plate thickened to 49 mm on the turret front. All but the initial Crusader Is were fitted with a bulbous, better-protected mantlet; close support versions of both types were also produced.

The first Crusaders were sent out to Egypt in 1941. One regiment of Seventh Armoured Division took part in the Battleaxe offensive in June with them, but their armour proved vulnerable to the 88-mm anti-aircraft guns and 50-mm anti-tank guns the Germans effectively used to stop the offensive. More were available by the end of the year, including a complete new Armoured Brigade, the 22nd, of three regiments of Crusaders, part of First Armoured Division. The offensive to relieve Tobruk was named 'Crusader' in honour of these tanks, and, in the heavy fighting that finally led to Rommel's withdrawal, the Crusader's combination of speed, firepower and protection was at a premium. Losses were heavy and these tanks acquired a bad name for vulnerability although the British tank compared adequately with its major German opponent, the *PzKpfw* III *Ausf* G. The main enemy of the Crusader was the anti-tank gun and against such a weapon the two-pounder (40-mm) was of little use. Only with the coming of the American Grant did the British Army acquire an effective long range, dual high explosive/anti-tank weapon.

The advent of the *PzKpfw* III *Ausf* J and *PzKpfw* IV *Ausf* F2, with better long range anti-tank capability, compounded the Crusader's armour piercing problem, but a Crusader III with six-pounder (57-mm) gun in a redesigned turret to some extent redressed the balance. These vehicles were available by mid-1942 and formed a significant proportion (105 tanks) of the 300 Crusaders that took part in the Second Battle of Alamein that began the drive to push Rommel out of Egypt in October. The forces that landed in Tunisia also included Crusader IIIs but with the end of the North African campaign the type was phased out of service as a battle tank.

The Crusader was also used for a number of specialized roles. There were turretless armoured recovery vehicles and bulldozer versions. Some lost their guns and gained extra radios as artillery observation posts and command vehicles while other became tractors for 17-pounder (76.2-mm) anti-tank guns. A series of Crusader III anti-aircraft tanks were specially designed for use in Normandy.

Some 5,300 Crusaders were built from 1940–3, 4,350 as tanks and 1,373 for use in specialized roles. The Crusader was Britain's major operational battle tank of the 1941–2 period and proved equal to the task, if a little under-armoured as time went on.

Below: *A Crusader III AA Mark III in service with a Sherman regiment in Normandy*
Bottom: *A few Crusader IIIs, like this example, were armed with the longer thinner Mark V, with prominent muzzle counterweight, in place of the Mark III six-pounder (57-mm) gun*

Cruiser Tank Mark VI Crusader I
Weight 19 tons (19.3 tonnes)
Crew five
Armament one 2-pounder (40-mm) Mark IX or X (L/50) gun with 110 rounds and two 7.92-mm Besa machine-guns with 4,500 rounds
Armour hull nose 33 mm, glacis 20 mm, driver's plate 40 mm, front 30 mm, sides 14 + 14 mm, decking 7 mm, belly 10 mm, tail 28 mm; turret front 49 mm, sides 24 mm, top 12 mm, rear 30 mm
Engine one Nuffield Liberty Mark II V-12 liquid-cooled petrol, 340-hp
Speed 27½ mph (42.5 km/h)
Range 200 miles (124 km)
Trench crossing 7 feet 6 inches (2.29 m)
Vertical step 2 feet 6 inches (76 cm)
Fording 3 feet 3 inches (1 m)
Overall length 19 feet 8 inches (6 m)
Width 9 feet 1 inch (2.77 m)
Height 7 feet 4 inches (2.24 m)

The tank illustrated is a Crusader Mark I in Eighth Army colours. Note the extra machine-gun turret which was deleted in the following mark

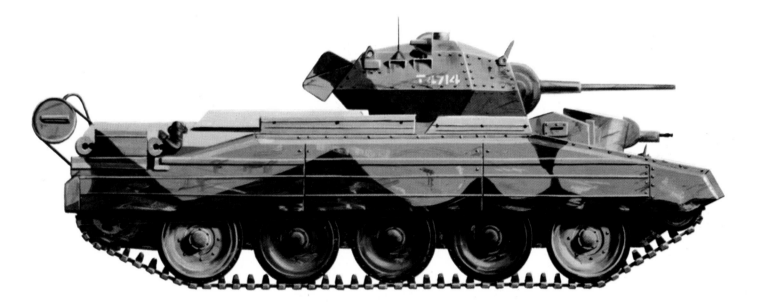

Cruiser Tank Mark VIII Cromwell and Cruiser Tank Comet

Early combat experience in France and North Africa showed that British cruiser tank design needed revision. By the beginning of 1941 a new specification was issued calling for improved reliability, heavier 75-mm turret armour and 65-mm hull protection, the new six-pounder (57-mm) gun with wider 60-inch (152-cm) turret ring, a weight of not more than 24 tons and a more powerful engine to give a speed of 24 mph (39 km/h). A production order was lodged with Nuffield in June 1941 for 500 such A24 tanks based on the Crusader design with an up-rated 410-hp engine. Designated 'Cavalier', they were not a success and only saw action as armoured recovery vehicles and artillery observation posts.

Leyland had begun an A27 project, also based on Crusader to utilize the superior Rolls Royce Meteor derivative of the Merlin aero engine, although the first vehicles were completed with Liberty power units. The chassis was similar to the Cavalier's but fitted with a new gearbox. The first A27(L) Centaur I appeared in June 1942. Like the Cavalier, it was only used for training as a battle tank despite the eventual fitting of an improved Liberty engine modified by Leyland. However, those vehicles modified for specialized roles as 95-mm howitzer armed Centaur IV close support tanks, anti-aircraft tanks, observation post vehicles, ARVs and bulldozers, did see action in North-West Europe.

Mass production of the Cromwell I began in 1943. The first tanks mounted six-pounder (57-mm) guns as did the later Cromwell II which was fitted with widened 15½-inch (39 cm) tracks. During 1943 the first Centaur Is were also re-engined being designated first Cromwell X and then Cromwell III.

Experience in the desert had shown that a better tank weapon was needed with an adequate dual high-explosive/anti-personnel capability. The six-pounder (57-mm) was therefore re-bored to take American 75-mm ammunition and the new weapon fitted to the Centaur III which,

when re-engined, became the Cromwell IV. Others were built new, some as Cromwell Vw with welded hulls instead of riveted construction. The performance of the 75-mm gun was only slightly inferior to that of the M3 of the Sherman and superior to the Grant's M2 75-mm. There was also a close support version, Cromwell VI, with 95-mm howitzer.

Cromwell IV was on the standard British cruiser tank pattern with Christie suspension of five large independently-sprung road wheels each side. The Meteor engine drove through the rear sprockets and delivered more than enough power to give the tank excellent performance both on roads and across country. Drive was through a Merritt Brown Z5 gearbox with fully regenerative differential steering. There was a 7.92-mm Besa in a hull mounting, while a second machine-gun was mounted co-axially with the 75-mm. Armour protection of 63-mm on the hull front was felt to be insufficient, so many tanks received extra appliqué plates welded on to increase thickness up to 101 mm. (Cromwell IV, Vw and VI vehicles so converted became Cromwell VII, VIIw and VIII.) Cromwells equipped Seventh Armoured Division and armoured reconnaissance regiments in 1944–5.

Cromwell chassis were lengthened to take the 17-pounder (76.2-mm) high velocity gun. One of these A30 vehicles, designated Challenger, were allocated to each Cromwell troop to stiffen their firepower. Mechanical problems delayed development, and, when it became clear that the Sherman could be fitted with the 17-pounder (76.2-mm), Sherman Fireflies provided the heavy gunfire support of the armoured divisions.

Cromwell needed the Challenger's heavy anti-tank support although the smaller tank made up in speed and agility for what it lacked in firepower. The 75-mm had great difficulty in penetrating the *Tiger* or *Panther* frontally, even at quite close range, but a good commander could often get in a flank or rear shot using his

superior manoeuvrability and fast traversing turret. Most important of all the reliable Cromwell kept going and its speed allowed it to exploit break-throughs even better than the Sherman. Seventh Armoured Division could advance at a rate of 70 miles (112 km) a day after the Normandy break-out. With its combination of speed, reliability and range, Cromwell was an especially good tank for reconnaissance purposes. Some Cromwell chassis became, in addition, turretless armoured recovery vehicles while others became observation post and command tanks.

Cromwell was developed into the last and most powerful British tank to see service in the war, Comet. Challenger had not been a great success and, in July 1943, Leyland presented a new up-gunned design. It would mount the largest gun easily compatible with an improved Cromwell chassis without undue modification. This was a shortened version of the 17-pounder (76.2-mm), originally called the 'High Velocity 75-mm' but later redesignated '77-mm'. It had a length of 49 calibres, as against the 17-pounder's (76.2-mm) 55, and a new chamber that allowed the use of shorter ammunition. The 77-mm had a penetration capability of 109 mm of 30° plate at 500 yards (457 m), slightly inferior to the 17-pounder's (76.2-mm).

The first prototype appeared in February 1944. This had a strengthened Cromwell suspension as, with the heavier gun and additional armour (76–101 mm), weight had been increased by almost five tons over the Cromwell IV. In production versions the suspension was still further modified with 18-inch (46 cm) tracks and four return rollers.

The first Comets were not available for service until November 1944 and 11th Armoured Division employed them from the Rhine to the Baltic. Comet was considered an interim type until the new heavier 'Centurion' came into service but it continued in service until 1960 with the British Army and even later in reserve.

Cruiser Tank Comet
Weight 32.7 tons (33.2 tonnes)
Crew five
Armament one 77 mm Mark II (L/49) gun with 61 rounds and two 7.92 mm Besa machine-guns with 5,175 rounds
Armour hull nose 63 mm, glacis 32 mm, driver's plate 76 mm, upper sides 32 mm, lower sides 29 + 14 mm, decking 25 mm, belly 14 mm, tail 32 mm; turret front 101 mm, sides 63 mm, top 25 mm, rear 57 mm
Engine one Rolls Royce Meteor Mark III V-12 liquid-cooled petrol, 600-hp
Speed 32 mph (51.5 km/h)
Range 123 miles (198 km)
Trench crossing 8 feet (2.44 m)
Vertical step 3 feet (91 cm)
Fording 3 feet 8 inches (1.12 m)
Overall length 25 feet 1½ inches (7.66 m)
Width 10 feet 1 inch (3.07 m)
Height 8 feet 9½ inches (2.68 m)

Left: *The Comet, note the new gun, turret and suspension as compared with the Cromwell illustrated on the opposite page*

Cruiser Tank Mark VIII Cromwell IV
Weight 27.5 tons (28 tonnes)
Crew five
Armament one 75-mm Mark V or VA (L/36.5) gun
with 64 rounds, two 7.92-mm Besa machine-guns
with 4,950 rounds
Armour hull nose 57 mm, glacis 30 mm, driver's
plate 63 mm, sides upper 32 mm, lower 25 mm
+14 mm, decking 20 mm, belly 8 mm, tail 32 mm;
turret front 76 mm, sides 63 mm, top 20 mm, rear
57 mm
Engine one Rolls Royce Meteor V-12 liquid-cooled
petrol, 600-hp
Speed 38 mph (61 km/h); with modified final
drive 32 mph (51.5 km/h)
Range 173 miles (278 km)
Trench crossing 7 feet 6 inches (2.29 m)
Vertical step 3 feet (91 cm)
Fording 4 feet (1.22 m)
Overall length 21 feet (6.4 m)
Width 10 feet (3.05 m)
Height 8 feet 2 inches (2.48 m)

The Cromwell IV illustrated is typical of those
which fought in North-West Europe in 1944–5

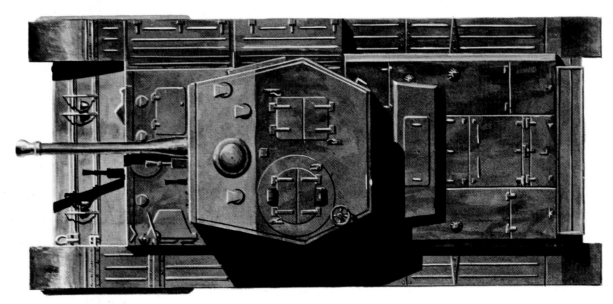

FRANCE

The French tanks produced in the inter-war years were impressive both in quality and quantity but French military thinking was inflexible and remained centered around the infantry, who had gained control of all tanks in 1920. As a result, full potential of the new weapons was never realized. This limited concept of armoured warfare was reflected in the deployment and in the design of French tanks throughout the period leading up to the *débâcle* of 1940.

General Estienne, the head of tank development, fought hard to change this short-sighted policy but, despite his powerful position, the new gospel of the tank's supremacy in future warfare went largely unheeded. To the military, looking back to World War I, static fortifications seemed a better investment, while for the politicians the new ideas on armoured warfare were mixed up with the unpalatable concept of an all-regular army necessary to provide the skilled and highly trained personnel.

Four main tanks were developed in France during this period: the heavy *Char* B, the medium Somua 35 and the light Renault 35 and Hotchkiss 35. But all four were intended as support vehicles only and this was reflected in such design features as short range, slow speed and poor communications systems. Despite superior numbers and often superior armour and gun-power these disadvantages proved fatal weaknesses in the new blitzkrieg warfare of the highly-mobile and co-ordinated forces of the *Panzer* divisions. Deployment was as important as design. The standard tank formation was the small *bataillon organique* of about 45 light *chars d'accompagnement* allocated to the various armies for close infantry support and not as independent fighting units; in 1940 almost half France's available tank strength in Europe remained in these limited formations or the even smaller *compagnies autonomes*. Paralysed by indecision, conflicting opinions and by delays in tank production, a separate armoured division, the *Division Cuirassée de Réserve*, had not been formed until September 1939. This was composed of two demi-brigades of the new, heavy *Char* B1s, (four battalions – 132 tanks), designed to smash a way through enemy defences with two battalions of *chasseurs* (motorized infantry), artillery, engineers and other support troops. It was planned to transport as much of the Division as possible on *Chenillette* Lorraine tracked carriers, but production delays made this impossible.

In January 1940 the Division was divided to form two new *DCR* but insufficient *Char* B1s meant that one battalion in each demi-brigade was replaced by one of the lighter and less powerful Hotchkiss H-39 tanks. Two months later a third *DCR* was assembled. The official divisional establishment of these formations was impressive: an HQ Company, the *brigade de combat* of 156 tanks, a single battalion of *chasseurs*, an artillery regiment, an anti-tank battery and a company each of engineers, signallers and transport – a total of 6,510 officers and men and 1,400 vehicles. In theory a squadron

of reconnaissance aircraft was also allocated to each division but, like much of this ambitious complement, these never appeared.

Without proper logistic or air support or organic anti-aircraft protection the *DCR* could never operate as independent formations, and without adequate radio communication even limited tactical co-operation between these slow, short-ranged tanks was difficult. Badly trained, equipped and deployed, it was not surprising that the *DCR* failed in action. The first was caught refuelling near Flavion, the second, scattered piecemeal on the roads leading to the front, had little chance of success, and the third was cut in half while deploying.

A fourth *DCR* was formed under General Charles De Gaulle after the Germans struck in May 1940. Initially it consisted of a mixed battalion of 20 *Char* B1s and 15 *Char* D2s (47-mm gun mediums developed in the early 1930s and procured in limited quantities from 1938 to 1940), and a reduced demi-brigade of about 50 R-35s with two battalions of motorized infantry and a weak artillery regiment. Without proper training or communications little success attended its two major operations near Laon and Abbeville even though at the latter it had been reinforced to about 140 tanks, including 40 Somua S-35s (two squadrons), and with an armoured car squadron, two more infantry battalions and more field and anti-tank artillery.

In addition to the *DCR* the French Army had another major armoured formation, the *Division Légère Mécanique* or Light Mechanized Division. In the early 1930s the French Cavalry showed increased interest in mechanization, and, after joint exercises with armour, issued specifications for new *automitrailleuses* (machine-gun cars) that were in reality tanks. In 1934, First *DLM* was permanently established with a *brigade de combat* of two regiments (four squadrons) of *automitrailleuses de combat* (from 1935 *chars de cavalerie*) and a reconnaissance brigade that included armoured cars and motorcyclists with a three-battalion regiment of *dragons portés* (mounted infantry), each of which had an organic squadron of 20 light tanks (*automitrailleuses de reconnaissance*). In support was an artillery regiment and an engineer battalion. The formation had 10,400 officers and men, and over 3,000 vehicles and motor-cycles, of which about 275 were AFVs.

But as with the *DCR* the main weakness of this impressive formation was its limited, traditional cavalry role of screening, reconnaissance and exploitation; it was not designed to win battles in its own right. Two more *DLM* were formed in 1938 and 1939 and excellent new equipment, notably the Somua S-35, was adopted but without tactical co-ordination and, dissipated across the front of the Allied advance into the Low Countries, the three divisions achieved little.

Two more *DLM* were formed before France finally fell: the Fourth and Seventh from the refitted mechanized remains of the First and Fourth Light Cavalry Divisions (*DLC*) which

had been badly battered in the initial German offensive. Five *DLC* had been formed the previous winter from the traditional cavalry, pairing a horsed brigade with a mechanized brigade of 22 Hotchkiss H-35s or -39s, along with motorcyclists, armoured cars and two *dragons portés* battalions each with an *AMR* squadron. A stronger Sixth *DLC* was deployed in Tunisia. The French cavalry also included seven individual *Groupes de Reconnaissance Motorizés* which together deployed 154 *AMR* in addition to a similar number of armoured cars.

In all 3,500 new tanks of all types were constructed by June 1940. Over 3,400 vehicles, almost 2,900 new types, 534 Renault *FT*-17s and six old 68-ton *Char* 2Cs, were deployed against the 2,574 German tanks that struck on 10th May,

but superior numbers, and often armour protection and gun-power were no defence against superior strategy, tactics and organization.

French tanks survived after 1940 in the armies of the Axis both as tanks and as chassis for self-propelled guns. About 300 remained in French hands in the Colonies: some fought the Allies in Syria and North Africa and the Axis in Tunisia. At the liberation many used by the Germans were turned again on their temporary owners, though by this time there were new French armoured divisions, *divisions blindées*, organized and trained in North Africa on progressive American lines and equipped with modern American armour. Two helped liberate their own country, while a third co-operated in the final defeat of Germany. It had been a long and bitter lesson in the principles of armoured warfare.

Below: *Hotchkiss H-39 light tanks on exercise. These are early models with the short SA 18 37-mm gun. Together with the earlier H-35, the H-39 was used in all three French armoured roles; as a cavalry tank, infantry support vehicle and a major component of the armoured divisions. Its mobility and good protection were vitiated by poor tactics and inadequate communications – note the flag being used in lieu of radio. Five of these tanks were used in the operations to capture Narvik in May 1940. A total of 821 H-35 and -39 tanks were deployed in France in 1940*

Char B Series

The *Char* B was the most powerfully armed and armoured tank available in quantity to any army in 1939. Instigated by General Estienne, the 'father of the French tank', work had begun in 1921 on a *char de bataille* to provide heavy support for the *chars d'accompagnement* of the infantry and to deal with difficult enemy defences including tanks. The new tank was to be heavily armed and armoured and equipped with radio to achieve some tactical co-ordination in its semi-independent operations, though its role was still basically one of infantry support and not independent attack.

After the construction of mock-ups, authorization was given at the beginning of 1926 for three prototypes to be built. It was decided to use the suspension of the design from FCM (Forges et Chantiers de la Méditerranée), the engine from Renault and the transmission from Schneider. In 1927 orders were placed with FCM, Renault and FAMH (Forges et Aciéries de la Marine et d'Homécourt). The Rueil Arsenal (ARL) co-ordinated the project and eventually the vehicles were completed between 1929 and 1931, two at ARL and one at FCM.

These tanks carried a short 75-mm gun in the hull front with two machine-guns, and two further machine-guns in a small turret. Armour protection was 25-mm and the tank weighed 25 tons. A 180-hp engine gave it a very limited speed of 12.5 mph (20 km/h), though its range was 160 miles (257 km). Trials during 1930 and 1931 were successful and development of what was now the *Char* B continued. Spurred by German rearmament and the occupation of the Rhineland in 1935, a modified version went into immediate production. A new cast turret carrying a short 47-mm gun was added, armour was increased to 40-mm, and a 250-hp engine was fitted to move the 30-ton vehicle at over 17 mph (27 km/h), which reduced the range of this slow, heavy tank to 125 miles (200 km).

The first 35 tanks, usually known as *Char* B1s, were followed by a further modified B1 *bis* with a more heavily-armoured APX4 turret with 34-calibre 47-mm gun, hull armour increased to 60 mm and weight to 32 tons. But a more powerful, and thirsty, engine of 307 hp reduced endurance to a mere 87 miles (140 km), which although not too important for infantry operations was a vital strategic drawback in long-ranging mobile war. Late production vehicles had auxiliary fuel tanks fitted to help solve this problem.

The B series had a frame of two girders and cross members upon which were bolted armoured plates and castings. The suspension was a modification of the Holt tractor type with three four-wheel bogie assemblies each side controlled by combined coil and compressed leaf springs. Three independently sprung wheels at the front and one at the back helped control each track, the tension of which could be adjusted from inside the vehicle using the spring-mounted front idlers. The rear-mounted engine worked via a synchromesh, double-differential transmission. The auxiliary differential was controlled from the steering wheel by a Naeder hydrostatic system, developed by Batignolles, for precision aiming of the fixed hull-mounted main armament. This concept is reminiscent of the principle of the modern Swedish turretless S Tank, which uses a sophisticated control system to aim the whole tank at the target.

The duties of the four-man crew were complex and even with a skilled and highly trained team the distribution of jobs did not lend itself to tactical efficiency in action. The driver of the tank also doubled as main gunner, elevating the 17.1-calibre 75-mm using a hand crank, while also usually controlling the single-hull machine-gun. A separate loader fused the 75-mm ammunition and passed 47-mm shells to the electrically-traversed turret, where an overworked commander/gunner attempted to direct the tank and/or formation and also work the high-velocity armament. The four-man crew was completed by a wireless operator.

In 1936 the four-year rearmament plan had aimed at 12 battalions of *Char* Bs (about 400 tanks) to equip two *DCR*. The mechanical complexity of the B1 *bis* delayed mass production, however, and only 365 had been constructed by the French collapse, despite the use of five manufacturers: Renault, Schneider, FCM, FAMH, and from 1939, AMX (Atelier de Construction d'Issy-les-Moulineaux). In the early months of the war a maximum of only 15 B1s *bis* per month were being produced. About 300 B1s and B1s *bis* were available to meet the Germans when the struck on 10 May 1940: 66 were on the strength of each of the three *DCR*, and 57 were scattered in various small *compagnies autonomes*. Up to 30 more formed the nucleus of De Gaulle's Fourth *DCR*.

The B1 *bis* had overwhelming strength in armament and armour. With its 47-mm it could out-gun the *PzKpfw* III and IV and could only be disabled by shooting off its tracks, putting a shot through the vulnerable engine grille on the left-hand side or bringing up an 88-mm AA gun. Yet the tank was largely a failure in action. Badly-trained crews found the complexities of the B too much for them, and, more importantly, the shortness of the tank's range coupled with stopping and starting on refugee-clogged roads, led to anxiety about fuel and numerous refuelling stops. First *DCR* never recovered from being surprised by German armour with its tanks refuelling. It is true that many *Char* Bs were dispersed by ignorant higher commanders and never had a chance to be employed *en masse* in the general confusion, but these crucial design weaknesses, which also reflected French limited strategic concepts, did not help matters.

After June 1940 *Char* Bs were used by the Germans for occupation duties (for example in the Channel Islands) as the *PzKpfw* B1 *bis* 740 (*f*). Some lost their turrets and armament to become *PzKpfw* B1 (*f*) driver training tanks, 24 had the 75-mm gun replaced by a flame-thrower to become *PzKpfw* B1 *bis* (*f*) *Flamm* and a small number were used as the chassis for a 105-mm SP field howitzer mounting, the

Opposite page: *A Char B painted in the standard 1939 camouflage of 'ochre, marron et vert-gris', although much of the brown on the side is mud carried by the tracks*
Below: *Three PzKpFw B1 bis tanks and a B1 bis Flamm on occupation duty in Jersey*

10.5-cm *le FH* 18 *Ausf Gw* B2 (*f*), used after conversion by Rheinmetall-Borsig with the occupation troops in France. A number of *Char Bs* back in native hands saw action during the Liberation.

A further modification of the B1 had appeared in 1937, the B1 *ter* with improved armour (75-mm), a five-man crew and a 75-mm gun with 5° lateral traverse. Only five were made, the first a prototype B reworked. The need to concentrate on the production B1 *bis* effectively killed the project although further theoretical development took place. It continued secretly during the occupation to form the basis of a new design, begun in earnest after the Liberation in 1944. This ARL-44 had a turret-mounted long 90-mm gun and 60 of these tanks saw service in the post-war French Army.

Char B1 bis
Weight 31.5 tons (32 tonnes)
Crew four
Armament one 75-mm SA-35 (L/17.1) gun with 74 rounds, one 47-mm SA-35 (L/34) gun with 50 rounds, and two 7.5-mm Model 1931 machine-guns with 5,100 rounds
Armour hull front and sides 60 mm, tail 55 m, decking 25 mm, belly 20 mm; turret front 55 mm, sides and rear 45 mm, top 30 mm
Engine one Renault inline six-cylinder liquid-cooled petrol, 307-hp
Speed 17½ mph (28 km/h)
Range 87 miles (150 km)
Trench crossing 9 feet (2.75 m)
Vertical step 3 feet 0.5 inches (93 cm)
Fording 4 feet 10 inches (1.47 m)
Overall length 21 feet 9 inches (6.52 m)
Width 8 feet 3 inches (2.5 m)
Height 9 feet 4 inches (2.79 m)

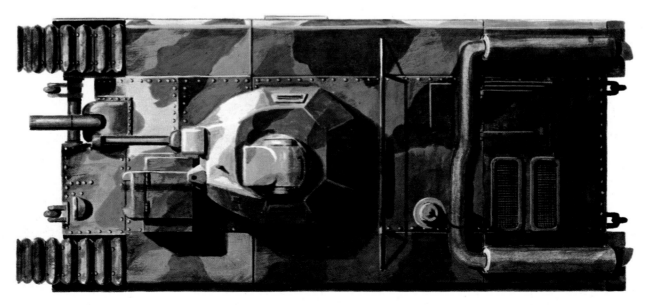

R-35 Light Tank

It was recognized in the 1920s that the World War I Renault *FT*-17 infantry support light tank would eventually require replacement, and design work culminated in the 14 to 20 ton *Char* Ds. In August 1933, after combined exercises, these Ds were reclassified as mediums and a new requirement for a *char léger* issued. As Germany began to rearm, more detailed specifications were drawn up in May 1934, calling for an eight-ton, two-man tank with thicker 40-mm armour to protect it from anti-tank guns and armament of either machine-guns or a 37-mm gun. Speed was to be only 9 to 12½ mph (15 to 20 km/h) and radius of action 25 miles (40 km) owing to the tank's traditionally limited role of infantry support.

Renault were the first to answer the original requirement, with a new ZM tank at the end of 1934, based on the design of their latest *AMR* for the Cavalry. This prototype had armour of only 30 mm, but up-armouring to the new detailed specification brought the weight to 10 tons. As a result of the deteriorating international situation this modified design, the *Char Léger Modèle 1935R* was ordered before it could be fully tested. Two other designs were offered from Hotchkiss and FCM, whose interesting, if expensive, diesel-engined 36 was procured in limited quantities (100 tanks).

The Renault R-35 was of composite construction with three superstructure castings mounted on a lower armoured plate. Side plates carried the suspension which consisted, on each side, of five rubber-tyred wheels bearing against each other through bell cranks and rubber springs. Power was transmitted to the front sprockets from the rear-mounted engine through a gearbox on the right of the driver in the fighting compartment. Steering was on the Cletrac principle with brake bands in a single differential, controlled by steering levers. From 1938 unditching tails were fitted to increase cross-country performance. The speed was the specified 12½ mph (20 km/h) but, with additional fuel tanks, range turned out greater at 87 miles (140 km).

The prototype had two machine-guns but production tanks had a 37-mm gun and co-axial machine-gun in an APX-R cast turret. The gun in production tanks was a short (21-calibre) SA 18, either the original version in earlier production vehicles, or the later M 37. A few were still later fitted with the 33-calibre SA 38 gun of higher velocity. At least two R-35s were experimentally fitted with FCM turrets, one cast, the other welded.

A new version of the R-35 appeared in 1940. Usually designated either R-40 or AMX-40, the new tank was a product of the Atelier de Construction d'Issy-les-Moulineaux – a branch of Renault until nationalization. The new R-40 suspension was developed from the *Char B* and the AMX-38 experimental medium tank. On each side six pairs of small bogie wheels were mounted on coil springs connected to three centre pivoting beams which gave better ground clearance and cross-country performance. Two battalions of the R-40, 90 tanks, were in service during the Battle of France. Some mounted the SA 18 M 37 gun and others the SA 38.

Between 1935 and 1940 1,600 of the standard

Above: *R-35s on parade. These are early models with diascope vision ports*
Top right: *A German R-35 based 47-mm tank destroyer converted to a flamethrower in Jersey*
Bottom right: *An R-35 outflanked and abandoned in 1940*

R-35 were built and about 850, more than any other individual type, were on first-line strength to deal with the German onslaught. Sixteen *bataillons organiques* were R-35 equipped, at least one with each of the nine armies. Although superior to both the *PzKpfw* I and II in firepower and to all German tanks in armour, the impact of the R-35 was limited. The low-velocity (1,273 fps or 388 m/s) gun fitted was not a good anti-tank weapon, while the R-35 was penetrable by both the 50-mm gun of the latest *PzKpfw* III and the 75-mm of the *PzKpfw* IV. Designed as an infantry tank both speed and range were limited and radio, felt to be unnecessary for close co-operation with infantry, was only fitted as an afterthought to some vehicles in 1940. Normal communication was slow and carried out using small triangular flags exposed through a hole in the turret next to the cupola. The difficulty in efficient communication must have been a particular drawback to the 50 to 70 R-35s from two battalions which formed a coherent armoured force as the major numerical strength of De Gaulle's *ad hoc* Fourth *DCR*.

In co-ordinated armoured operations the one-

man turret for the commander/gunner was a special liability. Observation was limited and, in a complex situation, it must have been impossible both to command the vehicle properly and work the hand-trained turret and armament. It was difficult enough even in the slow, infantry support operations for which the tank had been designed. When fitted, the turret-mounted radio only further overburdened the commander. Sure enough, spread out among the various armies, in accordance with the outdated doctrine which their design reflected, their counter-attacks were doomed to failure and the R-35s achieved nothing in a new kind of war.

Following the surrender, R-35s survived in the French Colonies and were used to defend both Syria and North Africa against the Allies. Many were modified with new opening hatch cupolas and hull-mounted radios for use by the *Wehrmacht*. Some 200 were issued for reconnaissance duties in Russia in 1941 – an indication of the acute German tank shortage as the slow, short range R-35 was totally unsuitable for this purpose. When the German advance foundered in mud and snow, a considerable number of R-35s lost their turrets to become ammunition carriers and tractors. In 1943 about 100 small 10-ton tank destroyers appeared using the Czech 47-mm AT gun in an open box-type superstructure on an R-35 chassis. A few were later converted to SP flame-throwers using the AT gun as the basis for the flame projector. Another version pro-duced in small numbers mounted the French 47-mm AT gun. The R-35 was also used in limited quantities as an SP carriage for the 105-mm field howitzer.

The Germans passed two battalions of unmodified R-35s to the Italians and these saw action against American forces in Sicily in 1943. The tank also saw service in various other armies. After tests with two R-35s in 1938 Poland received 53 of an order of 100 the next year. They were interned without seeing any action, in Romania, which also received others direct from France. Yugoslavia and Turkey also purchased a number; in all 240 were exported.

Renault R-35
Weight 9.8 tons (10 tonnes)
Crew two
Armament one 37-mm SA 18 (L/21) or SA 38 (L/33) gun with 100 rounds and one 7.5-mm Model 1931 machine-gun with 2,400 rounds
Armour hull front, sides and tail 40 mm, decking and belly 12 mm; turret front and sides 45 mm, top 30 mm
Engine one Renault inline four-cylinder liquid-cooled petrol, 82-hp
Speed 12½ mph (20 km/h)
Range 87 miles (140 km)
Trench crossing 5 feet 3 inches (1.6 m)
Vertical step 1 foot 8 inches (50 cm)
Fording 2 feet 7½ inches (80 cm)
Overall length 13 feet 4 inches (4.2 m)
Width 6 feet 2 inches (1.85 m)
Height 6 feet 8 inches (2.37 m)

H-35 Light Tank

Hotchkiss produced their prototype to meet the 1933 infantry *char léger* requirement at the beginning of 1935, but by this time the R-35 had been ordered in quantity and the Hotchkiss design was rejected. Although the trials commission at Mourmelon preferred some of the features of the new tank they were put off by the prototype's thinner armour and lack of power, coupled with poor suspension and weight distribution which marred its performance over difficult country. The Cavalry, however, were looking for a smaller but relatively heavily armoured *char de cavalerie* to accompany the S-35 in the new and projected *DLM*. They were more impressed by the Hotchkiss' higher speed, 17½ mph (28 km/h) and, despite the tank's disappointing 80 mile (129 km) range, it was put into production as the *Char* Hotchkiss 35-H.

As usual with French tanks the construction of the H-35, as it is normally called, placed great reliance on castings, six of which were bolted together and to a three-part under-plate to form the hull. The suspension consisted of six road wheels each side mounted in pairs on bell cranks, double coil-sprung against each other. The six-cylinder, 3½-litre, 75-hp engine was rear-mounted but drove through the front sprockets via a gearbox and single differential mounted to the left of the driver. Cletrac steering was used, as on the R-35.

The turret was also the same as on the infantry tank, the cast APX type with short SA 18 37-mm gun and co-axial machine-gun. Indeed, the two tanks looked very similar, being distinguished only by different suspensions, rear hull-shapes and driving positions. Recognition was made more difficult when *Char Léger* Hotchkiss 39-H appeared: this not only had increased armour protection but the new six-litre engine, which delivered 120 hp, necessitated a less sloping rear hull shape. With the new engine, speed was increased to 22½ mph (36 km/h) and range to 94 miles (151 km), slightly better for the tank's reconnaissance and screening role. Although early H-39s mounted the short, 21-calibre, 37-mm gun, later production vehicles were fitted with the higher-velocity (2,300 fps or 700 m/s) SA 38 gun of 33 calibres, an adequate anti-tank weapon.

With the heavier *Char* Bs in short supply, the infantry showed renewed interest in the Hotchkiss design and eventually adopted it, primarily for use in the new *DCR*. By 10 May 1940 each of the first three *DCR* had a Hotchkiss battalion as half of the two tank demi-brigades (90 H-39s in each division). Ninety more tanks equipped two infantry support *bataillons organiques*, the 13th and 35th attached to the First Army, and 30 were in independent companies.

The rest of the 821 H-35s and -39s deployed against the Germans were with the Cavalry. Each *DLM* had two battalions, while Third *DLM* apparently had another 60, replacing the three reconnaissance squadrons of *AMR* normally attached to the *dragons portés* battalions. Each of the five *DLC* had a 22-tank Hotchkiss squadron in its mechanized brigade combat group. More, along with S-35s and R-35s, were allocated to two of these brigades later in the campaign to form the weak *ad hoc* Fourth and Seventh *DLM*.

As with other French tanks maldeployment and design weakness vitiated H-35s and -39s effectiveness. The *DCR* were deployed with confusion and difficulty, caught in disadvantageous positions and dispersed as isolated strongpoints. In these actions and those of the *DLM*, the lack of a radio and the one-man turret, legacies of the limited strategic and tactical outlook, were severe drawbacks to co-ordinated action. The *DLM* were strung out across the Allied front in Holland and Belgium and were unable to fight more than a delaying action before destruction with the retreat to Dunkirk. The *DLC* formations were impossible to work effectively with their separate horsed and mechanized brigades, each of which had wildly different mobility factors and vulnerabilities. When remnants of the *DCR* and the new *DLM* attempted late counter-attacks, the armour of the H-35s and -39s, while better than that of German tanks, was insufficient to protect them from German anti-tank defences.

About 1,000 Hotchkiss tanks were constructed in all and the Germans made great use of them. H-39s, with the SA 38 gun, were used to equip the *Panzer* Divisions re-formed in France after the tank losses of 1942. The usual range of occupation police and second-line duties also fell to both types and an H-39 had the distinction of being the first tank captured by the Yugoslav partisans to form their armoured forces. Designated by the Germans *PzKpfw* 35-H 734 (*f*) and *PzKpfw* 39-H 735 (*f*), they usually had the normal German modifications of new cupolas and hull-mounted radios. At least one short-gun 39-H had four projectors for heavy 280/320-mm rockets fitted, two to each side of the hull.

As with the R-35, turretless Hotchkiss chassis were pressed into use as ammunition carriers and tractors on the Eastern front. Many were later fitted with revolving machine-gun turrets as mounted on the *SdKfz* 221 scout car. These vehicles would have been useful for limited reconnaissance duties. In 1942 some 72 39-H chassis were sent to the Alfred Becker factory in Krefeld for conversion to self-propelled guns. Forty-eight of these received *FH* 18 105-mm field howitzers, in which form they weighed 13

Hotchkiss H-39
Weight 11.8 tons (12 tonnes)
Crew two
Armament one 37-mm SA 38 (L/33) gun with 100 rounds and one 7.5-mm Model 1931 machine-gun with 400 rounds
Armour hull front, sides and rear 40 mm, decking 18 mm, belly 20 mm; turret front, sides and rear 45 mm, top 30 mm
Engine one Hotchkiss inline six-cylinder liquid-cooled petrol, 120-hp
Speed 22 mph (36 km/h)
Range 93 miles (150 km)
Trench crossing 5 feet 11 inches (1.8 m)
Vertical step 1 foot 8 inches (50 cm)
Fording 2 feet 9½ inches (85 cm)
Overall length 14 feet 1 inch (4.22 m)
Width 6 feet (1.85 m)
Height 7 feet 1 inch (2.14 m)

The tank illustrated is a late model H-39 with the longer gun. Note the distinctive Hotchkiss suspension with three pairs of road wheels

tons, had a crew of four or five and mounted the *FH* 18 in a high 12-mm armoured box with well-shaped, sloping sides. The remaining 24 received the 75-mm *PaK* 40, anti-tank gun, in a similar installation. Both types of SP were sent back to France to defend the Atlantic Wall. Incidentally, some 34 FCM infantry tanks received similar treatment by Becker: 24 were fitted with the old *FH* 16 model 105-mm field howitzer and 10 with the *PaK* 40.

After the war 12 H-39 tanks found their way into the hands of the Israelis who used them in the 1948–9 war. They were the first tanks possessed in any quantity by the Israeli army and were later, in typical fashion, up-gunned with British six-pounder (57-mm) weapons. These Super H-39s served until the 1956 Suez War, perhaps the last tanks of French pre-war design to see service anywhere in the world.

Left: *The H-35. Note the steeper slope of the rear superstructure with its smaller 3.5-litre engine as compared to the H-39 illustrated above. The short 21-calibre 37-mm gun cannot be used as a recognition feature as this low-velocity weapon was also fitted to early H-39s. The H-35 was widely deployed in French cavalry formations as a light battle tank and together with the H-39 saw considerable combat in the 1940 campaign. The short-gunned H-35s and H-39s proved disappointing in action as the low velocity weapon was unable to penetrate the armour of most German tanks*

S-35 Medium Tank

Among the specifications issued by the French Cavalry in 1931 was one for an *automitrailleuse de combat* to support the smaller *AMD* (armoured cars) and *AMR* (reconnaissance tanks) in its new mechanized formations. The original requirement turned out to be inadequate and the first two Renault *AMC* were built only in limited quantities. New specifications appeared in 1934 and these required a heavier 13,000-kg (12.8-ton) vehicle with improved 40-mm armour mounting a 47-mm or 25-mm gun.

The tank which met this specification was already under development by SOMUA (Societé d'Outillage Mécanique et d'Usinage d'Artillerie) based on the existing *Char* D mediums. The first prototype of the *AMC* Somua Type AC2 was demonstrated in August 1935 and was accepted for service as the *Char* Somua *Modèle* 1935-S.

The S-35, as it is usually known, was the first tank in the world to be of fully-cast construction. The well-shaped hull was in three parts: front and rear superstructure sections bolted to a lower casting containing the rear-mounted V8 engine and mechanical double differential transmission. The suspension, also bolted to the lower hull, consisted of nine, steel-tyred road wheels each side, protected by armour skirting, two pairs of four wheels on articulated arms with leaf springs, and a ninth on an independent coil spring at the rear. There were two return rollers and the track was guided by a central flange on the wheels and rollers fitting into a groove in the track. The transmission was at the rear and steering was via dry plate clutches and cables to a driver's wheel.

The prototype carried the APX turret of the *Char* D2 and B1 with short SA 34 47-mm gun, but the production vehicles had the APX 4 with thicker armour and 34-calibre SA 35 weapon. This was mounted co-axially with a 7.5-mm Riebel machine-gun and that had a limited degree of independent vertical movement. Although heavily-armed and armoured and rotated electrically, this one-man turret was the worst feature of the design. The tank had a crew of only three: driver, wireless operator and commander/gunner. No one man could command a tank, or worse a formation, while aiming and working the tank's weapons, but the French cavalry, like the infantry, had an essentially limited idea of the use of armour.

In all 416 S-35s were built and in May 1940 87 were allocated to each of the three *DLM*, providing the stronger of the two regiments of the *brigade de combat*. The Fourth *DCR*, formed from a mixed collection of cavalry and infantry units, also contained some 40 S-35s, two squadrons of the Third *Cuirassiers*, while about 50 were in Tunisia facing the Italian threat with the Sixth *DLC*.

The S-35 was arguably the best all-round tank of its period. Its gun, with a muzzle-velocity of 2,200 fps (670 m/s), was the equal of the latest *PzKpfw* III's 50-mm L/42, or the *PzKpfw* IV's short 75-mm L/24. The S-35's armour, while not impregnable, was 30 per cent or more thicker than the best of its opponents, while speed and radius of action were also good – considerably better than those of other French tanks.

Yet all this was of little avail when poor strategic and tactical employment prevented the S-35s presenting a real threat to the *Panzer* divisions. They were not in the right place and could not be redeployed in time. Their armour was not impenetrable and dispersion across a wide front exposed them as isolated sacrifices to the individually rather inferior, but more concentrated and experienced, German armoured forces. The turret and the weakness of the bolted joint in the hull must often have been decisive, while the lack of all-round observation facilities in the hull and a hull machine-gun assisted stalking by hostile infantry.

It was planned in 1940 to produce a diesel-engined S-40 with improved power and suspension but none appeared in service and plans for its production in the United States came to nothing. Produced only in prototype the same year was an assault gun on the S-35 chassis, the Somua S Au 40. A limited-traverse 75-mm gun was mounted beside the driver in the hull, and a new turret fitted for the commander.

After the fall of France the S-35 remained in service with the Germans. Owing to shortage of German tanks, particularly after the defeat at Stalingrad, they provided some of the equipment for *Panzer* divisions, for example the 21st when it was reformed from occupation forces in France in 1943. They were usually used as commanders' vehicles in mixed platoons of S-35s and H-39s. German S-35s were also used for occupation, police and training duties, including anti-partisan operations in Yugoslavia, where at least one

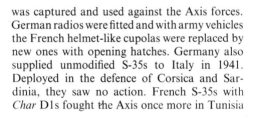

SOMUA S-35
Weight 19.7 tons (20 tonnes)
Crew three
Armament one 47-mm SA 35 (L/34) gun with
118 rounds and one 7.5-mm Model 1931 machine-
gun with 3,000 rounds
Armour hull front and sides 40 mm, tail 35 mm,
decking and belly 20 mm; turret front 55 mm,
sides and rear 45 mm, top 30 mm
Engine one Somua V-8 liquid-cooled petrol,
190-hp
Speed 25 mph (40 km/h)
Range 160 miles (257 km)
Trench crossing 7 feet (2.13 m)
Vertical step 2 feet 6 inches (76 cm)
Fording 3 feet 3 inches (1 m)
Length 17 feet 11 inches (5.45 m)
Width 7 feet (2.12 m)
Height 8 feet 10 inches (2.69 m)

*The S-35 illustrated is in standard 1940 'grise
armée/verte armée' camouflage.*

was captured and used against the Axis forces.
German radios were fitted and with army vehicles
the French helmet-like cupolas were replaced by
new ones with opening hatches. Germany also
supplied unmodified S-35s to Italy in 1941.
Deployed in the defence of Corsica and Sar-
dinia, they saw no action. French S-35s with
Char D1s fought the Axis once more in Tunisia

Left: *The S-35. Note the fine ballistic shape
of the cast hull and turret, the helmet-type cupola,
limited side vision facilities, powerful 47-mm gun,
large crew access hatch, engine inspection doors
and protected superstructure. Apart from a few
vital weaknesses this was the best tank in the west
in 1939–40 and soon won the Germans' respect.
Large numbers of these tanks were used to some
effect in Flanders and northern France during the
earlier stages of the 1940 campaign, but despite
their qualities were decisively outmanoeuvred.
Survivors formed the centres of small anti-tank
'Groupes Francs' in the closing stages of the
campaign*
Right: *The Char D2 from which the similarly
protected S-35 was developed. Only 100 of these
21.6 ton tanks were built. They were used in
General De Gaulle's Fourth DCR and in independent companies. The short SA 34 47-mm gun
was mounted, as in the proto-type S-35. The Char
Ds were intended as successors to the Renault
FT as a light infantry support tank, but proved
too large and was reclassified 'Char Moyen'
(medium tank) in 1935. Production was limited
due to concentration on development of the Char B*

CANADA

Canada had been a pioneer of armoured warfare, sending a motor machine-gun brigade, equipped with American-built armoured cars, to fight on the Western Front in World War I. A Canadian Tank Corps was formed in 1918 but this was disbanded at the end of the war. Although 12 Carden Loyd tankettes were purchased in 1930 as machine-gun carriers for the infantry it was only six years later, with the danger of a new conflict growing, that it was decided to begin a new Canadian tank force. Five officers and eighteen men under Major Worthington, who had served with the motorized machine-gun brigade in the Great War, formed the staff of a new Canadian Tank School. The twelve tankettes and two new Vickers Mark IV light tanks provided the vehicles. The school was later moved to Camp Borden in order to improve training facilities and in 1938 limited experimental tank exercises were held. In 1939 14 Vickers Mark VI lights were acquired.

In 1936 six militia cavalry regiments had been earmarked as tank units and they received some training in the following years. Although the rest were so designated on the outbreak of war, the first regiments were mobilized as cavalry and progress with mechanization was slow. The Canadians were misled by the initial course of the war and vehicles were also in very short supply, as it had been decided to rely on Britain for the provision of tanks; the Tank School was even closed at the end of 1939.

The German armoured success in the early summer of 1940 stimulated Britain to look to Canada for tank production facilities and forced Canada to revise her thinking on the importance of armour. Britain ordered 300 Valentine tanks from the Canadian Pacific Railway Company and on 13 August all the cavalry regiments were finally formed into a Canadian Armoured Corps with Colonel Worthington in command. The initial target was set at one three-battalion infantry support armoured brigade and one armoured division containing two armoured brigades (each with an organic motorized infantry battalion) and other units on the British pattern. A total of some 488 Valentine tanks were ordered from CPR to equip the army tank brigade and preparations were made to initiate production of a Canadian cruiser tank based on the American M3 medium. This eventually emerged as the Ram. Something more, however, was needed for immediate training and 229 American relics of World War I, about 90 Mark VIII heavies and the rest M1917 Six-Ton (Renault) lights, were purchased at scrap prices to train the new armoured battalions.

By June 1941 First Canadian Army Tank Brigade was ready to go to Britain, but it was not until that month that the first Canadian Valentines were produced. The Brigade's battalions were, therefore, equipped with British Matilda and later Churchill infantry tanks. Only the first 30 Valentines of the 1,420 finally produced by CPR by May 1943 saw service in Canada, where they were used for training. The rest went to Russia where they were some of the most popular western tanks used by the Red Army. This was probably due to Canadian design modifications, notably the more powerful six-cylinder General Motors diesel engine. They also had a modified gearbox, new electrics and, in all but the very first vehicles produced, a new, stronger, cast nose and Browning turret machine-gun. There were also abortive plans for a new cast turret mounting a six-pounder (57-mm) gun.

The Ram began to appear from the end of 1941 and entered service with the Fifth Canadian

Armoured Division. Arriving in Britain in Spring 1942 the Division's Rams were, at first, supplemented by American M3 Lees and Grants. The Fourth Canadian Armoured Division and an independent brigade had been formed in Britain at the beginning of that year. When they had all assembled the Canadian Armoured Corps was reorganized to bring the divisions' armour into line with the new British pattern of a single-armoured brigade and a tank-equipped armoured reconnaissance regiment. Although some units were disbanded, the Corps' basic structure remained the same, with First and Second Canadian Armoured Brigades (only the former the original formation) and Fourth and Fifth Canadian Armoured Divisions.

The first Canadian armoured troops to see service were from the Calgary Regiment of the First Army Tank Brigade whose Churchill Is, IIs and IIIs took part in the Dieppe raid. With Shermans, the Brigade fought in Sicily and Italy, where they were joined by others from the re-equipped Fifth Canadian Armoured Division. After acquiring a second infantry brigade the Division, together with First Canadian Armoured Brigade in First Canadian Corps, joined the other two major Canadian armoured units in Holland during March 1945.

Second Canadian Armoured Brigade, again with its Rams replaced by Shermans (including DD models) landed in Normandy and, together with Major-General Worthington's similarly re-equipped Fourth Canadian Armoured Division, fought as part of Second Canadian Corps from Caen and Falaise through Belgium to the Netherlands. Here, joined by First Canadian Corps to form First Canadian Army, the Canadian armoured forces finished the war.

When the Ram ceased production after 2,042 tanks, a slightly modified M4A1 Sherman, known as the Grizzly, was constructed at the Montreal Locomotive Works. The only important differences were more resilient Canadian tracks and a modified turret with a British-type radio set, a new stowage box on the rear and a two-inch (50-mm) smoke mortar in the roof (a feature which later became standard on US-built M4s). By the end of 1943, after only 188 tanks had been built, production ceased as enough American spare construction capacity became available to concentrate all Sherman production in the USA. Grizzlies were used by Canadian forces on both sides of the Atlantic and some were also passed to Britain.

A modification, the Skink anti-aircraft tank, appeared early in 1944, developed by the Waterloo Manufacturing Company. This mounted a new turret with four 20-mm Polsten automatic guns on a slightly-modified Grizzly hull. Conversion kits were also developed to alter existing Shermans/Grizzlies to the new configuration. Production orders were given but, with Allied air superiority, only three actual vehicles and eight conversion kits were finished.

MLW continued to produce Sexton self-propelled guns until the end of 1945 – a total of 2,150. In all, Canada had constructed almost 5,800 tanks and SPs, a significant achievement.

Below: *A Ram Kangaroo advances through heavy going in North-West Europe. The Canadian Ram saw no combat service as a battle tank but was widely used as a Kangaroo armoured personnel carrier. Troop capacity was about 10 with a driver and commander/wireless-operator as crew. Two regiments of Kangaroos, one Canadian, one British, gave valuable service from September 1944 until the end of the war in Europe*

Cruiser Tank Ram

The decision to form the First Canadian Armoured Division in the summer of 1940 raised the problem of procuring the faster and longer-ranged cruiser tanks. British production was fully absorbed and British orders had taken up American capacity so a new Tank Arsenal was set up at the Montreal Locomotive Works, a subsidiary of the American Locomotive Company (Alco).

It was planned to produce the American M3 medium but the armour was limited, the silhouette high, the radio not in the turret and, worst of all, the main gun was hull-mounted. By the beginning of 1941 it was decided to construct virtually a new tank which would be lower, better protected and have a turret-mounted radio and gun. Colonel Worthington, the head of the tank force, wanted a 75-mm weapon, but a standard British two-pounder (40-mm) and then six-pounder (57-mm) was eventually specified, allowing the use of the standard M3 60-inch (152-cm) diameter turret ring.

Worthington's interest in the design was reflected by the tank's name, the Ram, which formed the centre of his family crest. Owing to shortage of six-pounders the standard two-pounder mount of the Canadian Valentine was adopted for the prototype, completed in July 1941, and early production vehicles. The hull was of composite construction with a riveted plate chassis, a three-piece bolted cast nose and a cast hull top. The turret was also cast with a bolted-on front, easily replaced by a six-pounder (57-mm) fitting when required. On the left hull front was a small machine-gun turret mounting a 0.30-inch (7.7-mm) Browning and a similar weapon was mounted co-axially with the two-pounder (40-mm). A third could be carried for AA purposes. The engine, as in the M3, drove through a controlled differential gearbox and the front sprockets. Steering was by levers and the driver sat on the right, as usual in British practice. Suspension was also of the M3 pattern.

The tank went into production in November 1941. After 50 vehicles, Canadian Mark III six-pounder guns became available and were fitted, with an elevation stabilizer, to new production Ram IIs. Various design alterations later took place: notably the deletion of the hull doors to strengthen the hull and simplify production, the replacement of the small turret by the more versatile ball machine-gun mounting, the adoption of a new longer British Mark V six-pounder (57-mm) and a new engine which used lower octane fuel. In very late Rams the return rollers were modified to the trailing Sherman pattern and Canadian Dry Pin track adopted, being lighter and cheaper than the American equivalent.

Ram production ended in July 1943 after 1,908 Ram IIs. By that time, however, the chassis were being used as a self-propelled artillery carriage. In 1942 the SP concept was proved in British service in North Africa with the American M7 Priest and an SP version of the 25-pounder (88-mm) was required. A modified American M7 was built, but production facilities were unavailable. After some design problems the gun was fitted to the Ram chassis and the first Sexton arrived for British trials at the

beginning of 1943. By the end of the year MLW had produced 424 and the SP, together with a gunless GPO (gun-position officer vehicle), saw wide service after D-Day replacing Priests in British and Canadian hands. Later vehicles had the new-style return rollers and stronger one-piece noses.

The original Ram did not see action. It was used for training by the Canadian armoured formations from 1942, but an experiment with a British gun showed that it was not altogether suitable for up-gunning to 75 mm and the Canadians were re-equipped with Shermans before seeing action in 1944. Eighty-four Rams were used as observation post vehicles with dummy guns, partial-traverse turrets and extra observation and communications equipment. These saw active service with Sexton batteries in Europe.

Perhaps the most significant Rams to be used in action were the Kangaroo armoured personnel carriers. After operational experiments with redundant gunless Priests, the First Canadian Armoured Carrier Regiment was formed in September 1944 with Rams that had lost their turrets to provide space for 8 to 11 infantrymen on benches. After Kangaroos had been successfully used in the capture of Boulogne, 49th Royal Tanks was converted with 120 more to become 49th APC Regiment. The APCs saw considerable use for the remainder of the war and after.

Turretless Rams were also used as Wallaby ammunition carriers for Sexton batteries and as tractors for 17-pounder (76.2-mm) anti-tank

guns. Others became Badgers fitted with hull-mounted Wasp II flame-throwers and were used by the Canadians in Operation Veritable during the spring of 1945. Later, turreted Ram Badgers were used in similar fashion. A few Ram Kangaroos were fitted with searchlights in early 1945.

There were two versions of the Ram Armoured Recovery Vehicle (ARV): Mark I, a normal tank with tool boxes and a front-mounted winch, and Mark II with dummy turret and gun and an electric winch in the space. Two Rams were converted as engineer assault tanks in 1943 but it was decided to use the more heavily armoured and more mobile Churchill for this role. There was also an experimental SP anti-aircraft mounting, using first a 3-inch and then a 3.7-inch (94-mm) gun, but it proved high and unstable and was abandoned after tests.

The Ram was a good vehicle for its time; only limited armament restricted its operational usefulness. The Sexton, however, saw considerable service both during and after the war.

Below: *One of the first 50 Rams completed with two-pounder (40-mm) guns as the Ram 1. The rest of the production run carried a six-pounder (57-mm) main armament*
Bottom: *The Sexton self-propelled 25-pounder (88-mm) based on the Ram chassis was widely used both during the war and in the years following. Shortly after D-Day it completely replaced the Priest in the British and Canadian self-propelled artillery battalions fighting in North West Europe*

Cruiser Tank Ram II
Weight 29 tons (29.5 tonnes)
Crew five
Armament one 6-pounder (57-mm) Mark III (L/43) or Mark V (L/50) gun with 92 rounds and two or three 0.30-inch (7.62-mm) Browning M1919A4 machine-guns with 4,400 rounds
Armour hull nose 38 mm, glacis and driver's plate 44 mm, sides 38–63 mm, decking 38–76 mm, belly 25 mm, tail 38 mm; turret front 88 mm, sides 63 mm, top and rear 38 mm
Engine one Wright Continental R-975-CI or R-975-EC2 radial nine-cylinder air-cooled petrol, 400-hp
Speed 25 mph (40 km/h)
Range 144 miles (230 km)
Trench crossing 7 feet 5 inches (2.26 m)
Vertical step 2 feet (61 cm)
Fording 3 feet 4 inches (1.01 m)
Overall length 19 feet (5.8 m)
Width 9 feet 6 inches (2.9 m)
Height 8 feet 9 inches (2.67 m)

The vehicle illustrated is a Ram Kangaroo armoured personnel carrier – a turretless Ram II

THE SOVIET UNION

The Soviet Union produced more tanks in the inter-war period than the rest of the world put together. In a revolutionary environment and with Stalin's commitment to military expansion, the way was open for a more whole-hearted acceptance of mechanized warfare. And despite Russia's lack of technological resources and expertise, the ideas of progressive Western military thinkers fell on fertile ground.

In 1927 the Soviet Army possessed 90 infantry support tanks; two years later the first Five Year Plan aimed at an armoured force of 3,500 tanks – this number was later expanded due to ominous international developments. New tractor plants were set up that doubled as tank arsenals and foreign technology was exploited. Co-operation with the Germans on tank design and testing had been taking place since 1921 but this proved insufficient and British and American vehicles were also purchased. From 1931 the results of this technological treasure hunt led to the appearance of a whole range of vehicles from the *T*-27 tankette to the *T*-35 heavy tank.

Light tanks were to be used in the traditional direct support role in *NPP* (Close Infantry Support) battalions allocated to infantry divisions and in mechanized regiments with cavalry divisions. Medium and heavy tanks were used in break-through formations of up to brigade size, while 'Fast Tanks' in independent *DD* (Long Range) mechanized brigades were to follow up and strike deep behind enemy lines. By 1934 there were two 500-tank mechanized corps each of two or three *DD* mechanized brigades with additional motorized infantry brigade and artillery regiment plus six other independent *DD* brigades of 90 tanks each.

By the mid-1930s there were over 30 plants engaged in the production of tanks and, with the second Five Year Plan in full swing, the number of tanks in service topped the 20,000 mark. However, the growth of such a powerful mechanized force, based on principles of technocratic efficiency rather than ideological reliability, stimulated Stalin's political paranoia. Reaction set in: doctrines of armoured warfare were denounced as reactionary and bourgeois: Marshall Tukhachevski, the most senior supporter of progressive mechanized warfare, was replaced as Deputy Commissar of Defence and soon afterwards executed, and some 35,000 other Soviet officers were shot, imprisoned or dismissed.

In 1939, despite the decisive use of armour by Zhukov against the Japanese in the Far East, the mechanized corps, now seven in number, were broken up and their vehicles fused into divisions to be distributed as brigades along with the existing conventional units for infantry

support. But the malaise went deeper still. With armoured warfare politically dangerous any ideas on the improvement of the efficiency of the Soviet armoured forces were put forward at peril of one's career – or worse. As a result tank crews deteriorated in quality and production of new vehicles did not take place at the pace demanded by the international situation.

Soviet armour was employed with mixed success in the Winter War of 1939–40 with Finland but with the victories of Germany in Western Europe orders were issued in November 1940 for the reformation of armoured divisions and mechanized corps. However, it was a grandiose and impractical scheme and the Soviet armed forces were still in the throes of reorganization when the Germans struck. Despite greatly outnumbering their opponents in numbers of tanks the Soviet armoured troops were abysmally handled; in the opening months of the war 17,500 Soviet tanks were lost.

Such casualties could not have been borne by

other nations, but the Russians were able to make them good within a year, in a burst of production equalled only by the United States. In addition, the USSR had to cope with the loss of many of its industrial areas and as these were threatened, and/or overrun, their equipment had to be moved east to the existing plants at Nizhny Tagil and Chelyabinsk to form major tank production complexes. Together with over 40 new and existing plants these factories increased Soviet tank production from 6,590 in 1941 to 24,668 in 1942 and kept it at about that figure for the remainder of the war.

These tanks were, moreover, of new types, better than any foreign counterparts. The *T*-34 medium and the KV heavy tank series, designed in the immediate pre-war years, provided the Russians with a vital technological edge. This, if it did not make up for Soviet operational deficiencies, at least gave added impetus to the initial counter-attacks that first brought the Germans to a halt, and which from late 1942 began to turn the tables. Even when better German tanks appeared, both basic Soviet types could be progressively modified to keep pace.

Soviet tanks, however, were always crudely constructed with precision only being used where absolutely necessary. Their technologically unsophisticated crews worked in very basic conditions by Western standards. Radios, for example, were only issued to company commanders' tanks and the cut and thrust of blitzkrieg had to be replaced by a meticulously prepared attritional offensive. As the *T*-34 evolved into the *T*-34/85 and the KV into the JS, the Germans were steadily ground down by superior numbers.

After their monstrous losses of 1941 the Russians turned back to the individual brigade as their major armoured unit: two or three battalions – about 50 tanks in all – being grouped with a motorized infantry battalion and other support elements, including anti-tank and anti-aircraft units. Together with individual tank battalions these were the formations that were most easily handled by the inexperienced Soviet armoured leaders, although *débâcles* still occurred when the Russians tried premature counter-attacks in 1942. Despite the losses of that year, the tank brigades were reorganized on a more homogeneous basis with 53 modern *T*-34s and *T*-70s while independent battalions were doubled in size to regiments of 39 light and medium tanks. Heavy tanks were also concentrated into regiments of 21 vehicles each. Larger formations were reorganized: tank corps with three tank brigades and one motorized infantry brigade, and mechanized corps with three motorized infantry brigades (each with its own tank regiment) and one tank brigade. Both deployed 180–200 tanks and had their quota of reconnaissance, motor-cycle, signals, engineer, anti-tank and anti-aircraft units.

In 1943 *SU* (self-propelled mount) assault gun regiments were formed. These were allocated to both infantry and armoured units to provide mobile direct heavy gunfire support. *SU* regiments were often joined with tank brigades or regiments to form joint Tank-*SU* Groups.

By 1944 the standard Soviet tank brigade had grown to a strength of 65 tanks, while independent regiments now had 43 each, usually all *T*-34s. Heavy tank brigades contained 23 JS tanks. With up to two heavy tank and two *SU* regiments attached, a tank or mechanized corps might how have up to 300 tanks and assault guns. When the war ended the Soviet armoured force had grown to a peak of 302 armoured and mechanized brigades grouped into 25 tank corps, 13 mechanized corps, about 60 independent tank brigades, 180 independent tank regiments and 150 assault gun regiments.

An impressive AFV production fed these numerous formations. Russia produced the staggering total of 87,200 tanks and 25,300 *SU* vehicles in the period 1940–5, a total second only to the USA. She also received 4,260 tanks from Britain, 5,258 from the USA and 1,188 from Canada, a contribution which, if inferior in technology to Soviet armour, proved vital at the time of Russia's major losses and useful for the remainder of the war. No amount of superior skill could save the *Wehrmacht* from annihilation by an armoured steamroller of such proportions.

Apart from the basic type numbers, Soviet tank designations are usually Western and are often mixed up by their external origin and the existence of several systems from various intelligence sources. The nomenclature used in the following is that which has the greatest consensus and which seems least confusing. The multiplicity of building plants and the standards of Soviet tank construction also made for significant variations in armour thicknesses etc and all such figures should be taken as approximations.

Left: *A company of T-34s, the most significant tank of World War II, advancing towards the front. Each vehicle is carrying a 'tank descent' of infantry – a tactic commonly used by the Red Army. Note the tanks' different wheel types*

T-26 Series

The *T-26* was based on one of the foreign designs purchased during the Soviet Army's first Five Year Plan; this was the British Vickers 'Six-Ton' tank, newly developed as a private venture in Great Britain. Despite maximum armour thickness of only 15 mm, these seemed suitable tanks for the direct support of infantry, and six of the Model A type with twin turrets, each mounting a water-cooled 7.62-mm machine-gun, were purchased in 1930. Redesignated *T-26* the model was put into production the following year with DT air-cooled machine-guns. Some had a 12.7-mm machine-gun in the right-hand turret to provide limited armour-piercing capability. To give heavier fire support, others were completed with either 27-mm, or, more usually, 37-mm guns in the right-hand turret, and commanders' tanks *T-26* (*V*) had a large frame-aerial mounted around the hull.

In 1933 the desire to mount a more powerful 37-mm high velocity weapon in order to improve the tank's capability against enemy armour led to redesign. The larger gun was tested in the left-hand turret of a tank from which the right-hand turret had been removed, but this arrangement was found to give insufficient room for the new weapon. A larger single turret was, there-fore, adopted, off-set to the left. The single-turret vehicles are usually known as *T-26B* and the earlier twin-turreted tanks *T-26A*. Fuel capacity was also increased to improve the range from 87 miles to 140 miles (136 km to 219 km), which made the tank suitable for cavalry as well as infantry use. Later *T-26B*s mounted the improved 45-mm gun. The early *T-26B* had no machine-gun as secondary armament and was used to provide heavier gun support for the *NPP* battalions. They were also issued to *DPP* break-through armoured units and to the mechanized regiments attached to cavalry divisions.

The *T-26* had the normal layout of the Vickers 'Six-Tonner' with rear-mounted air-cooled engine, a licence-built version of the original Armstrong Siddeley unit with front sprocket drive and clutch and brake steering. Suspension was on the classic Vickers pattern with two pairs of leaf-sprung twin rollers each side. The tanks were of simple riveted construction, with some welding being used in the turrets of the *T-26B*. The crew of both types of *T-26* was three. The weight of the standard *T-26A* was 8.4 tons, while the *T-26B* weighed 9.1 tons.

The *T-26B*'s maximum speed of 17.5 mph (27 km/h), reduced from 22 mph (35 km/h) in the *T-26A*, proved rather slow for the more mobile armoured roles, so experiments took place with a 35 mph (56 km/h) development, the *T-46* with Christie type drive and suspension as in the *BT* tanks. This proved complex and made little advance on the existing *BT*. To keep tank output at high levels, therefore, only a few were built and the *T-26* was kept in general production with a new version appearing in 1937, sometimes called *T-26B-2*. More welding was used in the construction and armour protection was increased slightly on the new model to 25 mm on the turret and 16 mm on the hull, increasing weight to 9.4 tons. Range was also up to 215 miles (336 km). A 7.62-mm machine-gun was mounted co-axially with the 45-mm weapon and occasionally there was a second machine-gun in the turret rear. As with the *T-26A*, radio-equipped command versions of both variants were also built.

Early combat experience on both sides, in Spain, and in Soviet and Chinese hands against the Japanese, proved the power of the 45-mm armament but showed that more protection was needed. A new *T-26S* version appeared in 1938 with welded 25-mm armour of improved shape which improved this situation. A new turret

mounted the same armament as the *T*-26B-2 and an anti-aircraft machine-gun, sometimes fitted to earlier models, could also be mounted. Weight of the new model was increased to 10.3 tons, and the suspension and transmission both had to be strengthened. Speed was reduced to 16.8 mph (27 km/h) in this version, which was sometimes called the *T*-26C by foreign observers. The turret of the *T*-26S could also be mounted on the older *T*-26B-2 chassis.

Soviet *T*-26 tanks were used against the Finns during the Winter War of 1939–40, where they faced similar tanks, British-built 'Six-Tonners', 32 of which were bought by the Finns in 1938–9. The general failure of Soviet forces in the severe weather conditions led to large numbers of *T*-26s falling into Finnish hands and these were pressed into service, so many being captured that the standard designation for the type in the Finnish Army became *T*-26, their own type becoming *T*-26E.

About 4,500 *T*-26s of all marks were produced and large numbers remained in service with the Soviet Army when the Germans attacked in June 1941. The firepower of the later versions should have stood them in good stead against the German armour, but, strung out in disorganized groups, the lightly protected tanks stood little chance against concentrated German tanks or anti-tank guns. The Germans outflanked and captured many *T*-26s intact and used them in anti-partisan operations, some being converted into light tank destroyers with 75-mm *PaK* 97/38 anti-tank guns, modified from captured French 75-mm artillery pieces.

The *T*-26 was taken out of combat service by mid-1942, although the type remained for secondary duties on the now quiet Far Eastern borders. Others were converted into radio-controlled demolition vehicles or gun tractors, some with box-type central superstructures. Other variants included a number of not very successful flame-throwers, the *OT*-26, *OT*-130 and *OT*-133, smoke-laying vehicles designated DT-26 and *IT*-26 bridging tanks. There were several self-propelled guns including the *AT*-1 fitted with a 16.5-calibre 76.2-mm *PS*-3 tank gun in the rear of a modified chassis for use as an artillery tank in support of cavalry formations.

The *T*-26 was a good reliable tank for its time, generally well suited to Soviet requirements. It was simple and robust, well enough armed to be highly successful in its early combats. If it had been handled with more skill it might have done better against the Germans, although by 1941 its combination of firepower and protection was far inferior to later Soviet armour. A replacement infantry support light tank, the *T*-50, had a 45-mm gun and well-sloped 37-mm armour and utilized torsion bar suspension, like the larger KV. But such a tank cost as much to construct as the larger medium now required for the infantry support task on an increasingly dangerous battlefield, and only 65 *T*-50s were produced.

T-26S
Weight 10.1 tons (10.3 tonnes)
Crew three
Armament one 45-mm M-32 (L/46) gun with 165 rounds and two 7.62-mm DT machine-guns with 3,654 rounds
Armour hull front 25 mm, sides and rear 16 mm, decking and belly 10 mm; turret front and sides 25 mm, top 10 mm
Engine one GAZ *T*-26 horizontally opposed 8-cylinder air-cooled petrol, 88-hp
Speed 16.8 mph (27 km/h)
Range 215 miles (346 km)
Trench crossing 5 feet 8 inches (1.73 m)
Vertical step 2 feet 4 inches (71 cm)
Fording 2 feet 6 inches (76 cm)
Overall length 15 feet 3 inches (4.65 m)
Width 8 feet (2.44 m)
Height 7 feet 8 inches (2.33 m)

Opposite page: A T-26S. Comparison between this tank and the earlier T-26B below immediately reveals the great improvement in the shape. This tank is being inspected by British officers and men following the joint occupation of Iran in 1942; the standing figures offer a good key to the size of the vehicle
Below: A T-26B, the successor of the twin-turreted T-26A, captured by Franco's forces during the Spanish Civil War. The German tank crews fighting for Franco were so impressed by the Soviet tanks used by the Republicans that they offered rewards for their capture. The Soviet tank is being followed by an inferior PzKpfw 1

T-28 and T-35 Series

These two tanks formed the most powerful component of the Soviet armoured forces of the 1930s. Both were intended for the *DPP* (Distant Infantry Support) 'break-through' role, for which powerful armament and protection were required. The *T-28* and *T-35*, classified as medium and heavy tanks respectively, were both large vehicles for their day.

The *T-28*, which first appeared in 1932, was the more important numerically. Its design owed a great deal to contemporary foreign thought. The multi-turret layout was chosen, with a large central turret mounting a 45-mm gun together with a 7.62-mm machine-gun to the right. Two smaller auxiliary turrets on each side at the front mounted another machine-gun each. Armour was 30 mm maximum on the hull front and 20 mm on the hull sides and turret. Production tanks mounted the 16.5 calibre 76.2-mm gun as main armament.

The suspension was based on that of 15 Vickers Mediums, bought in 1930, with twelve small road wheels each side, each individually coil-sprung. Early *T-28*s were fitted with rear-mounted 375-hp Hispano Suiza engines driving through the rear sprockets, but most tanks had the 12-cylinder M-17L improvement of the Liberty aero-engine which increased available power to 500-hp and drove the 28.1-ton tank at 23 mph (36 km/h). In 1933 a modified 30.5-ton version (*T-28A*) appeared, which had hull armour thickened to 35 mm and a strengthened suspension. The crew of both types was six, and some vehicles had one of the auxiliary machine-guns replaced by a 45-mm weapon. This 2,350

fps (717 m/s) high-velocity gun had better armour-piercing performance than the 1,190 fps (363 m/s) weapon of the main armament which had a superior high-explosive capability. At first only some tanks were fitted with radio as *T-28(V)* commanders' vehicles, but later on most tanks of this type were so equipped.

In 1938 a version appeared (*T-28B*) which had the new 26-calibre L-10 76.2-mm gun as main armament. The improved armour-piercing capacity of this weapon made the fitting of extra 45-mm guns unnecessary.

A few *T-28*s went to Spain, but the tank's first major combat use was against the Finnish fortifications during the 1939–40 Winter War. Early battles showed that what had been adequate protection in the early 1930s was no longer enough against the new anti-tank weapons. Extra armour was fitted to some vehicles (sometimes called *T-28C*), bringing hull and turret protection up to 80 mm with side-armour increased to 50 mm.

Production of the *T-28* continued into 1940 and the vehicle remained in service when the Germans invaded. They proved easy targets, being deployed piecemeal and thus allowing their thin side armour to be exploited by the more manoeuvrable and better-armed German tanks, while their high silhouette made them easy to spot. Even the superior protection of the *T-28C* was no help against ineffectual use and strategic isolation. For their time, however, *T-28*s had been good tanks with an adequate combination of firepower, protection and speed coupled with good cross-country performance.

The *T-28* was used for a number of specialized variants – the *IT-28* bridge-layer and an *OT-28* flame-thrower – while a number of experimental 76.2-mm and 152-mm self-propelled gun projects of the 1930s also utilized the chassis.

The *T-32* heavy assault tank which appeared in 1931 was designed to give greater strength for break-through formations than the *T-28* medium could provide. Based on the Vickers 'Independent' project of 1925, it had five turrets – a raised central one for the main armament of a 16.5-calibre 76.2-mm gun and 7.62-mm machine-gun, two auxiliary turrets each containing 37-mm high-velocity guns with co-axial machine-guns, and two other machine-gun turrets. Armour was of 25 mm maximum. The tank weighed 44.3 tons, and a 345-hp M-17L engine drove it at 18 mph (28 km/h).

In 1933 an improved *T-35* appeared which replaced the troublesome hydraulic transmission of the *T-32* with a more conventional mechanical unit. The other features of the tank were retained, however, including the suspension of eight wheels per side, grouped in pairs and protected by 10-mm armoured skirts. Maximum hull

Below: *An early T-28 with its short 16.5 calibre 76.2-mm gun up-armoured to T-28C standard. There is heavy extra protection around the turret and on the hull front. Two auxiliary turrets can be seen in front of the main one. The T-28s were classified as medium tanks and their performance was adequate but wasted by poor strategy at the beginning of the hostilities on the Eastern Front. The turret is the same as the T-35's opposite*

armour was increased to 30 mm and the more powerful 500-hp V-12 M-17M engine fitted. Armament was the same as the T-32 but 45-mm guns began to replace the 37-mm weapons from 1935. A few tanks were fitted with flame-throwers instead of forward machine-gun turrets. Some T-35s were fitted with radios as commanders' vehicles, and very late tanks were of all-welded construction with 50-mm armour and reshaped conical turrets replacing the earlier cylindrical versions.

Not more than 30 of these 44.3–49.2 ton monsters were constructed and they were of limited fighting value, the multiplicity of armament preventing any coherent fire control. Some tanks had their two machine-gun turrets deleted for this reason. Armour protection was weak for a vehicle of such size. The T-35 was also troublesome mechanically, the clutch and brake steering being unable to cope with the weight. Range was also limited, and all those T-35s encountered by the Germans in 1941 were captured, either broken down or run out of fuel. None actually saw combat, a sadly futile end for a rather impractical vehicle.

T-35

Weight 44.3 tons (45 tonnes)
Crew ten
Armament one 76.2-mm PS-3 (L/16.5) gun with 96 rounds, two 45-mm M-32 (L/46) guns with 220 rounds and five 7.62-mm DT machine-guns with 10,000 rounds
Armour hull front 30 mm, sides and rear 20 mm, decking and belly 11–14 mm, turret fronts and sides 20 mm, top 11 mm
Engine one M-17M V-12 liquid-cooled petrol, 500-hp
Speed 18 mph (30 km/h)
Range 94 miles (151 km)
Trench crossing 15 feet (4.6 m)
Vertical step 3 feet 11 inches (1.2 m)
Fording 3 feet 11 inches (1.2 m)
Overall length 31 feet 6 inches (9.6 m)
Width 10 feet 6 inches (3.2 m)
Height 11 feet 3 inches (3.42 m)

The tank illustrated is an early T-35 with the usual complex multi-turret arrangement. The system of dark markings which can be seen on the turrets was often used during the 1930s but its purpose is not known. Note the distinctive form of suspension partly protected by armoured side shields

BT Series

The Soviet government's technical mission, sent out in 1929 to inspect foreign developments for possible utilization by the Soviet Army, was very impressed by the new fast tanks built by J Walter Christie in the USA with their powerful aero-engines and ability to run on both wheels and tracks. With a maximum speed of 40 mph (63 km/h) on tracks and almost 70 mph (109 km/h) on wheels, coupled with a range of 150 miles (234 km), the Christie seemed very suitable for the role of 'Fast Tank' (*BT*) in the *DD* (Long Range) mechanized formations designed for deep penetration independent operations. As a result two of Christie's M1931 tanks were purchased.

A *BT*-1 prototype and two simplified *BT*-2s were constructed and mass production began at the end of 1931. The first prototypes had been armed with twin machine-guns, like their American predecessors, but the Soviet production *BT*-2 mounted the M-30 37-mm gun together with a machine-gun in a ball mounting on the right-hand side of the turret. The 10.8-ton Soviet *BT* tanks also adopted a simpler riveted construction instead of welding. Otherwise the vehicles were identical to the US tanks, with the distinctive suspension of four, large, rubber-tyred, independently coil-sprung wheels each side, and a licence-built version of the 12-cylinder Liberty aero engine of 400 hp. The tracks were driven via the rear sprockets, with clutch and brake steering. Drive could also be connected to the wheels and the tank steered by moving the front wheel pair. The driver, who sat centrally in the hull front, used a steering wheel to control both systems. The other two crew members, commander/gunner and loader, occupied the turret which was set at the front of the vehicle.

Some vehicles were completed as *BT*-3s with M-32 45-mm weapons replacing the 37-mm guns and new type solid wheels instead of the spoked variety. Experiments took place with a *BT*-4 with twin turrets along the lines of the *T*-26A, but the next major model was the *BT*-5. This carried a new circular turret, mounting the 45-mm gun with a co-axial 7.62-mm machine-gun. There was provision for radio in an extended turret rear and this was fitted in *BT*-5(*V*) command tanks. The other major development of the new 11.3 ton model was the fitting of a Soviet-designed aero engine, the 12-cylinder M-5 of 350 hp. Some tanks were completed as *BT*-5As with short, 16.5 calibre 76.2-mm tank guns to give artillery support to the *DD* tank groups and cavalry units.

Production of the *BT*-5 had begun by the end of 1932 and it was not until 1935 that a major new version appeared, designated *BT*-7. This had the 450-hp M-17T engine, a Soviet modification of the original Liberty unit. The hull was of welded construction, and frontal armour protection was increased from a maximum of 13 to 22 mm. New shorter pitched tracks were fitted, which had less of a tendency to shed, and speed was reduced to a more practicable 45 mph (72 km/h) on wheels and 33 mph (53 km/h) on tracks. Fuel capacity was increased, boosting the range from 187 to 310 miles (292 to 499 km).

The first tanks (*BT*-7-1s) retained the *BT*-5 turret, but the later vehicles (*BT*-7-2s) had a new version with better-shaped protection slightly thickened from 13 mm to 15 mm. Radio-equipped *BT*-7 command tanks were built with *BT*-5(*V*) turrets, and *BT*-7A artillery tanks with short 76.2-mm guns. Some *BT*-7s had extra machine-guns mounted in the turret rear and later tanks had stabilized 45-mm guns. The *BT*-7 proved a popular vehicle in service and more tanks of this type were produced than any other in the Soviet Union during the 1930s.

The final, and most powerful, of the *BT* series to see service was the *BT*-7M. This was fitted with the new 500-hp 12-cylinder V-2 tank engine, fitted in a redesigned hull with enlarged front. The armament was increased with a hull-mounted 7.62-mm machine-gun, a similar weapon in each side of the turret, together with a powerful new 30.5-calibre 76.2-mm gun. Also sometimes designated *BT*-8, the tank was first displayed in 1938.

BT tanks were usually deployed in *DD* mechanized brigades in three battalions of 32 tanks each. They were also issued to the mechanized components of cavalry formations. With both these types of unit, mobility was at a premium, and some *BT*-5s were converted to *BT*-5 *PK* configuration for deep wading. There were also bridge-laying versions of both *BT*-3 and *BT*-5 while other tanks of this type were fitted with fascines. Older *BT*s were converted into crane tanks and others to *BT-DT* smoke-layers.

However, with Stalin's reaction against the independent use of armour, *BT*s were reorganized into infantry support brigades – a role for which they were unsuitable with their thin armour and which took no advantage of their good mobility. In the difficult conditions of Finland they were at a distinct disadvantage; many were destroyed and others captured, some to be converted into 114-mm assault howitzers. Large numbers of all types of *BT* still formed a major proportion of Soviet armoured forces in 1941, but handled by inexperienced commanders and opposed by well-handled German armour to which they were inferior in quality, heavy losses were sustained. By 1942 the *BT* had been replaced in front-line service by the *T*-34.

The *BT* series were, for their time, excellent vehicles. Their impressive mobility was demonstrated during manoeuvres in 1935 when they jumped 30 feet (9.14 m) over five-foot (1.52-m) steps at 30 mph (50 km/h). However, the ability to change from tracks to wheels was of little tactical usefulness. It took a 30-minute operation to effect the transfer, and tracks were necessary for any sort of cross-country movement. Wheeled speed, therefore, was not a facility that could be utilized during deep penetration of enemy lines, where all sorts of mobility were at a premium. Even on tracks, high cross-country speed was not practicable due to the effect of such manoeuvres on the crew. Nevertheless, the *BT* was the most mobile tank available in quantity to any army, suitable for experiments in progressive concepts of operations. It was the *BT*'s tragedy that this experience was thrown away in Stalin's purges and, when the time came for major combat, its crews and commanders were unable to exploit the remaining mobility advantages of what was now an obsolescent vehicle.

Below: *Late model BT-7s (BT-7-2s) advancing down Gorky Street in Moscow on their way to the front on 7 November 1941. The battles around Moscow were probably the last occasion on which BT tanks were used in large numbers*

BT-7-2
Weight 13.8 tons (14 tonnes)
Crew three
Armament one 45-mm M-32 (L/46) gun with 188 rounds and two 7.62 mm DT machine-guns with 2,394 rounds
Armour hull front 22 mm, sides and tail 13 mm, belly and decking 6–10 mm, turret front and sides 15 mm, top 10 mm
Engine one M-17T V-12 liquid-cooled petrol 450-hp
Speed wheels on road 45 mph (72 km/h); tracks cross-country 33 mph (53 km/h)
Range wheels on road 310 miles (499 km); tracks cross-country 220 miles (354 km)
Trench crossing 6 feet (1.83 m)
Vertical step 2 feet 6 inches (0.76 m)
Fording 4 feet (1.22 m)
Overall length 18 feet 8 inches (5.69 m)
Width 8 feet (2.44 m)
Height 7 feet 6 inches (2.29 m)

The tank illustrated is the BT-7-2, the last of a highly mobile series built on a large scale

T-34 Series

Few armoured fighting vehicles have had a greater historical impact than the *T-34*. The finest tank in the world at the time of its introduction, it provided the central instrument of Soviet survival and final victory in World War II. It also set the pace of armoured development on a world scale, spurring advances in German tanks which called for similar moves among the Western Allies. Its descendants equip the Soviet Army to this day.

The *T-34* was developed from the BT series of fast tanks which were based on the designs of J Walter Christie. M I Koshkin, of the design bureau at the Komintern Factory in Kharkov, modified the original fast tank to improve protection and increase firepower. This resulted eventually in the *T-32*, which with its modified suspension of five large road wheels each side, well-sloped welded hull and turret and powerful 30.5-calibre 76.2-mm gun was the immediate predecessor of the *T-34*.

Trials in 1939 soon showed the qualities of the new design to be much greater than those of any comparable machine in the size range, and it was accepted as the model for future medium/ cruiser tank construction. With armour thickness increased to 45 mm and modified transmission the resultant *T-34* weighed over 25.6 tons. Speed was slightly reduced from 35 to 32 mph (55 to 52 km/h), although this was still high, and tracks widened from 10.25 to 19.1 inches (26 cm to 48.5 cm) kept ground pressure at a very low level, so retaining the remarkable mobility of the *T-32* over soft ground. When these characteristics were combined with a relatively low profile, the heaviest protection of any tank in its speed range and firepower as great as any contemporary tank, the result was formidable.

Despite the drawbacks of a badly laid out interior, an overworked commander and an unreliable transmission, the *T-34* was the finest tank in the world; and with a deteriorating international situation was ordered off the drawing board in December 1939. However, due to the disorganization of the Soviet Army's armoured affairs, only 1,100 had been built by the time the Germans struck, and few had been issued to combat units.

The *T-34*, first encountered in the southern sector of the front, came as a most unpleasant surprise for the advancing *Panzer* forces. But used in ones and twos the *T-34* proved little more than a nuisance, though more importantly the new tank shattered German illusions of technical superiority, causing some problem with morale. As the German advance weakened and slowed in the vastness of Western Russia so it became more vulnerable to armoured counter-attacks, operations in which the *T-34's* technical superiority gave a crucial added edge.

As the Germans advanced so the Russians moved their tank production facilities east to join those already set up in the Urals. The Kharkov plant joined the Nizhny Tagil industrial complex, so forming the Ural Tank Building Establishment which was to be the major single source of *T-34s*. By the end of 1941, various improvements had been made in the design of the *T-34*. A new, mainly cast, turret was developed with maximum protection improved to 60 mm and this gradually superseded the welded version in production at those plants with the facilities. More importantly, half the 2,810 *T-34s* produced in 1941 had the new M-40 41.2-calibre, 76.2-mm gun with penetration capacity of about 65-mm of 30° plate at 500 yards (457 m), more than enough to deal with the latest *PzKpfw* IV.

In 1942 two major operational shortcomings of the tank were overcome by further redesign. The original turret was so constructed that when the single hatch was lifted up the commander had to peer round it to get forward view, thus making an excellent target for German snipers.

Below: *An early T34/76A put out of action during the German advance in 1941. This exceptional tank was the first to really shake the confidence of German tank crews, but the strategic mistakes made by the Soviets during the first year of the war meant that T-34s were often thrown into battle in isolation and were overcome by the inferior but more numerous German tanks*

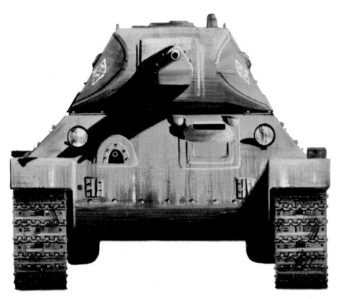

T-34/76B
Weight 27.6 tons (28 tonnes)
Crew four
Armament one 76.2-mm M-40 (L/41.2) gun with
77 rounds and two 7.62-mm DT machine-guns
with 2,394 rounds
Armour hull nose, glacis, sides and tail 45–47 mm,
decking and belly 20 mm; turret front, sides and
rear 45 mm, mantlet 20–46 mm, top 16 mm
Engine one V-2 V-12 liquid-cooled diesel, 500-hp
Speed 32 mph (52 km/h)
Range 188 miles (302.5 km)
Trench crossing 9 feet 8 inches (2.95 m)
Vertical step 2 feet 4 inches (71 cm)
Fording 4 feet 6 inches (1.37 m)
Overall length 21 feet 7 inches (6.58 m)
Width 9 feet 10 inches (3 m)
Height 8 feet (2.44 m)

*The tank illustrated is typical of those T-34/76Bs
produced in 1941–2. Note the long 76.2-mm gun,
the earlier hull machine-gun mount and early
rubber-tyred wheels*

In order to cure the problem, therefore, a new turret was designed with twin hatches and this was also reshaped to delete the troublesome rear overhang – German infantrymen had often taken advantage of the preoccupation of the over-worked crew to climb on the T-34 and wedge a mine between the over-hanging turret rear and the hull. The first version of this turret was of composite welded/cast construction, although by 1943 a fully cast version of improved ballistic shape had appeared. Both types could be fitted with turret cupolas to improve the observation of the commander when 'closed down'. Maximum armour thickness of the new turret was 75 mm on the front, with 52 mm on the sides.

Other modifications to the design of the T-34 were numerous, although with 42 different plants engaged in production these were often introduced on a rather haphazard basis. Extra appliqué armour was sometimes added, new style mantlets and wheels appeared, a more protected machine-gun mount was developed, an improved five-speed gearbox, more reliable than the older four-speed type, was fitted and external fuel tanks began to be carried which increased the T-34's maximum range to 270 miles (435 kilometres). Various designation systems, none of which were employed by the Russians, have been used to help identify the various sub-versions of the tank. Perhaps the least misleading is that which divides all early model T-34s or T-34/76s into three broad sub-types. Those with the short gun are called T-34/76A, those with the earlier turrets and the long gun T-34/76B and those with the later style 'hexagonal' turret, either composite or fully cast, T-34/76C.

By 1943, newer German tanks had emerged to challenge their technological position. First the Tiger and then the Panther asserted their superiority of firepower and protection, but quantity could now make up for quality and the massed use of T-34/76s proved very effective in halting the German offensive at Kursk in 1943. Even the Tiger could still be penetrated by the 41.2-calibre 76.2-mm gun at close range. Like the Sherman the T-34/76 provided an adequate vehicle with which to assert numerical advantage. However, the Russians were not satisfied and by the end of 1943 the design had been revised.

A more heavily protected T-34 with 110-mm frontal armour had been developed at the end of 1942 and produced in small quantities as the T-43, but the Soviet Army wanted an increase in firepower rather than protection. The M-39 85-mm anti-aircraft gun, developed as a tank gun for the KV-85 heavy tank, was fitted in a new, three-man cast/welded turret to the latest standard T-34 chassis to produce the T-34/85. This was a much improved vehicle: the 51.5-calibre D-5T85 (M-43) 85-mm gun had a muzzle velocity of 2,600 fps (792 m/s) and could penetrate 95 mm of 30° armour at 1,000 yards (914 m) with conventional armour piercing rounds. This was sufficient to deal with both Tiger and Panther tanks. More sophisticated armour piercing rounds improved performance further. Later tanks had the improved ZIS-S53 (M-44) gun of similar length. The addition of an extra crewman and the separation of the commander's and gunner's functions also greatly increased the tank's combat efficiency. Turret armour was increased to 75 mm on the front and sides, though hull armour remained 45 mm to keep the weight down to 31 tons. The result of these changes was a vehicle that retained all the mobility of its predecessors coupled with excellent firepower. What it lost in protection to the Panther the T-34/85 more than made up in mobility, and eventually, quantity. The tank had entered service by the end of 1943 and in 1945 most of the 11,758 T-34s built were of the improved type.

As a simpler solution to the problem of putting powerful guns on tracks the T-34 chassis was also utilized as the basis for a series of turretless assault guns. The first such vehicle was the SU-122. This mounted the 122-mm M-38 field howitzer in a limited-traverse mount in the sloping front of a fixed super-structure mounted forward in the chassis. Eight SU-122s were initially allocated with 17 SU-76s in each SU regiment to provide heavier fire support. They were later concentrated in medium SU regiments of 16 vehicles each. But the anti-tank potential of the 122-mm howitzer was limited and the advent of heavier German tanks led to the need

Left: *T-34/85 tanks in the East Prussian town of Heiligenbeil in January 1945. This tank was the Soviet answer to the introduction of the German Panther, retaining the mobility of the other T-34s but with added firepower. Note the extra track used to improve protection on the relatively thin hull plating*

to increase armour piercing capability. In 1943, production therefore began of a similar *SU*-85 mounting the same weapon as the *T*-34/85 tank. These were produced concurrently with early *T*-34/85s and were used to provide readily available additional firepower for the armoured formations which retained the earlier *T*-34/76. There were 21 *SU*-85s per regiment, together with a *T*-34 command tank, and they were allocated on this basis to tank and mechanized corps. In late 1944 an improved *SU*-100 appeared with 54-calibre D-10S 100-mm weapons. This could give valuable support to *T*-34/85 formations. The 100-mm gun could penetrate 160 mm of vertical armour at 1,000 yards (914 m). Low and inconspicuous, both *SU* assault guns were excellent for defensive fire from cover. In the attack, they were used for dealing with difficult targets, such as Tiger tanks, bypassed by the leading battle tanks.

Between 1940 and 1945 almost 40,000 *T*-34 tanks of all types were constructed, a record for a single type equalled only by the American Sherman. Development of both the *T*-34/85 and specialized types continued after 1945 but even before the war's end the tank had been radically redesigned with thicker 90-mm armour, modified suspension, new transmission and transverse engine layout. Some of these *T*-44 tanks armed with 85-mm guns may have seen action before the end of the war. Rushed into service the type had serious deficiencies and was soon replaced by the modified *T*-54, which, together with its later *T*-55 variant, has been the major Eastern Bloc battle tank of the post-war era. Like later *T*-44s, the *T*-54/55 had the 100-mm weapon. Gun size has been increased still further to 115-mm in the contemporary *T*-62; this, the latest tank in widespread Soviet service, still bears a distinct family resemblance to its ancestor, the most significant tank of World War II, the *T*-34.

T-34/85
Weight 31.4 tons (32 tonnes)
Crew five
Armament one 85-mm M-43 or M-44 (L/51.5) gun with 55 rounds and two 7.62-mm DT machine-guns with 2,394 rounds
Armour turret front, sides and rear 75 mm; top 20 mm
Range 220 miles (354 km) with auxiliary fuel tanks as fitted in the illustration below
Other details as T-34/76B

The T-34/85 tank illustrated is in post-war condition, in the colours of the Egyptian army, who used these vehicles against the Israelis in 1956, 1967 and 1973. Note the rear-mounted turret ventilator, a feature of early as well as post-war models of this type

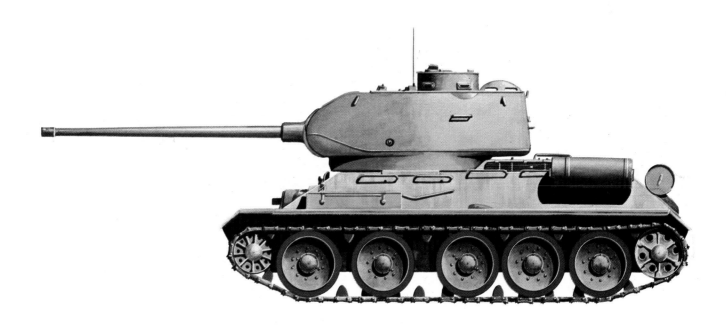

Soviet Light Tanks

In addition to the *T*-26 the USSR developed a whole series of light tanks primarily for reconnaissance purposes, although they were also used as battle tanks. The first of these light tanks was the *T*-27 based on the British Carden Loyd tankette. Some 4,000 of three basic variants were constructed between 1931–41, when they were classed as obsolete and relegated for use as artillery tractors and in other auxiliary roles.

Another British design adopted by the Russians was the A4E11 amphibious light tank, eight examples of which were purchased in 1931. Russian built *T*-33 prototypes were developed into *T*-37 production models, which had coil-spring Horstmann suspension, a rudder and propeller at the rear of the hull and a 40-hp GAZ copy of the four-cylinder Ford air-cooled engine. Armour was 9.5-mm on the hull and 6-mm on the turret which was mounted on the right-hand side. The *T*-37 was not a great success as the riveted hull let in water and some of the 250 constructed were completed to a design which used more welding, the *T*-37A.

A more radical modification, designed to decrease both weight and height while improving mobility and reliability, appeared in 1936. This was the *T*-38 with new final drive and steering, improved suspension, wider tracks and a new superstructure with the turret on the left-hand side. Both *T*-37s and 38s were used well into 1942 with tank and reconnaissance battalions and air landing corps but their vulnerability was soon obvious in action. They were only useful information gatherers, so long as serious opposition could be avoided.

A third amphibious reconnaissance tank appeared in 1940. This *T*-40 had a new boat-shaped hull of mainly welded construction, armoured to 13 mm, and was powered by an 85-hp GAZ 212 six-cylinder engine to give a maximum speed of 28 mph (44 km/h); buoyancy tanks were fitted to improve amphibious capability, and a single propeller drove the vehicle at four knots in the water. Weight was 5.4 tons and a 12.7-mm and a 7.62-mm machine-gun were mounted in the turret.

However, with experience against the Finns it became clear that protection had to be increased even at the expense of amphibious capability. An interim non-amphibious model, the six-ton *T*-40S, was constructed in 1941 with slightly thicker 14-mm armour and later that year the tank was completely redesigned as a non-amphibious vehicle. Redesignated *T*-60, it had a new hull with 20-mm armour and an off-set turret mounting a 20-mm ShVAK automatic gun, together with a co-axial 7.62-mm machine-gun. Six thousand were produced from December 1941 – later vehicles (*T*-60A) had 35-mm hull armour, 25-mm protection on the turret, a strengthened suspension with solid-type road wheels and weighed 6.3 tons.

But the *T*-60 also proved inadequate in combat and a new model, the *T*-70, with still heavier armament and protection appeared at the beginning of 1942. The new tank was armed with a 46-calibre, 45-mm high velocity gun with co-axial 7.62-mm machine-gun, armoured to 60-mm on the turret and on the hull and powered by twin six-cylinder ZIS-202 engines. This 70-hp power unit drove the 9.1-ton vehicle at 32 mph (50 km/h). The suspension was extended with five road wheels each side. Production of the new tank continued at the Gorki car factory until 1944; vehicles produced after 1943 having improved protection and more powerful engines were designated *T*-70A. A further improvement, the *T*-80, with heavier protection still was not produced in quantity. In all 8,226 *T*-70s were constructed but production was phased out as light tanks finally fell from favour. They could not be built with the strength to survive easily on the battlefield without becoming medium tanks

Below: A late T-70A, up-armoured from 60-mm to 70-mm maximum thickness. Note the squared-off, as opposed to rounded, turret rear
Opposite page, top: A T-37A light amphibious tank; this model used more welding in its construction than the original T-37 to keep out water. Its armament was a single 7.62-mm DT machine-gun. These vehicles were used against the Finns and then against Germans until 1942

and enough *T-34s* were now available to take over any light tank role where firepower and protection were needed. In cases where speed was required wheeled vehicles were sufficient. The *T-70* itself proved relatively disappointing in action, as the retention of the two-man crew of the earlier reconnaissance tanks prevented the overworked commander exploiting his heavier armament.

These light tanks were used side by side with heavier vehicles in the tank brigades and regiments. They also continued to be used by specialized reconnaissance units and by air landing corps, although it is doubtful if any of the latter used tanks operationally in airborne assaults. In the mid-war period *T-60* and *T-70* light tanks constituted a fifth of the armoured force, although by the end of the war their shortcomings had led to their removal from first-line combat forces.

The chassis of the light tanks proved useful for a variety of other roles. As *T-70s* and *T-60s* became redundant that they were used as light artillery tractors, while others lost their turrets to provide tracked mobility for the *NKVD Katyusha* rocket units. Standard *T-70* chassis were used as improvised mountings for anti-tank and anti-aircraft guns of various calibres, including captured weapons.

The *T-70* was also used as the basis for the first major purpose-built Soviet self-propelled gun of the war. This was the *SU-76*, which mounted a 76.2-mm ZIS-3 (M-42) gun in a protected rear superstructure on a chassis that utilized *T-70* components and fittings. The first of these vehicles, which appeared at the end of 1942, were very crude, with a separate engine for each track, but most production vehicles were on a redesigned chassis with engines in tandem and a normal common transmission to both tracks. This caused the gun and the fighting compartment to be offset to the left. The rear of the superstructure was cut down and straightened to simplify construction. Late model

SU-76 SPs had the rear of the vehicle heightened once more to improve protection for the commander, gunner and loader.

The *SU-76* was originally intended as a tank destroyer, but with the appearance of the *Tiger* and *Panther* neither its armour penetration capability nor its 25- to 35-mm armour was sufficient for use in the armoured battle and it was increasingly relegated to general infantry support, some 13 being included in the establishment of each infantry division. Despite its thin armour, vulnerable open top, and a bad reputation among its crews, who all had to work in cramped conditions, the *SU-76* was used up to the end of the war and remained in service afterwards with several countries.

Bottom: *An early model type SU-76 assault gun based on the T-70 light tank chassis but with an additional road wheel. Note the slope of the rear superstructure; the more numerous later models had straight backs*

T-70A
Weight 9.8 tons (10 tonnes)
Crew two
Armament one 45-mm M-32 (L/46) gun with 94 rounds and one 7.62-mm DT machine-gun with 1,008 rounds
Armour hull front 35–45 mm, sides 16 mm, decking and belly 10 mm, tail 25 mm; turret front 75 mm, sides and rear 35 mm, top 10 mm
Engine two GAZ-203 inline six-cylinder petrol, 85-hp
Speed 28 mph (45 km/h)
Range 260 miles (418 km)
Trench crossing 6 feet (1.83 m)
Vertical step 2 feet 2 inches (66 cm)
Fording 3 feet (91 cm)
Overall length 15 feet 6 inches (4.72 m)
Width 8 feet 1 inch (2.46 m)
Height 6 feet 8 inches (2.03 m)

SU-76
Weight 11 tons (11.2 tonnes)
Crew four
Armament one 76.2-mm M-42 (L/41.5) gun with 60 rounds
Armour hull nose 35 mm, glacis 25 mm, sides and tail 16 mm; decking and belly 10 mm; superstructure front 25 mm, mantlet 14 mm, sides 12 mm
Engines two GAZ 202 liquid-cooled petrol, 70-hp
Speed 28 mph (45 km/h)
Range 280 miles (450 km)
Trench crossing 6 feet 7 inches (2.00 m)
Vertical step 2 feet 11 inches (90 cm)
Fording 2 feet 11 inches (90 cm)
Overall length 16 feet 6 inches (4.88 m)
Width 9 feet (2.74 m)
Height 7 feet 2 inches (2.20 m)

KV and JS Series

Work on a new heavy break-through tank to supplant the *T-35* began in 1938 at the design bureau of Kirov Tractor Factory in Leningrad under Z Y Kotin. The multi-turret concept of the earlier *T-35* was retained, but due to the need to armour the vehicle to 60 mm, to resist 37-mm anti-tank guns, the number of turrets was reduced to two in order to keep weight within bounds. Two very similar prototypes were produced, the *T-100* and the SMK named after Sergei Mironovich Kirov, the assassinated Soviet leader. Both mounted a 24-calibre, 76.2-mm gun in the upper turret, set centrally on the chassis, with a 46-calibre, 45-mm gun in a forward auxiliary turret. A new torsion bar suspension was adopted with eight road wheels each side. Both vehicles had 400-hp BD-2 V-12 petrol engines developed from German BMW units.

The *T-100* was the heavier vehicle at 55.1 tons against the 44.3 tons of the SMK, but even the lighter tank proved too heavy for up-armouring against the increasing power of anti-tank weapons. The development of higher velocity 76.2-mm guns with good armour piercing capability made the retention of a special high-velocity armament and turret superfluous, so the SMK was redesigned with a single turret to take heavier armour at no increase in weight. By September 1939, Kotin's team had prepared the new tank which was selected for mass production as the Klementi Voroshilov, named after the Soviet Peoples' Commissar for Defence.

The new KV was of welded construction and had an armour thickness on the hull of 75 mm, enough to protect it against all enemy calibres up to 76.2 mm. Maximum turret thickness was also 75 mm with an additional 25 mm welded to the front. The standard KV-I tank mounted a 30.5-calibre 76.2-mm gun as in the contemporary *T-34*, but on some tanks equipped with a radio for the command function this was replaced by a more powerful 41.5-calibre M-40 weapon. This larger gun later became standard for all vehicles (usually called KV-IA) often with thicker 35-mm additional frontal turret armour and extra armour added to the hull. There was also a massive artillery support version, KV-II, with a large high turret mounting either a 122-mm howitzer in earlier versions or, more commonly, a 20-calibre 152-mm weapon. A rear mounted V-2 diesel engine in an up-rated 550-hp K version drove the 42.8-ton KV-I at 22 mph (35 km/h) and the 51.2 ton KV-II at 16 mph (25 km/h). Range was 140 miles (225 km) and 110 miles (177 km) respectively. Drive was through the rear sprockets and steering by clutch and brake. A shortened version of the torsion bar suspension with six road wheels each side was adopted for both models. Crew numbered five in the KV-I, with an extra loader in the KV-II to handle the heavy ammunition.

Isolated SMK/*T-100* tanks saw service in Finland in 1939 and the first KV models, both

Below: A captured KV-II artillery tank pressed into service by the Germans. Their passion for size evidently overcame any reservations about these vehicle's clumsiness and high silhouette
Bottom: Despite their ability to stand up to more than 70 armour piercing hits without effect, the KV-I heavy tanks were eventually isolated and destroyed. Note the early model 76.2-mm gun

KV-IA

Weight 42.8 tons (43.5 tonnes)
Crew five
Armament one 76.2 mm M-40 (L/41.2) gun with 111 rounds and three 7.62 mm DT machine-guns with 3,024 rounds
Armour hull nose 70 mm + 25 mm, glacis 75 mm, driver's plate 75 mm + 35 mm, sides 75–77 mm, decking 25 mm, belly 35 mm, tail 75 mm; turret front 75 mm + 35 mm, sides 75 mm, top 35 mm
Engine one V-2K V-12 liquid-cooled diesel, 550-hp
Speed 22 mph (35 km/h)
Range 140 miles (225 km)
Trench crossing 9 feet 2½ inches (2.8 m)
Vertical step 3 feet (91 cm)
Fording 4 feet 9 inches (1.45 m)
Overall length 22 feet 3½ inches (6.48 m)
Width 10 feet 11½ inches (3.34 m)
Height 10 feet 7¾ inches (3.24 m)

The tank illustrated is a KV-IA with a long 76.2-mm gun. Note the up-armouring on the turret, hull front and superstructure sides

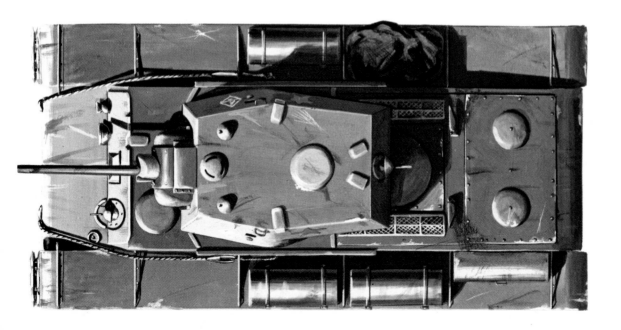

KV-85

Weight 45.27 tons (46 tonnes)
Crew four
Armament one 85-mm M-43 (L/51.5) gun with 71 rounds and three 7.62-mm DT machine-guns with 3,276 rounds
Armour hull front 60–70 mm, sides and tail 60 mm, decking and belly 30 mm; turret front, sides and rear 100–110 mm, top 30 mm
Engine one V-2K liquid-cooled diesel, 600 hp
Speed 26 mph (42 km/h)
Range 205 miles (330 km)
Trench crossing 8 feet 10 inches (2.7 m)
Vertical step 3 feet 11 inches (1.2 m)
Fording 3 feet 11 inches (1.2 m)
Overall length 28 feet 2 inches (8.6 m)
Width 10 feet 8 inches (3.25 m)
Height 8 feet 11 inches (2.8 m)

The KV-85 – a redesigned and greatly improved version of the KV with a new turret mounting an 85-mm gun. Note the rearrangement of the hull with a central driving position

118

KV-1 and KV-II, were also rushed into service. The new tanks were generally a success, their armour protection fulfilling its function and heavy armament proving effective against the fortifications of the Mannerheim Line.

A total of 508 KV tanks were on hand for the German onslaught in June 1941, like the *T-34* being used only in a support role for weaker tanks. Although even single KV tanks could inflict significant delays on the Germans, being virtually invulnerable to German anti-tank fire, their effect was neutralized. Lack of co-ordination allowed the Germans to employ desperate expedients, such as placing mines behind the turret or rolling hand-grenades down the gun-barrels, and problems with the gearbox, transmission and engine caused more setbacks.

Action experience resulted in extensive up-armouring to 110 mm on hull and turret sides while a new turret with cast sides armoured to 100 mm appeared in early 1942. Tanks with both sorts of improved turret armour, bolted on and cast, are called KV-IB. About the same time a still more heavily protected version with 120-mm turret armour was also developed and deployed (KV-IC). This latter had hull armour thickened to 90 mm basic, to which up to 40 mm of extra protection was added on the front and sides. The extra armour reduced speed to 18.5 mph (30 km/h), worsening difficulties already experienced in getting the heavier KVs to work efficiently with the faster *T-34s* in the mixed Soviet brigades and battalions. In order to aid co-ordination a new KV-I*s* (*s* for *skorostnyi* – fast) was built, with reduced armour thicknesses of 75 mm on the hull front, 60 mm on the

hull sides and 82 mm on the turret. Weight was reduced to 41.8 tons and maximum speed became 25 mph (39 km/h). A commander's cupola was introduced and modifications were carried out to the engine and transmission to improve reliability. KV-I*s* tanks were produced between August 1942 and June 1943 but the appearance of new types of German tank, and the creation of independent heavy tank regiments, caused the pendulum to swing once more to firepower and protection.

The role of the KV-II had been to provide heavy fire support, but its clumsiness and lack of success led it to be phased out by 1942. A large assault gun had already been produced in small quantities on the *T-100* chassis in 1939. These *SU-100Y* vehicles mounted a 130-mm gun in a central superstructure and were used in Finland and in the opening months of the war. The appearance of the *Tiger* put a new emphasis on such machines and a number of heavily gunned vehicles were produced by Kotin's bureau, now at the 'Tankograd' complex at Chelyabinsk, the major production centre for the KV series. The KV-II was modified with 85-mm and 122-mm high velocity weapons, but it still remained difficult to conceal. More serviceable and simple was the *SU-152* assault gun which Kotin designed and built within 25 days. This mounted the ML-20 (M-37) 152-mm gun-howitzer in a heavily protected mantlet in a low front super-structure. It was put into production in February 1943, and the first vehicles were in service with heavy *SU* regiments (12 per regiment) by the Battle of Kursk. The *SU-152* soon showed its capability against the new *Tiger* and *Panther*

tanks and became known as the Animal Killer. Thirty-five such vehicles were completed as *SU-122s* (not to be confused with the earlier *T-34* based model) armed with 122-mm A-19S high velocity guns.

The KV tank itself also received significant improvement in mid 1943 with the introduction of the KV-85. This mounted a new cast/welded turret armoured to 110 mm fitted to the modified hull of a KV-I*s*. The driver was repositioned in the hull front and the crew reduced to four. The new turret mounted the 51.5-calibre 85-mm D-5T85 (M-43) tank gun, a development of the M-39 anti-aircraft weapon of the same calibre. Some older up-armoured chassis also received the new turret.

The new tank could take on the largest German vehicles with some chance of success but the Soviets desired parity if not a clear technological edge and the KV-85 was only an interim design before a more thoroughly redesigned vehicle appeared. The suspension was lowered in this new tank altering the layout of the hull and increasing the size of the turret ring to allow

Below: *A KV-IB. Experience with enemy high velocity weapons soon led to further increases to even the KV's heavy protection. Some had heavy plates bolted onto the sides of the existing turret and others were fitted with cast turrets when production facilities were arranged. The more rounded shape of the turret created by the 100-mm cast sides can be clearly seen in this photograph. Both KV and T-34 tanks had diesel engines and wide tracks making them highly mobile vehicles, both in terms of distance and across country*

heavier armament. Cast armour of improved shape, which gave a 50 per cent increase in protection, was used in the construction of the hull and the larger cast/welded turret had its protection slightly reduced to 100 mm. This helped to keep weight down to 43.3 tons (overall), despite an increase in armour protection on the hull front to 120 mm with 90-mm armour on the hull sides. Weak transmission had been a common KV defect and a lighter and more flexible synchromesh was adopted together with regenerative steering which improved the new tank's manoeuvrability and reliability. The engine was derated to 513 hp, also to improve reliability, but speed remained relatively high at 23 mph (37 km/h) and range at 150 miles (241 km). The crew was again reduced to four: commander, driver, gunner and loader.

The new model, called JS-I (after Joseph Stalin, who had reputedly taken a great interest in tank design), and sometimes JS-85, appeared in late 1943 with 85-mm main armament. This gun calibre was soon increased to 100 mm (JS-100) and finally in 1944 the 43-calibre 122-mm D-25 (M-43) gun was adopted in a 102-mm mantlet. The new weapon was also retro-fitted in older vehicles. The 122-mm armed JS-I could challenge the *Tiger* on even terms, and although the Soviet tank's ammunition supply and rate of fire was inferior, due to the 122-mm shell's larger size, its reliability and mobility were considerably superior because of the automotive improvements and the JS-I's 25.6-inch (65-cm) tracks.

The first JS-I tanks with 122-mm guns were in action in the spring offensives of 1944 and soon demonstrated their formidable fighting potential. As the new tanks replaced earlier KV models in the heavy tank regiments, so the older vehicles were relegated to tractor and recovery vehicle duties. About 10,000 KV tanks were built before production shifted to the JS.

An improved JS-II with a revised turret and reshaped hull front of still better ballistic shape appeared in 1944, when some 2,350 JS tanks were built. They were issued to heavy tank regiments which were kept for independent use in the assault role often being grouped into three regiment heavy tank brigades. As a more easily produced means of heavy armoured gunfire support, the number of heavy assault gun regiments also increased, now equipped with new vehicles based on the JS chassis. There were three types of JS-based assault gun, all with a rather higher superstructure than their KV-based predecessors. Two JSU-122 variants were developed, the more numerous early model with the A-19S gun, a simple conversion of the artillery piece, and the later type with D-25S

Below: *A late model JSU-122 tank destroyer advances over the River Spree in Germany in April, 1945. This machine is equipped with a D-255 tank gun and displays the distinctive low suspension and high superstructure of the JS chassis, so different from the KV predecessors*

weapon, similar to the gun mounted in the JS-I and JS-II tanks. The advantage of the tank type gun, with a muzzle brake and sliding breech block, was its higher rate of fire, up to six rounds per minute in place of the earlier screw breech weapon's three. Both guns had a muzzle velocity of 2,625 fps (800 m/s) and fired 55-pound (25-kg) shells up to 14,200 yards (13,000 metres). The guns were mounted in heavily protected mantlets (190 mm) with 90 mm of armour on the super-structure front and 110 mm on the hull nose.

JSU-152s were also built with the M-37 152-mm weapon (1,814 fps or 553 m/s). Each type was produced in some quantity and issued to heavy assault gun regiments (grouped in 1944 into three regiment brigades). They often mounted 12.7-mm anti-aircraft machine-guns; this protection was also given to JS tanks. Over 2,000 JS-based assault guns had been built by the end of 1944.

The JS tank was still further improved in 1945 with the appearance of the JS-III. Both the hull and turret of this vehicle were reshaped to a new standard of ballistic excellence. The armour was also thickened, on the turret to 230 mm. Known as the 'Pike' because of its shape, the JS-III may have seen action in the closing days of the war, but it certainly came as a considerable shock to Western observers in the Berlin Victory Parade of 1945.

The KV and JS series provided a powerful supplement to the armoured strength of Soviet forces in World War II. Like all Soviet tanks they were crudely built compared with their German counterparts, but what they lacked in armament sophistication they made up for with the brute force of high calibre. A price had to be paid in ammunition storage but the JS tanks set a standard of reliability and mobility which their opponents could not approach. They were, therefore, able to provide the well-protected heavy fire support that was a vital part of the well planned Soviet offensives which won through to Berlin.

JS-II
Weight 45.27 tons (46 tonnes)
Crew four
Armament one L/43 122 mm D-25 (M-43) gun with 28 rounds, three 7.62-mm DT machine-guns with 2,330 rounds and one 12.7-mm DShK machine-gun with 945 rounds
Armour hull glacis 120 mm, sides 90 mm, decking 25 mm, belly 19 mm, tail 60 mm, turret front 100 mm, sides 90 mm, top 30 mm
Engine one V-2 IS V-12 liquid cooled diesel, 513 hp
Speed 23 mph (37 km/h)
Range 150 miles (241 km)
Trench crossing 8 feet 2 inches (2.5 m)
Vertical step 3 feet 3½ inches (1.00 m)
Fording 4 feet 2 inches (1.3 m)
Overall length 32 feet 2 inches (9.83 m)
Width 10 feet (3.07 m)
Height 8 feet 11 inches (2.73 m)

Below: *JS-II heavy tanks advance through Berlin's shattered streets. Note the white stripes on the turrets of the tanks, painted on many Soviet tanks as identification during the battle for Berlin*

THE UNITED STATES

Of all the major powers, the United States neglected armour the most in the inter-war period. A nation confirmed in isolationism saw little need for land forces of any type, least of all expensive mechanized units. Progress in the development of armoured vehicles therefore proceeded only haltingly, although the groundwork was laid for the massive armoured expansion that occurred from 1940 onwards. The American Tank Corps, founded in 1918, was abolished under the National Defense Act of 1920 which declared that armoured units would henceforth form part of the infantry. Some of the thousand or so tanks which had survived the cancellation of the massive armoured programme of World War I were organized into four tank battalions equipped with American built versions of the Renault *FT* 17 and the British Mark VIII. Doctrine was firmly infantry based, the battalions forming extra support strength to be used on the major lines of advance.

The British mechanized exercises of 1927 had some effect on American ideas and in 1930 a permanent regimental size mechanized force of all arms – infantry, cavalry and artillery – was established. But any trend to a specialized armoured force was stopped in 1931, when the newly appointed Chief of Staff, Douglas Mac-Arthur, stated that all arms were to be mechanized and that the cavalry would assume charge of the mobile role. Light tanks were designated 'combat cars', to get round the Congressional Act that had reserved 'tanks' for the infantry.

As a few new tanks and combat cars became available in the 1930s, and with the influence of progressive cavalry officers such as Colonels Adna R Chaffee and George S Patton, Seventh Cavalry Brigade (Mechanized) was slowly formed of two regiments and a total of 112 'combat cars'. Once the Brigade had been completed in 1939, pressure to form it into an armoured division on the German pattern grew, and there was some expansion of tank production following the outbreak of war in Europe. Successful combined exercises with the Seventh Cavalry and a motorized infantry regiment were held in 1940, but it was the German victories in Europe that year which proved decisive in the development of American armoured forces.

Congress now became willing to fund massive increases in armoured strength. Both cavalry and infantry units were merged in a United States Armoured Force under Brigadier General Chaffee. The initial strength of the new force was set at two armoured divisions and one independent tank battalion. Each division comprised three regiments (381 tanks). As there were only 464 serviceable tanks and combat cars on hand in the entire United States (almost all armed with nothing larger than machine-guns), more vehicles were urgently required.

The expansion of armoured vehicle production after 1940 was little short of phenomenal. In 1940, 330 new tanks were built: in 1941, 4,052; in 1942, 24,997 (more than the entire German tank output from 1939 to 1945); and in 1943, 29,487. America's unequalled expertise in mass production of motor vehicles was employed in the programme, while other heavy engineering plants also played their part. In addition, two new tank arsenals were built in a matter of months. Before the United States entered the war in December 1941, three more armoured divisions had been formed and eleven more followed up to 1943.

Against veteran German *Panzer* units, however, the Americans soon found that massed armour was not an answer to every tactical problem. A reaction set in and the emphasis swung more to all arms cooperation. The Armoured Force steadily lost independent status, and during 1943–4 all but two of the divisions, already reduced from eight to six tank battalions, had their complement halved to only three (219 tanks), each matched by an armoured infantry and artillery battalion. This reorganization swelled the numbers of individual infantry support tank battalions, which outnumbered those of armoured divisions by 65 to 52 by 1944.

The superiority of American tank output was based on the mass production of a few tried types, notably the M4 Medium tank. A constant battle was waged between the United States

Army's Ordnance Department and the Army Ground Forces Command over how far quality should be sacrificed to quantity. A series of new tank types were developed by Ordnance, always determined on technical excellence. Few new types were deployed, however, due to the restrictive attitude of the rest of the army, bent on standardization. This attitude could quickly change when more powerful enemy vehicles were encountered, but in a war increasingly dictated by numbers, it made sense not to interfere with the production of tried types that could later be modified to approach the capabilities of new enemy vehicles.

The destruction of enemy armour was the special task of the separate Tank Destroyer Force. At its peak the strength of this arm rose to 106 36-gun battalions, which were sometimes formed into brigades and groups for employment *en masse*. About half the tank destroyer battalions were equipped with self-propelled vehicles that were virtually lightly armed, heavily gunned tanks with open-topped turrets.

One American armoured division, the First, and eight individual tank battalions saw service in Italy. Six armoured divisions were committed in Normandy, where they proved their usefulness after the break-out, Patton's advance only being stopped by the exigencies of supply and inter-Allied politics. Nine more armoured divisions were available for the final defeat of Germany and about 39 independent battalions fought in North West Europe, some landing in the south of France. In addition twenty tank battalions and four independent companies saw service in the Pacific together with six tank destroyer battalions and tank battalions of the Marine Corps.

Between July 1940 and the end of the war, the United States produced a total of 88,276 tanks: 2,330 heavies, 28,919 lights and 57,027 mediums. A total of 43,481 self-propelled guns was built plus over 200,000 more AFVs of all types.

Left: *Built specially for British service the Grants were the first American medium tanks to go into action during the war*

Medium Tank M3 Lee/Grant

Medium Tank M3 Lee I
Weight 26.8 tons (27.2 tonnes)
Crew six
Armament one 75-mm (L/28.5) M2 gun with
41 rounds, one 37-mm M5 gun with 179 rounds
and three or four 0.30-inch (7.62-mm) Browning
M1919A4 machine-guns with 8,000 rounds
Armour hull nose, glacis and driver's plate 50 mm,
sides 38 mm, decking 13 mm, belly 13–25 mm,
tail 13–50 mm; turret front, sides and rear
50 mm, roof 25 mm
Engine one Wright Continental R-975-EC2 radial
nine-cylinder air-cooled petrol, 340-hp
Speed 26 mph (42 km/h)
Range 120 miles (193 km)
Trench crossing 7 feet 6 inches (2.29 m)
Vertical step 2 feet (61 cm)
Fording 3 feet 4 inches (1.02 m)
Overall length 18 feet 6 inches (5.64 m)
Width 8 feet 11 inches (2.72 m)
Height 10 feet 4 inches (3.15 m)

*The tank illustrated is a British Lee I – note the
distinctive high turret and hull-mounted radio*

When the German offensive against the Low
Countries began in May 1940, the United States
Army possessed only 18 modern medium tanks.
These were of the M2 type developed in 1937–38
by Rock Island Arsenal for infantry support.
The M2 weighed 19 US tons (17.2 tonnes), had
25-mm armour and was armed with eight
machine-guns. A 37-mm gun was mounted in a
high turret to engage enemy armour and the
engine was a nine-cylinder 350-hp Continental
R-975 radial. An improved M2A1 was also
developed with 400-hp engine, 32-mm armour
and other small modifications.

The German victory in France transformed
American armoured policy on medium tanks.
Some 1,741 mediums were immediately called
for and plans were soon approved for a new $21
million Tank Arsenal established by Chrysler at
Detroit.

The success of the *PzKpfw* IV in the campaigns
of 1939–40 led to demands for a 75-mm main
armament for US mediums and an interim

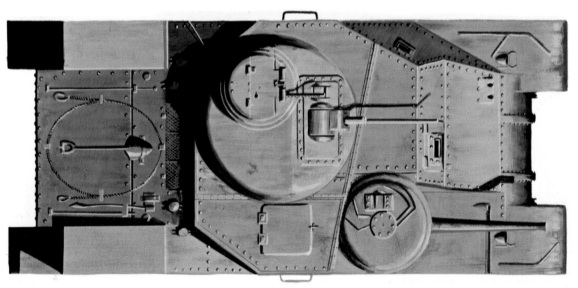

solution to this problem was offered by a T5E2 prototype SP gun built on the M2 chassis in 1939. This mounted a 75-mm pack howitzer in a limited traverse mount in the right hull front and it was used as the basis of the design of the new M3 Medium Tank. Three manufacturers – Chrysler, American Locomotive Company (Alco) and Baldwin Locomotive Company – had produced prototypes by April 1941, and by August production was in full swing.

The M3 kept the M2A1 layout with similar suspension and engine, derated to 340 hp. The hull was of riveted construction and maximum armour thickness was 56 mm. A cast hydraulically traversed turret, mounted to the left, retained the 50-calibre 37-mm gun, but a new M2 75-mm gun was mounted in the right hull front. This weapon had been designed from the standard American 75-mm field gun and was 28.5-calibres long with muzzle velocity of 1,860 fps (567 m/s). This was higher than that of the contemporary PzKpfw IV's 24-calibre 75-mm weapon and had

a similar armour penetration capacity to the later long L/60 50-mm gun of late model PzKpfw IIIs. The M2 could penetrate 60 mm of 30°-plate at 500 yards (457 m) and, just as importantly, had an adequate high-explosive capability also. The gun was mounted with limited traverse of 15° to each side, 20° in elevation and 9° in depression. This system had obvious tactical drawbacks, but a major leap in firepower had been achieved. In addition to the heavy weapons, a 0.30-inch (7.62-mm) machine-gun was mounted co-axially with the 37-mm, with a second weapon in the tank cupola and one or two machine-guns in the left-hand hull front. The M3's crew was six, a loader and a gunner for each weapon plus a commander and driver. A radio was mounted in the hull.

A major improvement with the M3 was gun stabilization and both larger weapons were fitted with gyroscopic systems to keep the gun at a given elevation. This allowed the tank to fire more accurately on the move and, more im-

portantly perhaps, to get its weapons into accurate action as soon as it had stopped.

Modified M3s, with lower turrets and turret-mounted radios, obtained by Britain were the first of the type to go into action. The new Grants (as they were dubbed by the British) were sent to the Western Desert in 1942: 167 were allocated to the Fourth Armoured Brigade of Seventh Armoured Division and to First Armoured Division's Second and 22nd Armoured Brigades. The Grants first saw action in the battle of Gazala in May, the firepower of their 75-mm guns holding off 21st Panzer Division in a long range fire fight. The Grants' merits were not enough to prevent eventual defeat, but in the retreat to Alamein the tank had a significant role in slowing the German advance. Heavy losses were incurred and by July First Armoured Division had all the Grants available to Eighth Army, a mere 38, to supplement about twice that number of Crusaders. Relief was on the way, however. With the passing of the Lend Lease Act in March, 250 standard M3s had been made available to the British and as the 'Lee' some were sent to Egypt. At the Battle of Alam Halfa the Eighth and 22nd Armoured Brigades fielded 164 Lee/Grants; with their heavy firepower, these played an important role in this defensive battle. By the Second Battle of Alamein there were some 210 M3s available to the Eighth Army; they were able to provide one of the most powerful elements in Montgomery's forces.

Production of the American M3 went on at Chrysler, Alco, Baldwin, Pressed Steel and Pullman until late 1942 when some 4,924 M3s had been built. Most were of the standard M3 type (Lee I to the British) some of which had Guiberson diesel engines. Alco produced about 300 M3A1s (Lee II) with a cast hull, some of which also had diesel engines. Twelve M3A2s were produced by Baldwin with welded hulls, and these were followed by 322 M3A3s, similar except for their General Motors 6-71 twin diesel engines of 375 combined hp. Some of these were later re-engined with Wright Continental units. The British called the M3A2 the Lee III, the Continental engined M3A3 Lee IV and the diesel-engined version Lee V. One hundred and nine M3A4s (Lee VI) built at Detroit had the 370-hp Chrysler A-57 multibank engine made up by putting five six-cylinder car engines on a common shaft. This necessitated a slight lengthening of the hull to 19 feet 8 inches (6 metres). Baldwin produced 591 M3A5s in 1942 which combined riveted hulls with the General Motors 6-71 engines. Although they retained their American turrets, these tanks received the British designation Grant II.

The various models were produced concurrently. Later tanks of all models had the longer

Top left: *A well-camouflaged British Grant converted for armoured searchlight (CDL) work. The searchlight was mounted behind a slit in the heavily protected turret which was fitted with a dummy gun to disguise the tank's specialized role*

Bottom left: *An M2 – the M3 was an up-gunned version of this pre-war medium tank*

M3 37.5-calibre 75-mm gun with 2,200 fps (671 m/s) muzzle velocity and a penetration capability against 30° armour at 500 yards (457 metres) increased by 10 mm.

United States Army M3s were used for training armoured forces, both in the United States and Britain, and they finally went into action with the landings in North Africa in November 1942. By then they were already only a 'substitute standard', following the adoption of the M4. Others were sent to the Pacific, but the newer tank quickly replaced the M3 in combat service with American forces in 1943. The older medium was finally declared obsolete in April 1944. M3s were also used for training British and Canadian troops but the type continued in first-line service until the end of the war with Commonwealth forces. As Lees and Grants were phased out of service with Eighth Army at the end of the North African campaign they were sent to the Far East. They formed a major part of Australian armoured strength while others fought with the 14th Army in Burma until the war's end. Unarmed Grant command tanks were also used by the Sherman-equipped Sixth South African Armoured Division in Italy until 1945. Other M3s were exported to Russia.

A number of other specialized types were developed on the M3 chassis. The Americans developed a T2 TRV (Tank Recovery Vehicle), later standardized as the M31. The M31B1 and B2 were similar vehicles based on the M3A3 and M3A5 respectively. M31s were supplied to the Free French armoured divisions and also to the British, who designated them 'Lee ARV'. The British and Australians also converted Grants into recovery vehicles. The Americans converted some of their M31s into M33 Full Tracked Prime Movers, which were used as tractors for heavy artillery, together with a similar M44.

The Lee/Grant's layout also lent itself to the CDL (Canal Defence Light) armoured search-light role. Following the advent of the Sherman, M3s were so converted by the British as Grant CDLs. First Tank Brigade took them to Europe with 79th Armoured Division and a few were used to illuminate the night crossings of the Rhine and Elbe rivers in 1945. Their guns proved useful in destroying mines floated downstream by the Germans.

The M3 saw use as a mine-sweeping tank, the British converting some Grant Mark Is into Scorpion flails for use in Tunisia, Sicily and Italy. The Americans produced a less satisfactory system of heavy rollers, with one set being pushed and the other being pulled by the M3, known as the Mine Exploder Device T1.

The M3 chassis played a vital part in the development of American self-propelled artillery, although an attempt to produce a tank destroyer on the chassis was abortive.

The M7 self-propelled 105-mm howitzer project began in 1941. The standard M1A2 American field howitzer was placed to right of centre in an open M3 chassis. Two T32 prototypes were built by Baldwin, and after certain modifications, including the addition of a pulpit-type cupola with 0.5-inch (12.7-mm) anti-aircraft machine-gun, the type was ordered into mass production. Alco built some 3,314 M7s until 1944, being joined by the Pressed Steel Car Company that year. After the latter had built 200 vehicles, however, production shifted to the M7B1 based on the Sherman chassis. Standard M7s which had the normal Continental R-975 engine of the M3, were issued to the artillery battalions of American armoured divisions. M7 battalions were also deployed separately and the gun was issued to the assault gun platoons of armoured infantry battalions.

British troops also received the M7, the first 90 arriving in Egypt in 1942 in time for the Second Battle of Alamein. Dubbed Priest by the British forces, due to the pulpit like superstruc-tures, M7s served with Eighth Army in North Africa and Italy. The British ordered a version mounting their own 25-pounder (88-mm) field gun and this led to the development of the Sexton which replaced the Priest in North West Europe after the initial fighting in Normandy. Free French forces also operated M7 self-propelled guns.

The largest of the M3 based SPs was the 155-mm Gun Motor Carriage M12. This originated as an experimental T6 carriage using M3 parts. In order to accommodate the heavy 155-mm gun the Continental R-975 engine was moved to the front and the standard M1917A1 gun was mounted in an open superstructure at the rear. A total of 100 were built during 1942–3 but due to mechanical problems and, doubts as to the general utility and reliability of such a weapon, it was not until 1944 that Baldwin was ordered to modify 75 M12s for service use. M12s then equipped six battalions, and they were used in North-West Europe from July 1944. A similar M30 cargo carrier without gun but with built up rear superstructure was also developed. Forty 155-mm shells could be carried by the M30, a useful supplement to the M12's stowage of only 10 shells.

The M3 medium tank was a stopgap weapon. It had severe tactical disadvantages but it did provide the first tank available to the western allies with an adequate dual purpose armament. Called 'the tank that surprised Rommel' and 'Egypt's last hope' it provided a vital boost to flagging Allied morale in the dismal summer of 1942 when it seemed that no Allied tank could approach a German in terms of quality.

Below: *The widely used M7 self-propelled 105-mm howitzer was based on the M3 chassis. Note the M3-type suspension of the leading vehicle in this American battery advancing through the snows of winter 1944*

Light Tank M3/M5 Stuart

The M3/M5 light tanks were the culmination of a series that dated from 1931. In that year General MacArthur, as Army Chief of Staff, had called for a new light tank armoured against small arms fire, relying on speed against larger weapons and suitable for service both as an infantry support tank and as a cavalry combat car for reconnaissance and exploitation. The existing T1 light tank series was too slow so a new T2 prototype was completed at Rock Island Arsenal in 1934. Its design owed a great deal to that of the Vickers 'Six Ton' light tank. The distinctive leaf-spring suspension and sloping hull front of the British tank were adopted; 0.30-inch (7.62-mm) and 0.50-inch (12.7-mm) machine-guns were mounted in the fixed turret with a further 0.30-inch (7.62-mm) gun in the hull. Armour was 16 mm maximum and the weight 6½ US tons (5.9 tonnes). A Continental radial aircraft engine of 250 hp, driving through the front sprockets, gave the required speed of 35 mph (56 km/h); steering was on the 'Cletrac' controlled differential principle. The Vickers suspension was ill suited to high speeds and the contemporary T5 Combat Car had a new arrangement of two vertical volute springs each side, each supporting a double bogie. Trials proved this layout superior with maximum speed being increased to 45 mph (72 km/h), and despite flirtation with more complex Christie suspensions the simpler system was adopted for almost all future light tanks and combat cars.

Limited production began of 19 M2A1 light tanks in 1936, and these were followed by Light Tank M2A2 with a twin-turret arrangement. The cavalry had produced a prototype Combat Car T5E2 with a small hand traversed revolving turret which was standardized as the Combat Car M1. Some 170 M1 combat cars and M2A2 tanks were completed by the end of 1937.

In 1938 an improved M2A3 light tank appeared with a longer wheelbase to improve the ride. The cavalry combat car was similarly improved and also given a new transmission, offset turret and radio as the M1A1. An alternative approach was tried with the diesel-engined Combat Car M2 which had a trailing idler to help improve the ride, a system also experimented with on M2A2E3 and M2A3E3 light tanks. The infantry, however, persevered with the raised idler in their next M2A4 tank of 1939, which was a major improvement over its predecessors with a single fully rotating turret mounting a 37-mm gun. With 25-mm armour weight was up to 12 US tons (10.5 tonnes) and speed was reduced to 37 mph (60 km/h). A 0.30-inch (7.62-mm) machine-gun was mounted co-axially with the 37-mm and another machine-gun was fitted in the nose and in each hull sponson. A fifth machine-gun could be mounted for anti-aircraft purposes. Most M2A4s had the 250-hp Continental W-670-9A seven-cylinder radial petrol engine but some later tanks had Guiberson (General Motors) diesel units.

Although only 50 M2A3 tanks and M2 combat cars had been built, the outbreak of war in Europe led to quantity production of the M2A4 light tank, 329 being ordered from the

Below: A US Army M3A1 of Seventh Armoured Division on exercise in the United States in 1942. Note the lack of turret cupola on the power-traversed cast turret. This particular tank has a welded hull but retains the side-mounted machine-guns usually deleted on this model

Light Tank M3 Stuart I
Weight 12.2 tons (12.4 tonnes)
Crew four
Armament one 37-mm M5 (L/50) gun with
103 rounds and three 0.30-inch (7.62-mm)
Browning M1919A4 machine-guns with 8,270
rounds
Armour hull nose 51 mm, glacis 13 mm, driver's
plate 38 mm, sides 25 mm, decking 10 mm, belly
10–12 mm, tail 19–25 mm; turret front 38 mm,
sides and rear 30 mm, top 13 mm
Engine one Wright Continental W-970-9A radial
seven-cylinder air-cooled petrol, 250-hp
Speed 36 mph (58 km/h)
Range 70 miles (113 km)
Trench crossing 6 feet (1.83 m)
Vertical step 2 feet (61 cm)
Fording 3 feet (91 cm)
Overall length 14 feet 10 inches (4.52 m)
Width 7 feet 6 inches (2.29 m)
Height 8 feet 3 inches (2.51 m)

*The tank illustrated is a Stuart I of British
Seventh Armoured Division, typical of the tanks
which fought in North Africa in 1941–2. Note
the deletion of the side-mounted hull machine-guns*

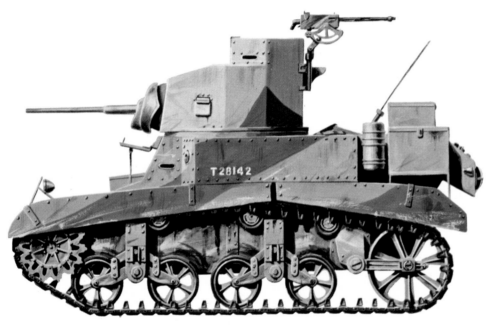

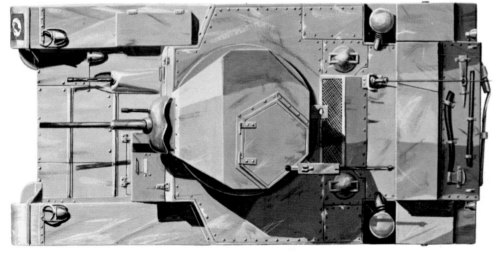

American Car and Foundry Company. The first
tanks were delivered in April 1940. The production order was later increased to 365 with 10 to
be built by the Baldwin Locomotive Company.

With the creation of the Armoured Force in
June 1940, the M1 and M2 Combat Cars were
redesignated Light Tanks M1A2 and M1A1,
respectively. The lessons of the French campaign
led to a major redesign of the M2A4 with thicker
51-mm armour and better distributed protection
to guard against air attack. The hull was also
lengthened to cover the exhausts, weight was
increased by two US tons (1.8 tonnes) and trailing idler suspension decided upon. The new
vehicle was designated Light Tank M3 and had a
crew of four, like the M2A4.

Like its predecessors, the original M3 was of
all riveted construction. A welded turret was
soon adopted to reduce weight and this was later
replaced with a partly cast turret. Gyro gun
stabilizers were also fitted. Later M3s were fitted
with Guiberson diesel power units and had
welded hulls. In all some 5,811 M3s were produced from mid-1941 until August 1942.

With the passing of the Lend Lease Act in
March 1941, M3s began to enter service with the
British Army, in whose service the M3 became
the Stuart I, diesel-engined versions being
designated Stuart II. Combat experience led to
various modifications, a new version entering
production in June 1942 as the M3A1. This had
power traverse for the turret, from which the
prominent cupola was deleted. The two hull
machine-guns were often removed, as they took
up valuable stowage space for very little offensive
return. Some 4,600 M3A1s, designated Stuart III
by the British, were built by American Car and
Foundry, the majority with welded hulls; 211
with Guiberson diesel engines became Stuart IVs.

The use of the Guiberson diesel reflected a
shortage of Continental aero engines because of
the demands of aircraft production, and this led
to the development of a new version of the tank,
the M5. The Cadillac division of General Motors
had claimed that twin V-8 Cadillac car engines
could replace the M3's standard Continental
engine. An M3E2 prototype was so fitted in
October 1941 together with the manufacturer's
Hydra-Matic automatic transmission, and after
a 500-mile (805-km) test trip the vehicle was
ordered into production as M5.

The new version retained the turret, chassis
and suspension of the M3A1, but the hull was
redesigned with a raised rear section and the
front maximum armour thickness was increased
to 67 mm which gave a weight of 16½ US tons
(15 tonnes). The two engines with a combined
output of 220 hp kept the maximum speed at 36
mph (58 km/h). Cadillac had the M5 in production by March 1942, and Massey Harris followed
suit later.

In August a prototype M3A3 appeared, with a
similar front hull shape to the M5. The radio was
moved to the turret which was extended at the
rear to accommodate it, while stowage and fuel
capacity were increased and sand shields fitted.
The following month an M5A1 prototype
appeared to bring that type up to the new
standard. Both M3A3 and M5A1 went into
production in December. In Britain the M3A3
became Stuart V; M5 and M5A1 were both
designated Stuart VI.

Despite an unfortunate tendency to catch fire

on starting, the Cadillac-engined tank was a generally superior vehicle to the Continental-engined version, with a more flexible power plant and automatic transmission. In August 1943, therefore, after 3,427 M3A3s had been built, the vehicle was replaced in production at American Car and Foundry by the M5A1. Production continued until June 1944, by which time some 6,810 M5A1 tanks had been completed. Total production figures for all versions of the M3 were 13,859 and for the M5 8,884.

The M1 to M5 light tank series played an important role in the United States Army. In the 1930s the early models provided virtually the only modern equipment of the infantry and cavalry armoured units. The old tanks continued in the early war years in a training role. The M2A4 was the only tank available in quantity in the early days of the Armoured Force. It was again employed mainly as a training tank. Some were used in action against Japan, still being deployed, together with the M3A1, by Marine Corps units at Guadalcanal in late 1942.

Although increasingly replaced by medium tanks in a major fighting role, M3 and M5 light tanks served throughout the war in the fighting, reconnaissance and headquarters echelons of the United States armoured forces and in USMC tank units. They saw action from the South Pacific and the Aleutians to North Africa and North-West Europe. The M3 was officially declared obsolete in the United States Army in July 1943, and the M5 was the major type in American service in 1944–5.

The Stuart saw action with British forces even before the United States was at war. With its 37-mm gun and 51-mm armour, the M3 was the equal of the British cruiser tanks in firepower and superior to them in protection. Although the American 50-calibre 37-mm gun was a little inferior to the British two-pounder (40-mm) it was still able to deal with Rommel's earlier model *PzKpfw* III and IV. Adopted as a cruiser tank before the later Grant M3 became available, the first 84 M3 lights arrived in North Africa in July 1941 and were soon nicknamed 'Honey' because of their reliability. Some 280 Stuart Is, more than half the 538 tanks produced in the initial three months of production, were sent to Africa and issued to the Fourth Armoured Brigade, Seventh Armoured Division which had 163 Stuarts on hand for the Crusader offensive of November 1941. The Stuarts proved ineffective when thrown against strong anti-tank defences but their manoeuvrability, speed and stabilized armament enabled them to outmanoeuvre more heavily armed and protected German tanks. Stuarts also served with British First Armoured Division and Australian and New Zealand units in North Africa. They saw further imperial service in Iraq, Europe and the Far East.

Left: *An M2A4, the immediate predecessor of the M3 light tank. These vehicles were mainly used for training by American and British forces though some saw combat service against the Japanese*
Below: *M3A3 light tanks of the Chinese Army advance against the Japanese. Note the redesigned hull of this Continental-engined model, based on that of the M5*

Medium Tank M4 Sherman

The M3 medium was always seen as an interim vehicle and in March 1941 a new project was begun at the Rock Island Arsenal for a tank with a turret-mounted 75-mm gun. The existing M3 was chosen as the basis for the new tank and by September a prototype had been constructed.

This T6 had a cast hull and turret which mounted an M2 75-mm gun and also contained a radio. The 28.5-calibre 75-mm gun was a provisional fitting until the longer 37.5-calibre M3 gun was available. There was a co-axial 0.30-inch (7.62-mm) machine-gun in the turret and three similar weapons in the hull front, two fixed and one in a ball mount (the twin guns were soon deleted in production tanks). Mechanically the new T6 was the same as the M3 with front sprocket drive, Cletrac steering, and a Wright Continental R-975 engine.

The tank was standardized as the M4, with a more easily produced welded hull, and the M4A1 with a cast unit. Initial targets were 2,000 vehicles per month and the first production M4A1 was produced in February 1942 by the

Sherman II (M4A1)
Weight 29.7 tons (30.2 tonnes)
Crew five
Armament one 75-mm M3 (37.5-calibre) gun, two 0.30-inch (7.62-mm) M1919A4 machine-guns with 4,750 rounds and one 0.50-inch (12.7-mm) M2 machine-gun with 500 rounds
Engine one Wright Continental R-975-C1 radial, nine-cylinder air-cooled petrol, 400-hp
Speed 25 mph (40 km/h)
Range 115 miles (185 km)
Trench crossing 7 feet 5 inches (2.26 m)
Vertical step 2 feet (60 cm)
Fording 3 feet (90 cm)
Overall length 19 feet 2 inches (5.84 m)
Width 8 feet 9 inches (2.66 m)
Height 9 feet (2.74 m)
Other details as Sherman VC Firefly

The tank illustrated is a Sherman II as used by the British Eighth Army in North Africa. Note the distinctive rounded cast hull, the M4-type trailing return rollers and the original style narrow mantlet and three-piece nose plate. Earlier British Shermans had M3-type return rollers

Sherman VC Firefly
Weight 34.75 tons (35.3 tonnes)
Crew four
Armament one 17-pounder (76.2-mm) Mk IV (L/55) gun with 78 rounds and one 0.30-inch (7.62-mm) Browning M1919A4 machine-gun with 5,000 rounds
Armour hull nose and glacis 51 mm, sides and tail 38 mm, decking 19 mm, belly 13–25 mm; turret front 76 mm, sides and rear 51 mm, top 25 mm
Engine one Chrysler A-57 Multibank 30-cylinder liquid-cooled petrol, 425-hp
Speed 22.25 mph (36 km/h)
Range 125 miles (201 km)
Trench crossing 8 feet (2.44 m)
Vertical step 2 feet (61 cm)
Fording 3 feet 6 inches (1.07 m)
Overall length 25 feet 6 inches (7.77 m)
Width 9 feet 6 inches (2.9 m)
Height 9 feet 4 inches (2.85 m)

The tank illustrated is the Sherman VC Firefly, the British conversion of the Sherman V and one of the most powerful tanks available to the Allies during the war. Note the extension of the turret caused by the 17-pounder (76.2-mm)

Lima Locomotive Company. All the firms which had produced the M3 – Detroit Tank Arsenal, Baldwin, Alco, Pressed Steel and Pullman – switched to the production of M4s and were soon joined by Federal Machine and Welder, Pacific Car and Foundry and the Fisher Body Division of General Motors, which built another tank arsenal at Grand Blanc, Michigan, based on Chrysler's Detroit plant. Production of M4s was on a massive scale, more M4s being produced than any other single type in World War II. In order to keep output high, different power installations had to be fitted.

The different engine units produced the following major variants in addition to M4 and M4A1: M4A2 with twin General Motors 6-71 diesels of 410 combined hp; M4A3 with purpose built 500-hp V-8 Ford GAA engine; M4A4 with 30-cylinder Chrysler Multibank engine of 425 hp; and M4A6 with Caterpillar RD-1820 nine-cylinder radial diesel (an unsuccessful type produced in very limited quantities). Both the M4A4 and M4A6 had hulls lengthened by 6 inches (15 cm) to accommodate the larger

engines with lengthened suspensions and tracks. (The term M4A5 was applied to the Canadian Ram tank.)

All types, except M4A1, had welded hulls, although M4A6 had an interesting composite hull with a cast front to improve the ballistic shape. These hulls were also applied to late M4s produced at Detroit at the beginning of 1944. All except the earliest M4A1s had the M3 75-mm gun, mounted in later tanks in a new wider mantlet to improve protection. Very early tanks also had the idler arrangement of the M3, but most M4s had the improved trailing idlers.

M4 tanks with 51-mm frontal armour, sloped at 56° from the vertical and with 75-mm guns, which could penetrate 60 mm of 30° armour at 500 yards (457 m), were the equal of most existing German tanks at their time of introduction. The appearance of more powerful German tanks and guns later created problems, however, and various improvements were called for in both firepower and protection as the tank had a reputation for combustibility when hit.

By 1944 improved versions of the M4 were coming into service. The new 76-mm gun developed for the T20 series of medium tanks was tested in a standard M4A1 but the turret was found to be unsuitable. Luckily, the entire turret of the experimental T23 medium tank was found to fit the M4's turret ring and belatedly began to be fitted to the M4A1, M4A2 and M4A3 production chassis. Up-gunned tanks all had (76 mm) added to their designations. At first the M1A1 gun was used, but later M1A1C and M1A2 weapons, both of which had muzzle brakes, were fitted.

Up-gunned M4A1, 2 and 3 tanks began to be produced in early 1944 and arrived in Europe from the middle of the year. Their improved armour penetration capability (the 2,600 fps – 693 m/s – gun could penetrate 110 mm of 30° armour at 500 yards or 457 metres proved useful against the heavily armoured German tanks they encountered.

Up-gunning went with the introduction of 'wet stowage' ammunition racks which had

M4A3E8
Weight 31.8 tons (32.2 tonnes)
Crew five
Armament one 76-mm M1A1C or M1A2 (L/52) gun with 71 rounds, two 0.30-inch (7.62 m) M1919A4 machine-gun with 6,250 rounds and one 0.50-inch (12.7-mm) M2 machine-gun with 600 rounds
Armour hull front 63.5 mm, sides and rear 38 mm, decking 19 mm, belly 25 mm; turret front and sides 63.5 mm, top 25 mm
Engine one Ford GAA-III V-8 liquid-cooled petrol, 450-hp
Speed 30 mph (48 km/h)
Length 24 feet 8 inches (7.51 m)
Width 8 feet 9 inches (2.66 m)
Height 11 feet 3 inches (3.42 m)
Other details as M4A1

The tank illustrated is a late model M4A3E8 (76-mm). Note the new turret and armament, stronger one-piece nose, 'clean' hull front, horizontal volute spring suspension' and distinctive new decking design. Such tanks were in service for the Ardennes fighting in late 1944

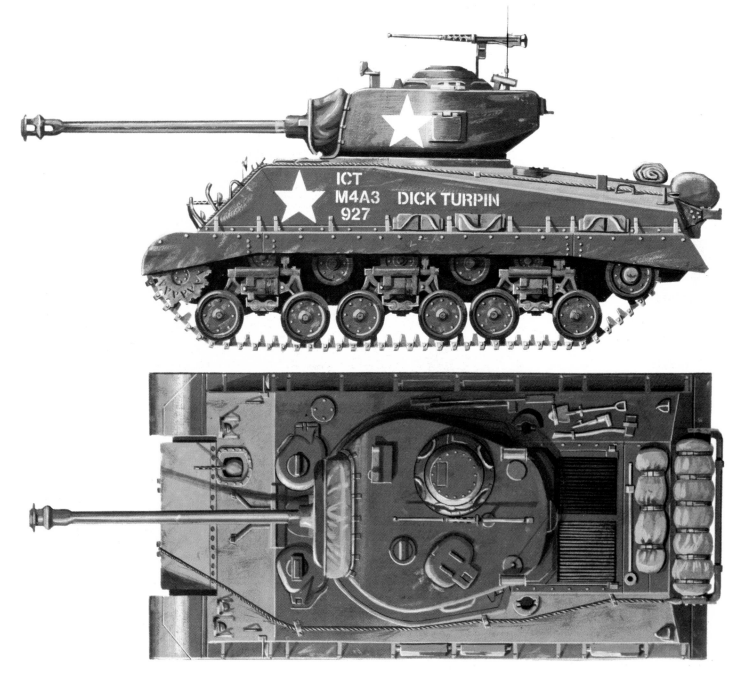

Below: *A British Sherman Crab Mark II mine-clearing flail. Earlier British mine-clearing attempts had used chain flails powered by auxiliary engines but in the Crab they were driven directly from the engine of the tank, a Sherman V, the most common British model. The drive was taken via chains and a drive shaft in the right hand boom. Once the mine-clearing was completed the vehicle could operate as a conventional gun tank. The arms could be raised and lowered to help stowage in the landing craft and the Mark II had a contour-following device to improve effectiveness over rough ground. The 'antennae' on the tank's rear are dim lights to guide following vehicles and the angled containers hold powdered chalk to mark the cleared path. The 30th Armoured Brigade used Crab Mark Is in Normandy and the rest of the North-West Europe campaign; the US Army also adopted and used the system*

hollow walls containing a mixture of water and glycerine that mitigated the fire risk when hit. The hull front was also redesigned to ease production with a new, slightly less sloping (47°) 'clean' front plate. The new hull and stowage system was also used on late 75-mm armed M4A3s built until March 1945. Earlier 75-mm gun tanks of all models except M4A6 were systematically reworked as part of a programme that began in 1944. Appliqué armour was added to the hull and new guns fitted in some cases. Spare track shoes, sandbags, wood and even concrete were often resorted to for improved protection in the field.

In late 1944 the final modification to the M4 took place with the fitting of improved, horizontal volute spring suspension (HVSS), together with wider tracks of 24 inches (61 cm). Instead of single road wheels with the track guide horns at the sides, the new track had centre horns and the road wheels were now double with return rollers being moved to the hull sides. The first prototype vehicle with this suspension was designated M4E8 and the E8 suffix was given to all the production prototypes of the HVSS M4A1, M4A2 and M4A3.

There were two other versions of the M4 tank which saw service. A special assault tank, the

M4A3E2, was designed quickly in 1944 as a heavily armoured, infantry support vehicle for use in North West Europe. The nose armour was increased to 140 mm and the frontal plating to 102 mm, while the side armour was increased to 76 mm. A new turret was fitted with an 178-mm mantlet and 152-mm sides. Although all M4A3E2s mounted the standard 75-mm gun, the new turret allowed the fitting of the 76-mm weapon by field workshops in Europe. The new armour increased weight to 42 US tons (37.4 tonnes), reduced maximum speed to 22 mph (35 km/h) and range to 100 miles (161 km). The extra weight also put greater strain on the suspension so the tracks were widened. M4A3E2s were first used during Operation Cobra, the breakout from Normandy in 1944, and became known as 'Cobra Kings' but later their more general name was 'Jumbo'. A total of 254 were produced.

In order to provide heavy fire support for the normal M4s in armoured units, two M4A4E1 prototypes were fitted in 1942 with 105-mm howitzers in place of the 75-mm guns. Two further M4E5 prototypes helped refine the concept and production of the M4 (105 mm) and M4A3 (105 mm) began in 1944; 800 and 500 of each type were built respectively before HVSS was adopted for the final production runs of 841

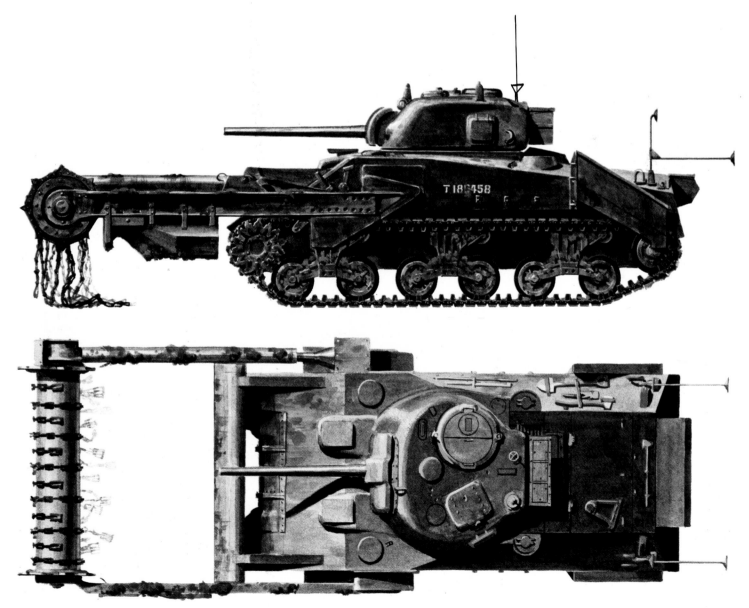

and 2,529. The howitzer was the 25-calibre M4 weapon, having the ability to fire a 33-pound (14.97-kg) shell over 6.9 miles (11.2 km).

Production figures for normal M4 battle tanks were as follows: M4 6,748; M4A1 6,281; M4A1 (76 mm) 3,396; M4A2 8,053; M4A2 (76 mm) 1,615; M4A3 3,071; M4A3 (76 mm) 3,370; M4A4 7,499; M4A6 75. When the M4A3E2, M4 (105 mm) and M4A3 (105 mm) tanks are taken into account this makes a total of 45,032 M4s produced, about twice Germany's production of all types of tank. With the M4 the United States became the tank arsenal of the Allies, large numbers of vehicles being supplied to Britain, Russia, the Free French and China.

The M4 became the standard battle tank of the British Army, who gave it its name, Sherman. Early Shermans, mainly M4A1s were rushed to the Western Desert to fight in the Alamein battles in September–October 1942 and they provided the Commonwealth armoured forces with a general superiority not known since the heyday of the Matilda. The turret-mounted 75-mm gun with its capacity to fire hull-down against a wide range of targets was a special advantage. Some 270 Shermans were used in the

Second Battle of Alamein and the tank soon became the most numerous in service with Eighth Army. The British, New Zealand and South African armoured forces in Italy in 1943–5 were almost entirely Sherman equipped, even Churchill units receiving the American tank.

The North-West Europe campaign began with 1,900 Shermans out of a total tank strength of 2,740 in 21st Army Group and Shermans continued to outnumber British tanks in the Group's British, Canadian and Polish armoured brigades by two to one. Indian and British troops also used the Sherman in Burma, while 4,000 of the vehicles went to the Soviet Union.

In February 1944 conversion began of Sherman Fireflies, equipped with the most powerful British high velocity gun, the 17-pounder (76.2 mm), which had an excellent performance (120 mm of 30° plate at 500 yards (457 m)) and made the vehicle the virtual equal of any German tank in firepower terms. About 600 were converted.

British designations for the various types of Sherman were: M4 – Sherman I; late production M4 with composite hull – Sherman Hybrid I; M4A1 – Sherman II; M4A2 – Sherman III; M4A3 – Sherman IV; M4A4 – Sherman V;

M4A6 – Sherman VII. If the tank carried a 76-mm gun the suffix A was used, B signifying 105-mm howitzer versions and C Fireflies. Y as a further suffix denoted HVSS. Most British Shermans were Sherman Vs.

The Americans carried out considerable work on specialized equipment for the M4, although with a standardization conscious United States Army, few saw service. An M19 swimming device was developed for use with standard wading gear which allowed the tank to fire whilst floating ashore: such vehicles were used by the USMC in the Pacific.

Two major types of American flame-thrower

Below: *The Sherman Duplex Drive amphibious tank. This vehicle was a basic Sherman III or V made watertight and fitted with a collapsible canvas screen which although it took 15 minutes to erect could be dropped immediately on landing. Two propellers gave a maximum speed through the water of about four knots and these could also be swivelled for steering, either by an hydraulic system or by means of a tiller operated by a crew member standing on the rear of the turret*

M4 were developed. The standard E4 series flame-gun could be fitted in place of the hull machine-gun while the Marines also had a version that used a long-range United States Navy POA Mark I flame-gun inside the normal 75-mm barrel of a standard tank or in an old 105-mm howitzer tube mounted in the turret. A version also existed with the tube mounted beside the barrel so that the gun capability was retained.

Another sort of firepower deployed with US Shermans was the rocket. The major type used in Europe was the T34 Calliope, which used a jettisonable 60-round projector for 4.2-inch (107-mm) rockets mounted on a frame above the turret. The projector was connected to the gun for elevation and trained by using the turret. There were variants on this standard theme – the T34E1 with extra tubes, and the 7.2-inch (183 mm) T34E2. Another 7.2-inch (183-mm) system was the T40 'Whizz Bang', a box-like launcher mounted similarly to the Calliope. The T99, which put a box launcher with 22 4.5-inch (114-mm) rockets on each side of an M4 turret, was used in the Pacific.

Some M4s were fitted in the field with bull-dozer blades and this conversion was so successful that a standard M1 bulldozer attachment was developed. A few United States mine-sweeping equipment variants also saw service with the Sherman. Most spectacular was the Mine Exploder M1 'Aunt Jemima', two large 10-feet (3-m) roller wheels pushed in front of the M4. Flails and ploughs were also used and a wide range of other equipment developed experiment-ally. The M32 Tank Recovery Vehicle was also sometimes used for mine-sweeping. This was a turretless M4 with a fixed superstructure con-taining a winch. Its large front-mounted jib could be used to support T1E1 Earthworm mine-sweeping rollers.

The M4 chassis also lent itself for use as a self-propelled gun. In 1944 M7 Priests began to be built by Pressed Steel on the Ford-engined M4A3 chassis. These were designated M7B1 and over 500 were constructed in 1944–5; 127 M7B2s with higher mounted howitzers were produced by Federal Machine and Welder in 1945. Pressure from Armoured Centre led to a successor for the M12 heavy self-propelled gun being developed using a widened version of the M4A3 chassis. Before the war ended, 311 were

built and designated M40 Gun Motor Carriage, carrying the M2 155-mm gun; 48 were produced as the M43 with 8-inch (204-mm) howitzers. All were constructed in 1945 and fitted with HVSS.

The Sherman chassis was also used to provide mobile anti-tank weapons for the tank destroyer battalions. The M10 Tank Destroyer used the M7 76-mm gun which could penetrate over 100 mm of 30° plate at 500 yards (457 m). Production began in June 1942 and 4,993 were produced, along with 1,413 M10A1s which had the V-8 Ford petrol engine of the M4A3. Both types weighed 33 US tons (30 tonnes), had 57-mm turret and 38-mm hull armour and a maximum speed of 30 mph (48 km/h).

The balance of the M10's turret was never entirely satisfactory and a new turret was developed which could take the M3 90-mm gun. The 90-mm turret was fitted to the M10A1 chassis, and the combination was standardized in June 1944 as the M36. Vehicles with the M10 chassis became M36B2, and with the normal M4A3 tank chassis M36B1. From late 1944 they increasingly supplemented and replaced the M10 in American tank destroyer battalions, and together with the 76-mm armed M18 'Hellcat' formed their basic equipment by the end of the war. The M10/M36 series proved a useful source of mobile anti-tank firepower, speed and conceal-ment making up for deficiencies in protection.

M10s and M10A1s were also issued to British and Free French forces. In British service the M10 became the 'Wolverine' self-propelled gun. From late 1944 Wolverines began to be up-gunned with 17-pounder (76.2-mm) guns as the 17-pounder SP Achilles, Mark IA if an M10 and Mark IIA if an M10A1.

The British used the Sherman as the basis for a number of special purpose vehicles of their own. One of the most important of these were the Duplex Drive (DD) amphibious tanks fitted with the flotation gear designed by Nicholas Straussler. In 1943, after experiments with Tetrarch and Valentine, the Sherman was chosen for use in the Normandy landings. The DD equipment consisted of collapsible canvas screen carried around the tank, erected by rubber tubing which could be filled with compressed air. The vehicle was waterproofed and with the screens

Top left: *M4 series tanks of the 40th Tank Battalion, part of US Seventh Armoured Division, during the Ardennes fighting. Note the 75-mm guns and the effectiveness of the vehicle's winter camouflage. On its introduction the Sherman was soon called by its respectful opponents the 'T-34 of the West'. Speer, the German armaments minister always used these manoeuvrable all-round vehicles as an example for the size-con-scious Wehrmacht with its passion for clumsy, unreliable monsters*

Bottom left: *One of the flame-thrower versions of Sherman fitted with the American E4 series flame-gun in place of the hull machine-gun mount. There were three variants E4R2, 3 and 4. Fuel was carried within the vehicle. Another similar device was the E6 which could be fitted above the co-driver's hatch. Both E4 and E6 flame-throwers were issued in kit form for fitting in the field. An E7 could be mounted in the turret. In addition to the POA some USMC M4s (and M3 light tanks) were fitted with turret mounted Canadian Ronson flame guns*

135

M7B1
Weight 20.8 tons (22.6 tonnes)
Crew seven
Armament one 105-mm M2A1 (L/22.5) howitzer with 69 rounds and one 0.50-inch (12.7-mm) M2 machine-gun with 300 rounds
Armour 12–62 mm
Engine one Ford GAA-III V-8 liquid-cooled, petrol 450-hp
Speed 26 mph (41 km/h)
Range 125 miles (201 km)
Length 20 feet 4 inches (6.19 m)
Width 9 feet 5 inches (2.87 m)
Height 8 feet 4 inches (2.54 m)
Other details as M4A1

The vehicle illustrated is the M7B1 self-propelled howitzer, based on the standard M4A3 chassis. Note the Sherman-style return rollers, later style cast one piece nose, and distinctive 'pulpit'

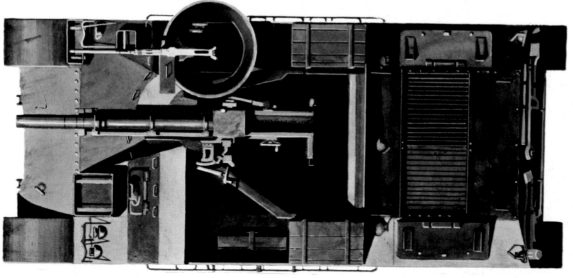

erected could float, being propelled through the water by two propellers powered by the tank's engines via the tracks and rear idler wheels.

A total of 573 Sherman III and V tanks were initially chosen for conversion as Sherman III DD and V DD. Others were converted for American use. The various DD units were used on 6 June 1944 with general success. The only major failure was on Omaha where 27 of the 29 tanks launched at 6,000 yards (5,486 m) sank in the heavy swell. Those that got ashore played a vital part in breaking down the initial German defences and supporting the first Allied troops inland. British DD Shermans were later used in the crossing of the Scheldt, Rhine and Elbe and also in Italy.

Another important British conversion used by the Americans was the Sherman 'Crab' flail mine-clearing tank. Sherman Crabs, best of the British mine-sweeping tanks, were such a success that the Americans procured the system also as the Mine Exploder T2 Flail.

Right: *An early M4A1, still in service with US First Armoured Division, moves up to attack the Gothic Line in Italy during the late summer of 1944. Note the early 'narrow' mantlet and three-piece bolted nose plate as well as the improvised frontal 'protection'. First Armoured Division was the only such US Army formation to fight in Italy*
Below: *Two British 'Achilles' tank destroyers – M10 series vehicles up-gunned with British 17-pounder (76.2-mm) guns. Note the different shape of the M10 hull compared to the basic M4 tank, and the open-top turrets*

Two British flame-thrower systems were developed for the Sherman but neither was used in action. Four Shermans fitted with British Crocodile equipment were used by the United States Second Armoured Division, however, and the United States Marine Corps fitted some M4s with Canadian-designed Ronson flame-guns as with the 'Satan' based on the M3 light tank.

Various types of armoured recovery vehicles were modified by the British – the Sherman III and V ARV Mark I without turret and with simple recovery equipment, and the more sophisticated Sherman V ARV Mark II with dummy turret and gun, two jibs and a 60 ton winch fitted. A beach armoured recovery vehicle (BARV) was also built, and used successfully in the Normandy landings and Rhine crossings in rescuing 'drowned' vehicles.

The British converted Shermans into OP tanks, some with dummy guns; during 1945 First (Armoured) Battalion the Coldstream Guards converted a number of their Sherman Vs and V Cs with an improvised rocket-launcher mounting, a 60-pound (27.2 kg) rocket and aircraft rack on each side of the tank. These gave remarkably effective additional firepower in the final battles in Germany. Other tanks were converted into fascine carriers while Commonwealth Shermans were used in Italy as bridging vehicles, gun tractors and armoured personnel carriers.

Sherman production ceased in June 1945 but development went on after the war in both the United States and Britain and a new M74 recovery vehicle was developed on the chassis. Shermans were widely distributed after World War II and they fought again in various major post-war conflicts, notably with the US Army in Korea, on both sides in the Indo-Pakistani War of 1965 and with both Israeli and Egyptian forces in the Arab Israeli Wars since 1948. The Israelis still keep the Sherman in service as the Super Sherman and Isherman with new engines and guns. The Sherman also remains in service with Latin American countries (some Fireflies still exist in the Argentinian Army), and in Portugal, South Korea, Uganda and Yugoslavia.

Below: A standard British Sherman festooned with extra front 'protection' in Normandy. The Sherman, mostly of the Sherman V type, provided the standard British medium tank from 1943 to the end of the war. The white star was used by all Allied forces in North-West Europe and Italy. Note the Sherman-based M10 Wolverine tank destroyers in the background

Bottom: The M1 Aunt Jemina, one of the most spectacular mine-clearance devices of the war, was used in conjunction with the M4 series. Note the chain drive from the sprockets to the 10-foot (3.4 m) 'indestructable' wheels. A total of 75 of these devices were built and the system was used in action by American forces, an extra M4 sometimes being necessary to push the heavy equipment along

Light Tank (Airborne) M22 Locust

The German conquest of Western Europe in 1940 dramatically illustrated the effectiveness of airborne forces and prompted the United States Army to explore the concept of a light tank to support such operations. In February 1941 the Ordnance Department held a meeting, also attended by General Staff, Air and Armoured Force representatives, which drew up the specification for such a tank. To aid air transport weight was to be 7½ US tons (6.8 tonnes) – this was later raised to 8 tons (7.2 tonnes).

This requirement was given to three manufacturers, and the design of Marmon Herrington finally chosen. Marmon Herrington had been constructing light tanks since 1935, both for the US Marine Corps and for export. The latest versions of these were the machine-gun armed CTLS and the larger CTMS and MTLS with single and twin 37-mm guns respectively. A number of CTLS tanks were put into service by the US Army as Light Tanks T16 and used for training. Later Marmon Herrington light tanks used the standard American vertical volute-spring suspension and this system was adopted for the airborne vehicles. There were two bogie units each side with large trailing idlers to improve weight distribution. This system soon proved weak and a large external girder was

added to strengthen it, soon being replaced by a lighter rod to reduce weight. A welded hull was used for the tank, armoured to 25 mm, with a power traversed cast turret mounting the standard M6 37-mm gun with co-axial 0.30-inch (7.62-mm) machine-gun. Two further machine-guns were mounted in the right hull front. A 162-hp six-cylinder, air-cooled Lycoming engine drove via the front sprockets.

The first T9 prototype was too heavy and the next T9E1 prototypes were reduced in weight. Both the hull and turret were redesigned, which also improved their ballistic shape, and the power traverse, gun stabilizer and hull machine-guns were deleted. The bogie frames were lightened and the external suspension rod retained. The new tank now weighed an acceptable 8.2 US tons (7.4 tonnes) fully laden, and in April 1943 the first tanks left the production lines. Production was terminated in February 1944 after 830 vehicles, by which time the vehicles had been designated M22.

As well as the mechanical defects, two fundamental problems caused the project to be curtailed. Firstly, it was doubted whether such a lightly armed and armoured tank could survive on the battle-field. Secondly, the United States Army Air Force had not developed a proper

means of delivery for armoured vehicles. They had no suitable gliders to deliver the tanks directly into a dropping zone. The only machine capable of carrying the tank was the Douglas C-54 transport aircraft and even then the turret had to be separated from the hull and valuable time later spent reassembling the vehicles. Consequently, M22s were never used in action by the Americans.

The new tank was of more use to the British, however, who had a large capacity glider, the Hamilcar, designed for their own Tetrarch light tank. The second T9E1 prototype was sent to Britain and it was followed by a large proportion of the production vehicles, which the British called Locust. To increase the power of the 37-mm guns Littlejohn Adaptors were fitted to the ends of barrels to impart added velocity. A few Locusts were used alongside Tetarchs in support of the Sixth Airborne Division during the Rhine crossing in 1945.

Below: *A British Locust emerges from a Hamilcar glider. Locusts were deployed in this way during the crossing of the Rhine, their only operational use in their intended role. Mechanical defects and lack of suitable transport meant that M22s were never used in action by the United States*

Light Tank (Airborne) M22 Locust
Weight 7.3 tons (7.4 tonnes)
Crew three
Armament one 37-mm M6 (L/50) gun with 50 rounds and one 0.30-inch (7.62-mm) Browning M1919A4 machine-gun with 2,500 rounds
Armour hull nose 25 mm, glacis 13 mm, sides 9–13 mm, decking 9 mm, belly and tail 13 mm; turret front and sides 25 mm, top 9 mm
Engine one Lycoming 0-435T horizontally opposed six-cylinder air-cooled petrol, 162-hp
Speed 40 mph (64 km/h)
Range 135 miles (217 km)
Trench crossing 5 feet 5 inches (1.65 mm)
Vertical step 1 foot 0.5 inches (31 cm)
Fording 3 feet 2 inches (96 cm)
Overall length 12 feet 11 inches (3.94 m)
Width 7 feet 1 inch (2.16 m)
Height 6 feet 1 inch (1.85 m)

The tank illustrated is an M22 supplied to the British Army as the Locust. They were never successful vehicles, remaining underpowered and unreliable; only 830 were built out of an order of 1,900

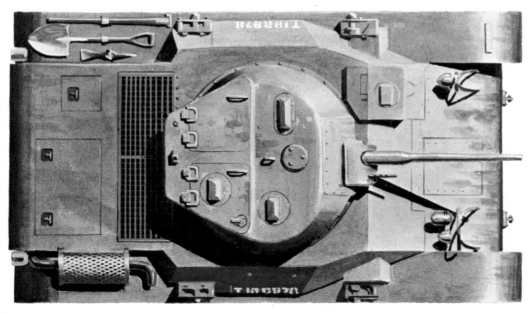

Light Tank M24 Chaffee

Although the M5 Stuart was in most respects a good light tank it was soon clear that its armament and protection needed improvement. After a number of unsuccessful projects, work began in April 1943, in conjunction with Cadillac, on a new light tank that would be within a 20-US ton (18-tonne) weight limit. This new T24 had the same Cadillac engines as the earlier M5 and similar Hydra-Matic automatic transmission with front sprocket drive and Cletrac steering. The new torsion bar suspension, increasingly favoured by the Ordnance Department, was adopted based on that of the M18 light tank destroyer with five road wheels each side. An enlarged hydraulically-traversed turret mounted a stabilized lightweight M6 75-mm gun based on a design for fitting in the B-24 Mitchell bomber. This 39-calibre weapon, weighing half as much as the old M3 gun of the M4 medium tank, had comparable performance; 0.30-inch (7.62-mm) machine-guns were mounted co-axially with the main armament and in the right hull front. In order to keep weight limited to the required 20 US tons (18 tonnes), armour was only 25 mm thick on the hull with a 38-mm mantlet.

The T24 proved so successful that 1,000 were soon on order and this figure was later raised to 5,000. Cadillac began production in April 1944, and in May the tank was standardized as the M24. When the end of the war caused production to cease Cadillac had produced some 3,300 M24s, with 770 more coming from Massey Harris from July 1944.

M24s began to be used with United States Army light tank battalions and cavalry reconnaissance units in North West Europe and Italy in late 1944 and the vehicle also saw service in the Pacific. The vehicle was a more powerfully armed tank than many earlier mediums. Although not very well protected (sandbags were often added), the M24 proved a good reconnaissance vehicle that could, if necessary, use agility and manoeuvrability to enable its adequate armament to inflict real damage on more heavily protected opponents. The M24 was also supplied to Britain where it was called 'Chaffee', a name adopted by the United States Army after the war.

In order to rationalize spares and maintenance a 'Light Combat Team' of gun carriages was developed on the M24 chassis. The first of these was the M19 self-propelled twin 40-mm anti-aircraft gun. In the M19 the engine was moved to the front of the chassis and a twin 40-mm M2 Bofors mount occupied the rear. The number of return rollers was increased to four. This anti-aircraft vehicle was originally to have been based on the M5A1 but the suspension was changed with the adoption of the M24.

Another development of a concept originally based on the M5A1 chassis was the M41 Howitzer Motor Carriage. The original T64 chassis, designed to mount the standard M1 155-mm howitzer was modified into T64E1 configuration with torsion bar suspension and standardized for production. The chassis layout was similar to that of the M19 with the howitzer carried on the rear of the vehicle with a large spade to help check recoil.

The final M24-based SP to see service was the M37 105-mm howitzer. This was designed as a more compact and economical mounting than the M7 Priest and kept the rear engine layout of the M24 tank. The howitzer was fitted in the front of a large open box superstructure with a prominent 'pulpit' in the right-hand side front. Both protection and ammunition were improved over that of the M7. Production had only just begun when the war ended. A T38 project to mount a 4.2-inch (107-mm) mortar on this vehicle was abandoned in August 1945. Other projects involving the M24 which did not see service were an amphibious version with M20 swimming device and a T24E1 with Continental R-975 engine, which was also eventually fitted with a longer 75-mm gun, and a T6E1 recovery vehicle.

Below: *M24's, like this example, were supplied to Britain who named them Chaffee and used them in the closing months of the war replacing the Stuarts in the reconnaissance troops of armoured regiments*

Light Tank M24 Chaffee
Weight 18.1 tons (18.4 tonnes)
Crew five
Armament one 75-mm M6 (L/39) gun with 48
rounds, two 0.30-inch Browning M1919A4
machine-guns with 3,750 rounds and one 0.50-inch
(12.7-mm) M2 machine-gun with 440 rounds
Armour hull nose and glacis 25 mm, sides
19–25 mm, decking 13 mm, belly 9–13 mm,
tail 13 mm; turret front, sides and rear 25 mm,
mantlet 38 mm, roof 13 mm
Engine two Cadillac 44T24 V-8 liquid-cooled
petrol, 220-hp
Speed 34 mph (55 km/h)
Range 100 miles (161 km)
Trench crossing 8 feet (2.44 m)
Vertical step 3 feet (91 cm)
Fording 3 feet 4 inches (1.02 m)
Overall length 18 feet (5.49 m)
Width 9 feet 8 inches (2.95 m)
Height 8 feet 1½ inches (2.48 m)

Top: *An M18 Hellcat – the torsion bar suspension
of the M24 was based on that developed for this
tank destroyer. This 17.9 US ton (18.18 tonnes)
76-mm armed vehicle was built by Buick and was
not based on any tank chassis. A total of 2,507
were built*
Above right: *The M24 only saw limited service
in World War II but remain in service with many
modern armies today*

Heavy Tank M26 Pershing

The success of German armour in May 1940 prompted a requirement for a heavy tank. A large 76-mm armed 60-US ton (54.4 tonne) M6 was produced but the project was cancelled because of the problem of shipping such a tank overseas and doubts about its reliability and weight. Only when the heavily armed and armoured *Panther* and *Tiger* tanks were encountered in quantity did opinion on heavy armour change.

An experimental T20 series of medium tanks was developed from 1942 and culminated in the T25 and T26, both with 90-mm guns. Armour on the T26 was 102 mm against the 87 mm of the T25. Most of the first pilot batch of these two vehicles had torsion bar suspensions and torque converter 'torquematic' gear boxes. Forty of these T25E1 and 10 T26E1 tanks were built between January and May 1944. Then in June, the Army Ground Forces and Armoured Command suddenly demanded priority development of the T26 to counter modern German armour. At 46 US tons (41.7 tonnes) the type was now officially a 'heavy tank'. Some 250 were eventually ordered, production vehicles being modified with improved stowage and muzzle brake on the gun. In January 1945 the first 20 crossed the Atlantic and the new tank was standardized in March as the M26, soon also known as 'General Pershing'.

This late start prevented the Pershing's wide deployment with combat units. Allocated to Third and Ninth Armoured Divisions, it saw only limited action. By the end of the war, some 200 were in service with the United States Army in Europe, with 110 more in reserve. The 53-calibre M3 90-mm gun almost equalled the German 88-mm in performance, while the Pershing's well-shaped armour gave protection from the majority of enemy projectiles.

The Pershing was of welded construction with rear-mounted engine driving through the rear sprockets. Cletrac controlled differential steering was used, as on all American armour. Suspension was by torsion bars, with six road wheels each side and five return rollers. Some 2,428 M26s were constructed by the two tank arsenals at Detroit and Grand Blanc from November 1944 until the end of the war. With increasing size standards, the Pershings were reclassified as mediums in 1946. They became the forerunners of the series of modern American medium tanks that led via the M46, M47 and M48 Pattons to the M60s of today.

Heavy Tank M26 Pershing
Weight 41.1 tons (41.7 tonnes)
Crew five
Armament one 90-mm M3 (L/53) gun with 70 rounds, two 0.30-inch (7.62-mm) Browning M1919A4 machine-guns with 5,000 rounds and one 0.50-inch (12.7-mm) M2 machine-gun with 550 rounds
Armour hull nose 76 mm, glacis 102 mm, sides 51–76 mm, decking 7–8 mm, belly 13–25 mm, tail 51 mm; turret front 102 mm, sides and rear 76 mm, top 51 mm
Engine one Ford GAF V-8 liquid-cooled petrol, 500-hp
Speed 20 mph (32 km/h)
Range 92 miles (148 km)
Trench crossing 8 feet 6 inches (2.59 m)
Vertical step 3 feet 10 inches (1.17 m)
Fording 4 feet (1.22 m)
Overall length 28 feet 10 inches (8.79 m)
Width 11 feet 6 inch (3.5 m)
Height 9 feet 1 inch (2.77 m)

Below: Two M26 Pershings advance through the remains of a German town; a few of these heavy tanks were used in action in the closing months of World War II